the new complete

German Shorthaired Pointer

Dual Ch./AFC Shill Rest's Impressive, CDX, MH, earned an impressive number of titles during his too-short life. This memorable dog was a wonderful example of the German Shorthaired Pointer's legendary ability to do many jobs and do them all wonderfully well.

the new complete

German
Shorthaired
Pointer

Robert H. McKowen

HOWELL
BOOK
HOUSE

Howell Book House
A Simon & Schuster Macmillan Company
1633 Broadway
New York, NY 10019

Macmillan Publishing books may be purchased for business or sales promotional
use. For information, please write: Special Markets Department, Macmillan
Publishing USA, 1633 Broadway, New York, NY 10019.

MACMILLAN is a registered trademark of Macmillan, Inc.

Library of Congress Cataloging-in-Publication Data
McKowen, Robert H.
    The new complete German shorthaired pointer / Robert H. McKowen.
        p.   c.m.
    ISBN 0-87605-149-2
    1. German shorthaired pointer.   I. Title.
SF429.G4M35   1998
636.752'5—dc21   98-17340
                                                           CIP
                      636.7525

Manufactured in the United States of America

10 9 8 7 6 5 4 3 2 1

This book is dedicated in fond remembrance to:
Harold Fuehrer, *my mentor and friend*
Bob Arnold, *my friend whose whole life was*
  the German Shorthaired Pointer
Ida Mae Jordan, *who mothered Adam as a puppy*
Ch. Adam v. Fuehrerheim, *who deserved a better owner*
And to all my many friends in the Shorthair world

Blueprint of the
German Shorthaired Pointer

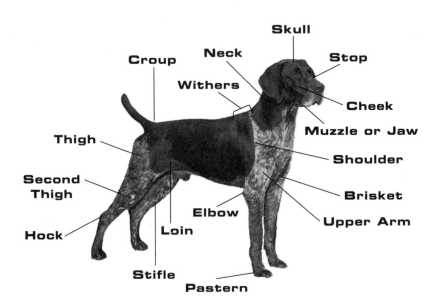

Skull, Neck, Croup, Stop, Withers, Cheek, Muzzle or Jaw, Thigh, Shoulder, Second Thigh, Brisket, Elbow, Upper Arm, Hock, Loin, Stifle, Pastern

Contents

Ch. Crossing Creek Homesteader, owned by Ken Marden, displays the Shorthair's love of water.

Introduction

On a crisp autumn evening in 1961, on the edge of Lancaster, Pennsylvania, I saw a dog running loose that I couldn't identify. Under the street light, I could see it had large liver patches, ticking and a short tail. I couldn't get it to come to me, and it ran off into the night, one hopes to where it had come from. I recognized it had to be a Pointer of some kind, but that was all I knew. That was the start of a quest that almost thirty years later would find me serving as president of the German Shorthaired Pointer Club of America and later as vice-president of Performance Events at the American Kennel Club in New York. However, it was not until July 1962, when my old Weimaraner died, that I began looking for a dog like the one I had seen that autumn evening.

The first place I looked was a newsstand in Lancaster, where I found a paperback book about the shorthair that had been authored by Richard S. Johns, of Benton, Pennsylvania, one of the early post–World War II importers of shorthairs from Germany. The photos matched the dog I had seen on the street the previous year. My next mission was to find out where I could see one. One of the few, if not the only, magazines on newsstands about dogs was *Dog World*. It was printed in black-and-white and had sections on various breeds. In it, I found out that an AKC dog show would be held in Williamsport, Pennsylvania, in a few weeks. On a hot July Sunday morning, I set out on the ninety-mile trip to Williamsport hoping to see some shorthairs. I had never been to a show before and had no idea how they were run. When I got there, I found that the breed had already been judged, and all but one shorthair had already left the grounds. The shorthair that was still there had the large liver patches that I had admired. He was owned by Robert Rudy and had come from the kennels of Harold Fuehrer in Mount Holly Springs, south of Carlisle, Pennsylvania, home of the Military War College and former Carlisle Football Team on which Jim Thorpe starred. What I wanted was a dark-pigmented dog like Bob Rudy's, and Harold Fuehrer's was the place I intended to stop in my search for a shorthair.

Harold Fuehrer was a maintenance engineer employed by a large manufacturer in the Carlisle-Harrisburg, Pennsylvania, area. His place looked like a little slice of Bavaria, with a stocked trout stream running through the center of it between his kennels and an area where he raised birds.

Harold told me that he knew of a litter in Richmond, Virginia, that was sired by a dog that had been recently imported from Swden called Adam, which had won show and field championships in Sweden, Norway and Denmark. The dam had been sold by Harold to a sporting goods store owner— Charles L. Jordan IV, who lived in Midlothian, Virginia, near Richmond. Harold had recommended that the owners of this bitch, which came out of his kennel, be bred to the import Adam, which was now owned by Mr. John Wilkins of Virginia, a coffee importer. He had bought Adam to be used on his own private hunting preserve at Chestnut Lawn, Virginia.

Harold had bought a male and a female out of the litter (Crista and Kreg), and I had a chance to see them when they were three months old. They were exactly what I was looking for. He showed me a color photograph of another dog left in the litter, and that was the one I really preferred. I put down a ten-dollar deposit to pick up the dog within the month when the Jordans were visiting Harold and would bring the dog with them. I paid a total of 100 dollars for Adam at four months of age. Looking back, it was a very low price for a dog that would ultimately be worth 50,000 dollars himself and probably either have sired or grandsired litters worth approximately one-half million dollars. The people who bred Adam to Fuehrenheim were able to command very large prices for their puppies. Unfortunately, only a handful of people bred dogs to the import Adam.

Harold had strong line breeding going back to the original imports from Dr. Charles Thornton in Montana, who is credited with bringing in the first shorthairs that were recognized in the United States in 1925. I spent three hours talking with him and in that period of time learned enough about the German Shorthaired Pointer, showing a dog and the sport of field trialing to last me a lifetime. As it proved many decades later, most of the information he gave me was right on the mark. The most basic and the best advice he gave was to read all I could about the shorthair and about training and adapt all that would best suit the dog that I owned. And he was so right!

Harold told me, when I picked up the dog a month later after visiting a number of kennels in the eastern United States, there was a field trial coming up in October at the Eastern German Shorthaired Pointer Club Championship in New Jersey. I entered the trial, not knowing what it was all about. I was wearing a pair of army combat boots from World War II and met a tall gentleman, named Ken Marden, wearing paratrooper fatigues and combat boots. Ken would become a lifelong friend and would have a great deal to do with my future, which came about several decades later. I also met Dick Johns, the man who had written the book on shorthairs and was handling several dogs for some people in addition to one of his own, and Tom Getler, who was handling, among other dogs, an outstanding performer called Field champion Tip Top Timmy. In this short period of time I'd run into many of the dominant factors in the field trial world in the eastern United States and dogs that would have bearing on the quality of future generations of the breed throughout the United States.

I didn't realize that I had entered into an era when the German Shorthaired Pointer was beginning to rapidly grow in field trials and in shows. In those days, we saw a variety of colors, sizes and shapes. My dog Adam was a very dark liver, not quite but almost to the point of being black. Many of the dogs that I saw at that time were faded brown or faded liver. They came in all sizes and shapes, and there was not a strong unifying force for the breed. That would come later. In an interview with Dick Johns in early spring of 1997, when he had reached the age of 82 and was still extremely sharp mentally and in good shape physically, I learned why there was such divergence in type and how that compared to what was happening in Germany.

So what is a German Shorthaired Pointer, and why did it become so popular in a relatively short period of time following World War II? First, let's take a look at the origin of the breed.

German Shorthaired Pointers generally get along peacefully with other household pets. Here an accomplished hunting dog relaxes at home with a seventeen-year-old friend.

What Is a German Shorthaired Pointer?

The German Shorthaired Pointer is a medium-size hunting dog used primarily on upland game in the United States for finding, pointing and retrieving birds. As developed in Germany, the Shorthair is also capable of trailing furred game and water retrieving. These dogs have also been used to pull sleds and can be trained easily to do many other jobs. However, the GSP in the United States is used almost exclusively for hunting game birds, in which it is equal or superior to any other breed.

The Standard calls for males to be twenty-five inches at the withers (top of the shoulder blades) and females to be twenty-three inches high, with an inch allowed above or below for both. Even though allowed in the Standard, however, a twenty-two-inch-high female is not often seen and would appear to be small. Its medium size places the GSP between the Brittany on the smaller side and the Pointer and Irish and Gordon Setters on the larger side in the bird dog community.

The Shorthair is compactly built with a fairly broad chest, though it is not so wide as to interfere with front movement. The topline slopes slightly from the withers to the croup, with only a slight drop where the tail is set on. The tail is cropped to about two-fifths of its length. The body has a moderate tuckup with a fairly short loin, although slightly longer in females. The legs are well-boned, dropping straight from the shoulder in front and well angulated in the rear. The shoulder slopes approximately 45 degrees to provide reach. Viewed from either front or rear, the legs are straight and the feet should turn neither in nor out. The dog is a little longer than tall and slightly more rectangular in profile than square. Proportion and balance are the key words to describe the ideal GSP. It should have the appearance of speed and endurance and be neither blocky nor rangy.

The coat is short and hard, a little softer on the neck. In America, the Shorthair can have a variety of color combinations, including white and liver, white ticking and liver patches, or solid liver. Most purebred Shorthairs in the United States have liver heads, sometimes with a blaze down the middle, and liver patches on the body interspersed with liver ticking over a white ground color.

The only acceptable colors are liver, liver and white, and liver and ticking. Pure white is a disqualification, as is a third color such as red, which is referred to as tri-colored. Brown is sometimes used to describe the color liver, and the Shorthair is frequently referred to as brown. Liver is a good word to describe the color since it runs the gamut from medium to very dark brown, almost black.

In the 1970s, when I served on the Board of Directors before being elected president of the German Shorthaired Pointer Club of America, an attempt was made to define color in such a way that it would prevent the practice of breeding a Pointer to a German Shorthaired Pointer to get greater range or speed in the resulting progeny. It was thought that a Pointer would pass its predominantly white color and if white could be made a disqualification, the practice could be halted. However, the project bogged down because agreement could not be reached on what proportion of white would be a disqualification. Rather than leave the issue up in the air, it was decided to simply change the Standard to read that all-white would be a disqualification. Of course, an all-white Shorthair, or a Pointer for that matter, would be a rarity indeed.

Black is another taboo color in America, again because it is felt that a purebred GSP cannot be solid black or carry any black marking, and that the presence of black in a GSP indicates Pointer infusion. The rest of the world accepts the color. The Prussian Shorthair has a lot of black and is used not infrequently abroad to put dark color back into the eyes and coat. In fact, black and black-and-white Pointers were said to be used for that purpose. Some livers in the United States are so dark as to appear almost black, but genetically a dog cannot be black if its nose is brown. Therefore, if a judge is examining a dog whose color is in question, he or she should check the nose before passing judgment. Dark liver comes from a few lines in America and where conformation is an issue, those lines are used to enrich the faded browns of some Shorthair families.

In discussing color, it should also be noted that certain lines of purebred Shorthairs have pure white background with or without some liver patches. Some of the progeny from clandestine breedings of Pointers with Shorthairs look more like Shorthairs than some of the purebred specimens, so color alone should not be the basis for determining impure breeding. Later, we will have a detailed look at the differences between a Pointer and a Shorthair. Always keep in mind that the German Shorthaired Pointer was developed as a hunting dog, and it was introduced to America for that purpose.

The German Shorthaired Pointer is virtually free of genetic faults even though many today are strictly family pets or show dogs. Their pleasant disposition and desire to please, as well as their handsome appearance and intelligence, have made them one of the most popular breeds in the United States.

But, first and foremost, they are wonderful bird dogs with great natural ability that makes them highly suitable for the average hunter.

After years of selective breeding, the type similar to what we see today was set in the latter part of the nineteenth century in Germany. There were a variety of types emanating from different regions of Germany, but the desired type was well established by the turn of the century. The Germans were trying for a dog that could do virtually every hunting function, from trailing furred game to retrieving waterfowl, and most of all hunting upland birds. While fast and able to cover plenty of ground, the early Shorthairs did not naturally range as far as the American Pointer and setters, but in later years they were fully capable of competing with them in gun dog stakes in field trials.

As Germans emigrated to America early in the twentieth century, they brought some Shorthairs with them, as is shown in certain documented evidence. But it was not until 1925 that the GSP was formally recognized in the United States, when Dr. Charles Thornton of Missoula, Montana, imported the first of many dogs from both Germany and Austria. Others followed and, although little known until recognized by the AKC, they began to get a foothold in American hunting circles in the 1930s. After World War II, with increasing entries in dog shows and field trials, GSPs became a strong nucleus as the dog of choice by many hunters. The Shorthair did the hunting, and the hunters did not have to hunt for the dogs.

The German Shorthaired Pointer is the product not just of the latter half of the nineteenth century in Germany, but of natural selection when dogs joined up with humans more than 10,000 years ago. Many of the characteristics so prevalent in the Shorthair today are the result of thousands of years of natural selection into various types and people's breeding to fix type for the traits that best served them. The Shorthair, then, is the result of taking the best of dogs that were available to form a great hunter with good looks and a pleasant personality. The Germans gained control over type with the formation of the first GSP breed club, and the Americans followed with the German Shorthaired Pointer Club of America as the parent club of the breed. Under AKC rules, parent clubs develop the Standards for their breeds and thus set the Standards by which their breeds are judged. Following is the official Standard approved by the AKC and a description written by the father of the breed in America.

REVISED STANDARD FOR THE GERMAN SHORTHAIRED POINTER
September 1992

General Appearance

The German Shorthaired Pointer is a versatile hunter, an all-purpose gun dog capable of high performance in field and water. The judgment of Shorthairs in the show ring reflects this basic characteristic. The overall picture which is created in the observer's eye is that of an aristocratic, well balanced, symmetrical animal with conformation indicating power, endurance and agility and a look of intelligence and animation. The dog is neither unduly small nor conspicuously large. It gives the impression of medium size, but is like the proper hunter, "with a short back, but standing over plenty of ground." Symmetry and field quality are most essential. A dog in hard and lean field condition is not to be penalized; however, overly fat or poorly muscled dogs are to be penalized. A dog well balanced in all points is preferable to one with outstanding good qualities and defects. Grace of outline, clean-cut head, sloping shoulders, deep chest, powerful back, strong quarters, good bone composition, adequate muscle, well carried tail and taut coat produce a look of nobility and indicate a heritage of purposefully conducted breeding. Further evidence of this heritage is movement which is balanced, alertly coordinated and without wasted motion.

Size, Proportion, Substance

Size—height of dogs, measured at the withers, 23 to 25 inches. Height of bitches, measured all at withers, 21 to 23 inches. Deviations of one inch above or below the described heights are to be severely penalized. Weight of dogs 55 to 70 pounds. Weight of bitches 45 to 60 pounds. *Proportion*—measuring from the forechest to the rearmost projection of the rump and from the withers to the ground, the Shorthair is permissibly either square or slightly longer than he is tall. *Substance*—thin and fine bones are by no means desirable in a dog which must possess strength and be able to work over any type of terrain. The main importance is not laid so much on the size of bone but being in proper proportion to the body. Bone structure too heavy or too light is a fault. Tall and leggy dogs, dogs which are ponderous because of excess substance, doggy bitches, and bitchy dogs are to be faulted.

Head

The head is clean-cut, is neither too light nor too heavy, and is in proper proportion to the body. The eyes are of medium size, full of intelligence and expression, good-humored and yet radiating energy, neither protruding nor sunken. The eye is almond-shaped, not circular. The preferred color is dark brown. Light yellow eyes are not desirable and are a fault. Closely set eyes are to be faulted. China or wall eyes are to be disqualified. The ears are broad and set fairly high, lie flat and never hang away from the head. Their placement is just above eye level. The ears, when laid in front without being pulled, should extend to the corner of the mouth. In the case of heavier dogs, the ears are correspondingly longer. Ears too long or fleshy are to be faulted. The skull is reasonably broad, arched on the side and slightly round on top. Unlike the Pointer, the median line between the eyes at the forehead is not too

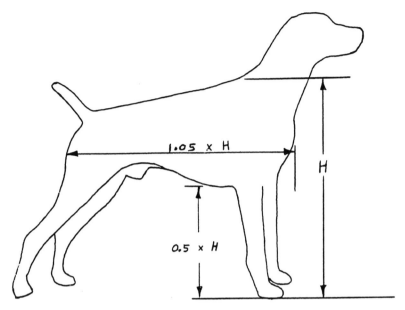

Correct Body Proportions for the German Shorthaired Pointer

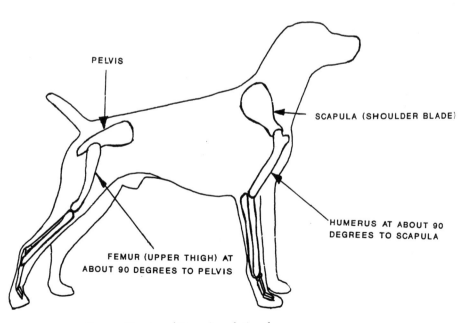

Correct Front and Rear Angulation for
the German Shorthaired Pointer

deep and the occipital bone is not very conspicuous. The foreface rises gradually from nose to forehead. The rise is more strongly pronounced in the dog than in the bitch. The jaw is powerful and the muscles well developed. The line to the forehead rises gradually and never has a definite stop as that of a Pointer, but rather a stop-effect when viewed from the side, due to the position of the eyebrows. The muzzle is sufficiently long to enable the dog to seize game properly and be able to carry it for a long time. A pointed muzzle is not desirable. The depth is in the right proportion to the length, both in the muzzle and in the skull proper. The length of the muzzle should equal the length of skull. A dish-shaped muzzle is a fault. Too many wrinkles in the forehead is a fault. The nose is brown, the larger the better, and with nostrils well opened and broad. A spotted nose is not desirable. A flesh-colored nose disqualifies. The chops fall away from the somewhat projecting nose. Lips are full and deep yet are never flewy. The teeth are strong and healthy. The molars intermesh properly. The bite is a true scissors bite. A perfect level bite is not desirable and must be penalized. Extreme overshot or undershot disqualifies.

Neck, Topline, Body

The neck is of proper length to permit the jaws reaching game to be retrieved, sloping downwards on beautifully curving lines. The nape is rather muscular, becoming gradually larger towards the shoulders. Moderate throatiness is permitted. The skin is close and tight. The chest in general gives the impression of depth rather than breadth; for all that, it is in correct proportion to the other parts of the body. The chest reaches down to the elbows, the ribs forming the thorax show a rib spring and are not perfectly round or barrel-shaped. The back ribs reach well down. The circumference of the thorax is about a hand's breadth behind elbows, so that the upper arm has room for movement. Tuckup is apparent. The back is short, strong, and straight with a slight rise from the root of the tail to the withers. The loin is strong, is of moderate length, and is slightly arched. An excessively long, roached or swayed back must be penalized. The hips are broad with hip sockets wide apart and fall slightly toward the tail in a graceful curve. A steep croup is a fault. The tail is set high and firm, and must be docked, leaving approximately 40% of its length. The tail hangs down when the dog is quiet and is held horizontally when he is walking. The tail must never be curved over the back toward the head when the dog is moving. A tail curved or bent toward the head is to be severely penalized.

Forequarters

The shoulders are sloping, movable, and well covered with muscle. The shoulder blades lie flat and are well laid back nearing a 45-degree angle. The upper arm (the bones between the shoulder and elbow joint) is as long as possible, standing away somewhat from the trunk so that the straight and closely muscled legs, when viewed from the front, appear to be parallel. Elbows which stand away from the body or are too close result in toes turning inwards or outwards and must be faulted. Pasterns are strong, short and nearly vertical with a slight spring. Loose, short-bladed or straight shoulders must be faulted. Dewclaws on the forelegs may be removed. The feet are compact, close-knit and round to spoon-shaped. The toes are sufficiently arched and heavily nailed. The pads are strong, hard and thick.

Hindquarters

Thighs are strong and well muscled. Stifles are well bent. Hock joints are well angulated and strong with straight bone structure from hock to pad. Angulation of both stifle and hock joint is such as to achieve the optimal balance of drive and traction. Hocks turn neither in nor out. Cowhocked legs are a serious fault.

Coat

The hair is short and thick and feels tough to the hand; it is somewhat longer on the underside of the tail and the back edges of the haunches. The hair is softer, thinner and shorter on the ears and the head. Any dog with long hair in the body coat is to be severely penalized.

Color

The coat may be of solid liver or a combination of liver and white such as liver and white ticked, liver patched and white ticked, or liver roan. A dog with any area of black, red, orange, lemon or tan, or a dog solid white will be disqualified.

Gait

A smooth lithe gait is essential. It is to be noted that as gait increases from the walk to a faster speed, the legs converge beneath the body.

The tendency to single track is desirable. The forelegs reach well ahead as if to pull in the ground without giving the appearance of a hackney gait. The hindquarters drive the back legs smoothly and with great power.

Temperament: The Shorthair is friendly, intelligent, and willing to please. The first impression is that of a keen enthusiasm for work without indication of nervous or flighty character.

Disqualifications: China or wall eyes. Flesh-colored nose. Extreme overshot or undershot. A dog with any area of black, red, orange, lemon, or tan, or a dog solid white.

Approved: August 11, 1992
Effective: September 30, 1992

chapter 2

Origin of the German Shorthaired Pointer

The one unquestioned fact about the origin of the German Shorthaired Pointer is its German development. The ingredients that went into what has evolved into the present-day GSP are, and no doubt will remain, a mystery, since so many variables went into the creation of the breed. In general, we can accept that the present-day GSP is a mix of one or (most likely) more pointing breeds and one or more scent hounds, with a lot of subsequent refinement. Whatever blends of other breeds were used to create the GSP, we can say with certainty that it is now a distinct and separate entity with a combination of attributes not found in any other breed.

We also know that in Germany, as in the United States, several people and the foundation of national breed clubs contributed greatly to the ultimate success and popularity of the GSP. Unfortunately, many of the breeders who contributed to the successful culmination of the ultimate goal will remain lost in the mists of history because their contributions were made anonymously. As an example, Herr Fritz Grueber breeds his Heidi to his neighbor's Rudy, and one of the pups is bought by a landowner who enjoys hunting. His male is seen by guests to his farm, and one of them breeds a female to the young male. On they go until one of the pioneer developers of the breed acquires one of the offspring, and gives it his kennel name. The kennel gets a reputation for winning at shows and field trials, and the family integrates with the best of other kennels, while continuing to be nourished by little breeders, until an outstanding line is established. The ultimate result is a Standard and the breed that a handful of individuals were seriously seeking to bring into being since the mid-1800s.

Probably the best answer to what made up the GSP is a combination of the German Pointer (if that can be defined), the old Spanish Pointer and a scent hound, but not the Bloodhound as currently defined by the official breed Standard. Added to this mix was a strong shot of English Pointer here and there, from France, England and Italy.

The question arises as to just what distinguishes the German Pointer. Where did it come from? How did it differ from French, Spanish or English Pointers? Why didn't the Germans simply refine the breed to get what they wanted, i.e., breed the desired specimens to other desired specimens? The answer to the last question is that they couldn't. They tried, hence the infusion of other breeds.

These questions all lead to another question: Where did the Pointer come from? Some say all Pointers were derived from the old Spanish Pointer and that the old Spanish Pointer always existed. No one has traced the Pointer further back than this.

One theory is that the old Spanish Pointer went to England, where the English sportsmen refined its abilities by introducing Foxhounds and maybe even Greyhounds to the ultimate pointing dog. Some say that the Pointer went to France, where it became less clumsy, and then to England, where the refinement continued. The old German Pointer, it is held by some, is a direct offshoot of the old Spanish Pointer with some of the French blood inherited en route to Germany. German breeders also maintained Pointer kennels, and one can assume some were used to develop the GSP.

It would appear that a pointing dog of some sort evolved from the dog family many centuries ago and scattered throughout the known world through traveling armies, explorers, tradesmen and royal families. What we do know about Pointers is that the old Spanish Pointer was rather clumsy and slow but had a good nose and would stand its game. Many pointing breeds do have direct lines to the old Spanish Pointer. It is likely that many of the pointing breeds derived from the same sources and became regionalized through selective or convenient breeding, and that they remained in a given area because of transportation difficulties or lack of transportation and territorial boundaries.

Thus we have the old German Pointer, which no doubt was crossed with the Spanish Pointer either directly or through its French cousins. The German Pointer appears to be a staple in German hunting dogs, and it was suitable for its purposes until a certain time in history when it was no longer considered satisfactory for prevailing hunting conditions.

Two conditions favoring pointing dogs existed throughout the world until the development of guns capable of shooting flying birds at a distance. A pointing dog was needed to locate game and point it until its owner or a group of men could slip up and throw a net over the quarry, usually a flock of game birds, or bludgeon them. Speed was not important; in fact, it was not wanted because of the method of hunting. This slow dog with a good nose that would hold its quarry was satisfactory and, outside of breeding good pointing dogs to other good ones, no real effort—as far as we know—was made to make it perform any better or improve its appearance.

The other situation was that most of the land was owned by the nobility and the very rich. The common man did not have access to much of the large land masses where game was plentiful. In fact, hunting as a sport was not

German Pointers of the early 1800s such as these exhibited a coarse, hound-like appearance the Germans sought to refine.

This illustration of Patti v. Reuden and Pommery v. Reuden appeared in *Les Races De Chiens,* published in 1897 in Deventer, Holland, by A. E. Kluwer. The author-editor was Heri De Bycandt. These dogs of 100 years ago are very similar to Shorthairs of today. Little has changed since the Germans perfected the type.

available to the commoner. Hunting, for him, was confined to more rugged areas and was more a matter of survival than sport.

When the shotgun was invented and hunting opened up for the average man, the needs in dogs changed. In addition to profits to be gained from the sale of game, the sport of hunting became widespread. Faster dogs were needed to cover vast stretches productively. Since the new dogs were faster and ranged farther from the hunter, they needed to be trainable so that they stayed on point, and they needed good noses to find game while going at a faster pace.

A number of individuals throughout Europe, and especially in Germany, wanted a dog that could do it all. The dog needed to be medium-size so as not to take up too much room in a kennel, in transport and in the home. It had to have a pleasing personality, since so many of the dogs lived in the home or in proximity to the family's everyday living style. Additionally, these people wanted a dog of pleasing appearance.

This movement began in the 1800s, advanced to a more concentrated effort in the middle of the century and pretty well reached the desired goals by the start of the twentieth century. Anyone interested in hunting game birds sooner or later came to the conclusion that the old German Pointer was not entirely satisfactory. These owners wanted to keep the tractibility of the German Pointer but improve on its speed and range and even its nose. Equally important was a dog with endurance, perseverance, courage and ferocity to stand up against wild animals while remaining gentle with people except when guarding the premises against strangers. The dog had to be able to retrieve from land and water and be equally at home with waterfowl as with upland birds.

Since most Germans were limited in their means, usually they had only one or two dogs, which had to be able to do everything. In addition to their work on flying game, they had to be good on hare, other furred game and large game. The dogs also had to be able to scent hot game and to trail cold to find furred quarry and large animals, both before being shot and afterward, when wounded animals escaped to die at a distance.

This was the objective, whether defined more closely, as with the more advantaged, or randomly by others. In the mid-1880s, transportation determined the extent of most breedings. Breedings were mostly confined to local areas. While this helped set type better than ranging all over the country, it also had limitations. Some of these dogs were better than others, but, except for word of mouth, a good dog might never be able to offer its genetic inheritance to the betterment of the breed in general. In the second half of the nineteenth century the objectives became clearer, but it was not until the last quarter of the century, with the formation of a Standard and a national breed club, that the GSP evolved pretty closely to what we have today, more than 100 years later.

By now, communications were improved and some knowledgeable and advantaged people added their influence to the breed's development. Two schools of thought emerged: one was to breed first for appearance and type; the other, to breed first for performance and then for type and appearance.

There lived in Germany at the time a handsome prince who maintained a Pointer/Setter kennel and was knowledgeable about pointing dogs and breeding. Prince Albrecht Zu Solms-Bronfels became interested in the process of developing a German Pointer and lent his considerable influence to that cause. When discussing the origin of the GSP, Prince Zu Solms-Bronfels is given credit as the major force behind the successful development of the German Shorthaired Pointer.

Although one of his early experiments resulted in a rather grotesque dog called Feldman I, Prince Solms started the process of developing a dog for function first and gradually moved toward appearance. Feldman I looked like an escapee from the Secret Island of Doctor Moreau, but, according to earlier works on the Shorthair, Prince Solms was pleased with his performance in the field. He resembled more closely the old Spanish Pointer, but his performance in the field exceeded that of the clumsier German Pointer.

The first German Pedigree Registry was formed in 1872 in Hanover, and the honor of the first dog to be listed in the registry went to Hector I, who was vastly improved over the earlier Feldman I. In 1873, Prince Solms established the Training School of Bronfels, where methods were developed to judge a dog's conformation and field ability. This was a real step forward in establishing the breed, because it was believed to have been the major influence in setting up a national breed club and a conformation and performance Standard.

Prince Solms, along with the Marquis Graf Wilcek, organized the first dog show with classes for the Shorthair, in Vienna in 1877. A breed Standard was approved in 1879. The breed was now on its way, acknowledged by Dr. Paul Kleeman, an early enthusiast inspired by Prince Solms. Dr. Kleeman, who was highly instrumental in the future progress of the breed, became president of the new breed club, ultimately called *Klub Kurzhaar,* formed in 1890. Although there were a number of individuals who played an important role in the development of the GSP, Prince Solms, by virtue of his position, experience and enthusiasm, is acknowleged as the leader. Close beside him is Dr. Kleeman, who took the breed from the evolutionary stages into the final development of the present-day German Shorthaired Pointer.

With the formation of a breed club and creation of a Standard, the GSP was now ready to move forward toward the long-sought goal of a dog with the unique characteristics suitable for modern-day hunting in Germany of all types of game. In Germany, breed Standard meant more than conformation. It included field ability as well as appearance. Prince Solms advanced the process with the creation of his training school, and Dr. Kleeman moved it forward with the creation of testing procedures embodied in the Derby in 1893. The Derby, first called Brauntiger (Brown Tiger), was renamed *Klub Deutsch-Kurzhaar* a year later.

The Derby is held each spring for dogs whelped the previous spring to test their natural instincts in the field. A set of tests must be passed in order to be certified. The dogs are further tested in the Utility Search held in the fall to evaluate both their learned and natural abilities. The fall event was renamed the "Solms-Memorial" in 1903 in honor of Prince Solms. The event is commonly referred to as the "Solms" or the "Kleeman-Solms." Dogs that qualify receive the title of Seiger. The Seigers must have both outstanding field ability and conformation that meets the Standard.

Finally, everything came together after more than fifty years of concentrated effort. Doctor Kleeman continued to upgrade the tests to meet the demand of greatly improved performances as the breed continued to progress into the twentieth century.

Shows and field trials were equally important in the development of the German Shorthaired Pointer. With the great concentration on shows throughout the world, it should never be forgotten that the GSP was developed for the purpose of hunting and not for appearance alone.

While the GSP was being developed in Germany, it is important to note what was taking place about the same time in England and America. On May 1, 1866, at the country estate of Cannock Chase, Staffordshire, England, the first recorded field trial was held. A scorecard type of system was used to place the dogs. Although an informal field trial had been held the previous year, the 1866 event is listed as the first pointing-breed field trial because it was recorded and was judged on a uniform basis. The trial was for Pointers and Setters, since other pointing breeds either were not in existence or were largely unknown. In whatever manner the English Pointer came into being, it was a different Pointer from those on the continent, certainly a far cry from the old Spanish Pointer or the old German Pointer.

Although Pointers and Setters in America were not unlike those in England, from where most of the stock had come, it took eight more years— until 1874—for the first field trial for Pointers and Setters to be held on this side of the Atlantic Ocean. The trial was held near Memphis, Tennessee, and attracted an entry of nine. The first dog to win an organized field trial in America was an English Setter named Knight, owned by H. C. Pritchett. From those inauspicious beginnings, field trials flourished in England and caught on like wildfire in the United States.

Thus field trials were well underway in England and America while the Shorthair was still in its formative stage in Germany. It took twenty-seven more years after the first trial in England before the GSP came under formal testing in the field with the creation of the Derby.

Early field trials in the United States were held under the auspices of the American Field Registry, and the first American Kennel Club trial was held in 1924 at the English Setter Club Grounds in Medford, New Jersey. The English Setter grounds are still being used for field trials in spite of the advancing developments marching ever outward from Philadelphia.

As the Germans concentrated on developing the ideal dog for hunters, the climate for such a dog was developing in England and America. Imported Ringneck pheasants had really taken hold in the United States along with all its natural game birds, and the sport of field trials was well on its way. Field trials were modeled on the big-going Pointers and setters used in plantation hunting in the South and dogs used in the grouse woods in the Northeast.

But, in the United States, as in Germany and England, the average hunter wanted a dog with a good nose and style that was more attuned to working with a man on foot. Unbeknownst to most Americans, such a dog was well on its way, but it would take several more decades before it reached the United States.

chapter 3

Coming to America

In his book *The Complete German Shorthaired Pointer,* published by Howell Book House in 1951, author Herr H. F. Seiger had this to say about the importation of the German Shorthaired Pointer to America:

It would be of great importance to all fanciers of our dog in America and to breeders as well, if all imported German Shorthairs with verified pedigrees were re-registered in the American Studbook, which is particularly advocated by the following reasons: Many interested American breeders, who are not yet sufficiently acquainted with this breed and its blood-lines in particular, had some Shorthair experts here in Germany to select a stud dog and a brood bitch to be mated to each other, with the greatest quality in their characteristics and similarity in their general appearance. To human knowledge, such matings should be successful. Against this stands the fact that pups out of such a mating should not be registered in America on account of the restriction, that an imported dog can only be paired with a consort, which has already been registered in U.S. Otherwise, it would not be eligible for registration. By this restriction many a good prospect is condemned to failure and as a consequence many less promising matings will be done.

We should also consider that in prewar time unscrupulous breeders certainly did not export their best breeding stock. It is quite sure, that dogs from former imports—with few exceptions—yield much to the quality of our dogs today. They were only the most passionate fanciers, who brought their breeding stock despite the great shortage of food through these hard times and there is no doubt that they exclusively kept their really outstanding stud dogs and brood bitches. Thus the years of want and need became the executor to what was but average. If such outstanding producers cannot fully display their eminent qualities in U.S.A. on account of the restrictions that have been imposed on the breed, immense preju-dice will be done to its improvement and dissemination. Still, I am of the belief, that our American Shorthair fanciers will very soon meet with consideration on the part of their authorities on breeding.

Herr Seiger, of course, was correct in his assumptions. Once clubs were formed and a Standard was accepted, and professionals lent their expertise to training, the German Shorthaired Pointer flourished in the United States. From about the time Herr Seiger's book was being published in English, America was already on its way with a strong nucleus of German imports, as well as outstanding dogs from adjacent countries, particularly Austria and Denmark.

Two years after the publication of Herr Seiger's important work on the development of the breed, an interesting book was published by the fledgling German Shorthaired Pointer Club of America (GSPCA) in Minneapolis. This book was titled *German Shorthaired Pointer Activities,* edited by George J. Ruediger, an important breeder and exponent of the Shorthair in his own right. The preface credits the National Breed Committee of the GSPCA as the organizing body for the book. The book contains sketches from major breeders of the time and provides an important link between the first importers of the GSP in America and the post–World War II importers. Several books on the German Shorthaired Pointer have appeared between then and now by highly respected authorities such as C. Bede Maxwell, Gertrude Dapper and Georgina Byrne of Australia. Much interesting information can be found in those books.

It is not the intention of this author to plow a lot of old ground other than to show linkage of some of today's outstanding dogs with those later and earlier imports. Many good dogs will not be covered in this book because of space limitations, and many outstanding fanciers will also be missing. However, it is the author's intention to provide a complete description of what a German Shorthaired Pointer is and where it stands today. Most of the noteworthy people involved in the success of the breed and many of the most outstanding dogs that have been developed will be covered. Some very important people involved with dogs from the past have been overlooked or afforded scant mention in earlier works. I believe these individuals and dogs deserve more than passing mention for their great contributions to the wonderful dogs we have today.

Let it be said from the outset that not all that glitters is gold. Some of the big-winning dogs are not necessarily what they are purported to be. The origins of some of these big winners are at the very least suspect. Standing staked out at a trial, some of them would defy imagination as to what breed they are. Color is not necessarily a determinant of breed. There are and always have been white Shorthairs. After all, in their development, the color of some of their ancestors was definitely white. We still have considerable white influence from Denmark. There is no reason to question a dog's purity solely on the basis of color—white or liver. But we can most certainly question some of the conformation.

I cannot tell you with any legal certainty that any German Shorthair has ever been outcrossed with a Pointer, as the AKC calls the breed, or the English Pointer as it is more appropriately described. However, many (of we) realists have fairly strong convictions that a great deal of outcrossing to English Pointers took place in order to get more run and an advantage over pure Shorthairs in field trials. We see some terrible examples of such clandestine breedings at field trials and we see terrible performances—simply outlaw runs that stop only when the erring dog crosses a game bird and remembers the threat of a shock collar to stop and remain on point. Even at that, they frequently have to be hammered into staying by strong verbal abuse from the handler, hard charging on his steed to where the pointing dog awaits implementation of the "riot act."

Despite these instances, there are still many wonderful purebred German Shorthaired Pointers performing beautifully in field trials, and some have held their own in highly respected Pointer/Setter trials. A good GSP, judged correctly on its hunting and bird-handling ability, can compete in AKC Gun Dog Stakes or American Field Shooting Dog Stakes with any dog.

The very real danger to the breed in America is the overemphasis on range at the expense of high-class bird work. We hear about "the drag of the breed" toward one mediocre center in performance, and criticism of anyone who cannot appreciate an outlaw dog running into the next county, never deviating into any likely cover along the way. The dog must run with purpose and under control. This is why the GSP was brought to America. We already had Pointers and Setters, but more on this situation in later chapters. Meanwhile, let's get back to some of the basics and to what was happening in the United States while the breed was beginning to reach its full potential in Germany.

There were three great waves of importations to the United States and, interestingly enough, those dogs came into areas of the country where upland game hunting was at its zenith. The first wave was almost singular in nature through the efforts of one man. The second wave began in the 1930s after Dr. Charles Thornton, then of Missoula, Montana, got his first imports, and extended to the beginnings of World War II. The third wave came immediately after the end of the war.

The Shorthair was brought to the United States to fill the need for a dog that could do what the Germans set out to accomplish seventy-five years before: to hunt to the gun with unflagging desire and style, move through the cover with intelligence and speed, stand on point with intensity and retrieve what was brought down from land or water. On top of that, the GSP offered an attractive appearance and pleasing personality.

In observing hundreds of photographs of dogs from the 1930s on, type was pretty well set, and present-day Shorthairs do not appear much different from dogs of that era. The main change is that there are more good dogs because of the greater awareness and acceptance of the breed. Inevitably, along with the greater numbers, there are also some pretty mediocre specimens. In general, however, the chances of acquiring a quality Shorthair are pretty high. Most continue to exhibit natural hunting abilities and, with a little training, make useful companions in the field that satisfy the needs and expectations of the average hunter. The good GSPs continue to demonstrate the high degree of performance envisioned by the breed's creators. As a breed, perhaps the basic difference in today's Shorthairs from those of earlier decades is that they are faster, cover more ground and have greater endurance. This is the result of the many trials in which the best are tested against the best in competition and the AKC hunting tests, where they are tested against a predetermined standard of performance.

chapter 4

Comparison of the German Shorthaired Pointer with the Pointer

Although the Pointer was used extensively in the development of the German Shorthair, the two breeds differ in several important ways, from the tip of the nose to the end of the tail and chest and feet. The Shorthair is an upland game specialist for all kinds of cover, while the Pointer is a coursing dog with the desire and equipment to carry it well over the horizon in quest for birds. Although the Shorthair can also run for a certain distance, it is more suited for closer work, with fast coverage of all the likely spots in which game may be found, whether in heavy brush or along hedgerows. The Shorthair's stockier build allows it to burst through the cover. The breed also performs well as a water retriever, having strong instinct and desire for water work. All dogs can swim, including the Pointer, but the Shorthair is expecially built for the task; its assets including a tight coat and webbed feet.

HEAD

German Shorthair

The skull is reasonably broad, arched on the sides and slightly rounded on top. The scissura (median line between the eyes at the forehead) is not too deep, and the occipital bone is only slightly pronounced. The line to the forehead rises gradually and is slightly pronounced. It rises gradually and never has a definite stop, but rather a stop effect when viewed from the side due to the position of the eyebrows. The foreface rises gradually from nose to forehead. However, the entire head never gives the impression of tapering to a point.

Pointer

The skull is of medium width, approximately as wide as the length of the muzzle, resulting in an impression of length rather than width. There is a slight furrow between the eyes. There should be a pronounced stop. From this point forward, the muzzle is of good length, with the nasal bone so formed that the nose is slightly higher at the tip than the muzzle at the stop. Parallel planes of the skull and muzzle are equally acceptable.

Ears are slightly longer than the German Shorthair's.

Eyes are rounded compared to the almond shape of the Shorthair's. Both should be dark brown, the darker the better.

CHEST

The Shorthair has a broader chest than that of the Pointer, which has more depth than breadth. The chest on both breeds leaves enough room for the legs to move freely. The Shorthair appears more compact than the Pointer and is approximately an inch shorter. The Pointer Standard says a good Pointer cannot be the wrong height or the wrong color, whereas the wrong color in a Shorthair is a disqualification and an inch over or under considered a serious fault.

Bones on the Pointer are oval, versus a more rounded shape for the Shorthair.

FEET

The Shorthair's feet are compact, close-knit and round to spoon-shaped. The Pointer's feet are oval with long, closely set arched toes.

TAIL

The Shorthair's tail is set high and firm and must be docked leaving 40 percent of the length. The Pointer's tail is left undocked; it is carried no higher than 20 degrees above the line of the back.

COLOR

German Shorthair

The coat may be of solid liver or any combination of liver and white, such as liver and white ticked, liver spotted and white ticked or liver roan. A dog with any area of black, red, orange or tan or a solid white dog will be disqualified.

Pointer

Pointers may be liver, lemon, black or orange, either in combination with white or solid color. A good Pointer cannot be a bad color. In the darker colors, the nose should be black or brown; in the lighter shades, it may be lighter, or flesh-colored.

The typical German Shorthaired Pointer.

The typical Pointer.

RUNNING STYLE

The two breeds also differ in their respective running styles. The Shorthair has strong drive off the rear quarters and has a long reach, though not as long as that of the Pointer, which runs more like a coursing hound.

In summary, there is a definite difference between the two breeds, although both are used for the same purpose. A Pointer would be a definite asset when hunting off horseback in southern fields, but for all-around hunting nothing can beat the Shorthair.

chapter 5

The "Everyuse Dog"

AUTHOR'S NOTE: The following article by C. R. Thornton, M.D., early breeder and importer of German Shorthaired Pointers, appeared in the July 1, 1929 issue of the *American Kennel Gazette*.

MEET THE "EVERYUSE DOG"

*Sold Abroad as the German Shorthaired Pointer,
Breed Wins Friends Here*

By C. R. Thornton, M.D.

There has been as much printers ink spread on the publication of the all-purpose dog as any other topic in dogdom, including everything from the Airedale to the Skye Terrier. We are living in the age of economic concentration. What would our farmer do, today, if he had to go back to the old grain cradle? What would we do without our automobiles, our modern linotype, presses, scores of electrical developments, and thousands of other conveniences that were unknown fifty years ago?

The styles in dogs change just the same as all other utilities of man. You who are speeding along toward your half century will remember the English Pug, with his tawny coat and doughnut tail. He was the popular house dog at that time. Today, he is almost a curiosity. Many other changes have come and gone among fanciers. There are, however, a few breeds that have stood the test of time and are still as popular as they were centuries ago; but with marked improvement. I refer to two or three breeds of hounds, Pointers and setters. Looking back at the old pictures of these breeds, you would hardly recognize them as compared with our dogs of today.

I am in a position to know that here, in the United States, we have a newcomer showing up on the horizon. It is none other than the new German

Pointer or "everyuse" dog, registered in Europe as the German Short-haired Pointer. Before entering into the merits of this breed, be it understood that I do not expect this dog to replace our Pointers and setters of field trial caliber. But as a companionable, intelligent, shooting dog, that will handle all varieties of upland game birds, water fowl, and most any game man cares to pursue, he is par excellence.

A sketch of the origin of this breed should be both instructive and interesting at this time. It is generally known that our English Pointer was developed from crossing the old Spanish Pointer with the English Foxhound. By selective, careful breeding the English Pointer has come into his own, and today occupies an enviable position in the eyes and minds of all admirers of this wonderful breed.

The Spanish Pointer when introduced into Germany was crossed with the Bloodhound. The Germans were well pleased with their product and stuck to this cross for years. They bred for intelligence and obedience first; placing type last. The color they chose was chestnut brown, as this color is not so noticeable and easily distinguished by game.

When, finally, they perfected the breed, they had a highly intelligent, obedient, flat-coated, chestnut brown heavy dog, that bred true to type, resembling more the bloodhound than the Pointer. With the exception of his slowness, he possessed some sterling qualities. He was absolutely fearless, and was a born retriever on land or water. The Germans worked him on all feathered game, furbearing animals, roe deer, bear, and wild boar.

The family tree is as follows: Spanish Pointer cross with Bloodhound made old German Pointer. German Pointer cross with English Pointer made German shorthaired Pointer or "all-purpose" dog.

By this breeding you will note, at a glance there is a double cross of the old Spanish Pointer and a single cross each of Bloodhound and Foxhound. This accounts for the superior scenting ability of this breed. I have seen them pick up a scent and work it out, time and again, that my setters, with good nose would pass up.

As we approach the present age of high speed, the Teutons began to realize their shooting dog was too slow. Fifty years ago, field trials were unknown in Germany and Austria. It has been about forty years since the sportsmen of those two empires organized and commenced these exhibitions with the express idea of improving their shooting dogs.

They began crossing the old German Pointer with the English Pointer of which there were many on the estates of the nobility in both Germany and Austria. With characteristic German thoroughness, they mated their choicest specimens, and we have, today, the *everyuse* or all-purpose dog. The coat of this breed is a little longer than that of our English Pointer, more wiry in texture, and compares closely to the coat of the harp seal, being very resistant to water.

They vary in color from solid brown to brown and white, and brown and white finely ticked with brown, known as tiger color. This color is also classified in those that are ticked as to light or dark tiger according to the amount of white or brown showing through the coat. They are never entirely white, and breed true to type and form. In short, they are built from the ground up to stand hard usage. Well muscled, deep chested, and weigh from fifty to seventh-five pounds. Ranging from eighteen to twenty-six inches at the shoulder.

The females, naturally, approach the minimum measurements. They have beautiful intelligent heads, expressive eyes, varying from various shades of olive to brown and long, low hung ears. They are essentially a family or one-man dog. Good disposition. Love to be caressed. Take kindly to children, and show almost human intelligence in looking after small tots. As companions and pals, they are next to man.

As hunting dogs they will hunt anything you care to hunt, from duck to deer. Primarily, they are bird dogs; but I have never attempted hunting anything from a mouse to a moose, that they were not ready and willing to assist. I have used them with equal success, here, in Montana, on all of our upland birds including quail, Chinese pheasants, Hungarian pheasants, prairie chicken, sage hen, blue grouse, brush pheasants, fool-hen and jack snipe. They point staunchly, and retrieve with passion. As duck retrievers, they are perfectly at home. With their superior nose, and with little experience they are as nearly non-slip retrievers as it is possible to develop on land or water.

My first season duck shooting over these dogs brought me many surprises. One stormy day, I was hidden among the jack pines, above a large dam. It was snowing, the river was afloat with slush ice. My only companion—a two-year-old female—Senta, her first season on ducks. Fortunately, both luck and ducks came our way. She handled them as if she had years of experience at the game, paying no attention to the icy water. Finally, I winged a large mallard, the daddy of them all. When he struck the water, Senta was ordered to "fetch."

The wise old bird put on all steam and was making full speed ahead. When overtaken, he was better than one hundred yards out. He ducked and dove and did all the stunts known to his kind. The race continued for thirty minutes. Mr. Mallard began to decide he was spending too much time under the water and began to maneuver for the shore. Finally, with a desperate effort, he came up on the bank and made for the brush.

I had to walk around a point which took several minutes. When I came up to the pair, Senta was frozen on point as staunch as a rock. The duck had crawled into heavy brush. I ordered her to "fetch." Instantly she obeyed and delivered the bird to hand. The most thrilling bit of retrieving I have ever witnessed. Repeatedly, I have had this breed point ducks when cover and conditions were right, just as staunchly as any other game bird.

Reports come to me from Cuba, of a puppy, less than a year old, retrieving eleven quail without fault, following a barrage. From old Mexico, I have reports of perfect work of this breed on wild turkeys, deer, wild pig, ducks, geese, bobcat and all upland game birds. The writer concludes his praises by saying: "Truly he is an all-purpose dog."

Differing from some Pointers and setters, their hunting of other game does not detract from their bird ability; but I am positive they should be broken on birds before they are put on other game.

For range and speed, they equal our setters and Pointers of shooting dog class, ranging, ordinarily, from two to four hundred yards and sometimes as much as a quarter of a mile away. However, it all depends on the cover. Heavy cover is hunted by them just as eagerly as is the open. Pointing and backing are natural with them. At the tender age of three months, if given a chance, I have seen them point and back like an old dog; and at four to four and a half months, they were almost perfect shooting dogs. Do not think, for a moment, that they just naturally knew this. In both instances these puppies, self-hunted, daily, with their mothers, from the time they were six to seven weeks old and were on game daily. If left in the drawing room or behind the kitchen stove, you cannot expect these results.

I have had a few of these dogs in my kennels that were just as adapted to handling stock as a German Shepherd. They were natural heelers, but I discourage this trait for fear of their becoming injured. Their value as breeding stock was too great to take such a risk.

The tail is docked at the age of six or eight days. The reason for docking is, the dogs are merry-tailed fellows when making game. When hunting in heavy cover, the tail soon becomes sore and bleeds freely, soiling the dog and everything he comes in contact with. The appearance is much improved by docking; as many of them have long, thick tails which gives them more of a hound appearance.

Some buyers have insisted that their puppy not be docked. In that case, we give careful study to the individuals and select puppies with keen, short, whip-like tails. Most, however, have thick, heavy tails, which is a trait carried over from their early ancestors.

They are not quarrelsome, and seldom pick a fight, but are capable of taking care of themselves against all comers when called upon the defend themselves.

We hear much about this breed and that breed being the real all-purpose dog. I am thoroughly familiar with all Sporting breeds. I have known an individual Airedale to point. I also knew a German Shepherd to do the same, but as a breed they will not do it. As a breed, the German all-purpose dog will do it all and do it well.

The breed is practically self-trained, if given a chance on game. I have used them in the coldest of weather, in snow and ice, alongside of long-haired retrievers and have never seen one bothered with ice balls between its toes or about its body or thighs. They are merry, busy hunters, body scenting and pointing birds with just as much style and staunchness as any Pointer or setter ever had.

The earlier they are worked on game, the better. During my early experience with them, I thought they did not begin to hunt as early as our setters and Pointers; but I soon found, if given a chance, they were just as adept at hunting as any of the Pointers.

I find it a mistake to give puppies any command or order when working them on birds. The word *steady* or *careful*, should not be given when they are on point, as they are over anxious to obey, and are very apt to quit their point and return to you. Hallooing or harsh commands are not needed, and whipping is liable to spoil your student.

You can praise or correct them in the same voice, and they thoroughly appreciate being told how well they have performed. With them, as with all other bird dogs, shooting over them should be the last and not the first lesson.

After they have become thoroughly familiar with handling birds, I have picked them up, when on point, and carried them twenty feet or more and dropped them. When they hit the ground they were still frozen on point. When thus handled, you cannot call them off point or force them on to their birds. They are past masters on crippled game.

In the auto or about the house you are not bothered with a mass of unsightly long hair. They are more than anxious to obey commands. As a rule they bark-treed on game that tree, and give tongue when trailing four-footed animals. I find them a sensible, intelligent watch dog.

After four years of breeding and handling these dogs, I have come to the conclusion that they are the greatest all-around dog ever produced.

chapter 6

Charles Thornton—Pillar of the Breed

Dr. Charles Thornton was a far greater influence on the establishment of the German Shorthaired Pointer in America than most fanciers realize. Almost everyone who cares to look into the background of their Shorthairs beyond the first generation knows that Dr. Thornton imported the first Shorthair of record to the United States in 1925. What most people don't realize is the extent of his importations and their impact on the breed then and today. Scratch the surface of a high percentage of big-winning show or field Shorthairs today, and you will find a Thornton dog behind it.

Dr. Thornton grew up on a farm in Ohio where all the animals, even his first dog, had to perform useful functions. The dog had to be able to kill rats as well as perform other farm chores before young Thornton could have the pleasure of his hunting abilities. Even then, the dog was expected to supply game for the table. In those days, any dog that could perform would do, and owning a purebred was considered a distinct luxury. The Setters were the kings of upland game dogs then, followed by Pointers, which, of course, have come to surpass the Setter breeds in popularity if not capabilities.

Not much was known about Dr. Thornton beyond his dog activities, and a study of his life would no doubt form the basis of an interesting biography. We know that he became a medical doctor and moved to Missoula, Montana, where he bought a farm and raised Swiss dairy cattle and draft horses. He had a kennel full of Setters, which he used to hunt the vast supply of native birds on the Montana hills and valleys. When he grew older, Dr. Thornton moved to Siloam Springs, Arkansas. He contributed greatly to the establishment of Chinese (Ringneck) pheasants in the United States as well as to dog breeding.

What sets Dr. Thornton apart from all others is the fact that he imported the first recorded German Shorthaired Pointer to America in the late spring of 1925. Although there may have been other Shorthairs brought to America by immigrants or their American relatives, there is no official record of them.

Pioneer breeder Dr. Charles Thornton (right) visits with George Ruediger of Minnesota, circa 1950.

Not only did Dr. Thornton import the first GSP, he built a whole family of Shorthairs that were widely distributed throughout the United States. They became the pillar of the breed in America in fact as well as fancy.

Consider the period and you realize how remarkable his accomplishments were. Airplanes were in their infancy. If you wanted to have a dog shipped in, you had to use the railroad or drive to your destination in an early, not always reliable, automobile over a poor network of roads more suitable for horses. By rail, you had to ship as freight and be dependent on the people who handled the freight. Now, consider importing a dog from Europe. The dog had to be shipped first by rail, automobile or truck to the port and then put on a ship that took weeks to cross the Atlantic. Then the dog was transshipped by rail to the nearest station of its final destination and finally transported by truck or auto to the buyer.

Shipping a dog all the way to Montana from the East Coast in 1925 took considerable time, and it would take many days, or even weeks, for a dog shipped from Montana to almost anywhere to reach its destination.

Simply from a logistical perspective, shipping a dog anywhere during the early part of the twentieth century was an arduous undertaking. Communications also were not nearly as sophisticated as they are today. How did people learn about breeders and dogs? The fact remains that, in spite of all these obstacles, they did, and they bought. From the very first, Dr. Thornton sold dogs all over the United States, and he sold a lot of them.

The first dog to arrive at Dr. Thornton's kennel was an in-whelp bitch named Senta v. Hohenbruck (Rih v. Hohenbruck ex Susi v. Hohenbruck). The white and liver, ticked bitch was bred by Eduard Rindt, of Bruck an der Leita, Austria, and was whelped on January 30, 1924.

Senta was bred to Treff v. Hohenbruck before leaving Austria, which resulted in a litter of four males and four females whelped on July 4, 1925. Certainly an auspicious occasion, it marked a grand Fourth of July celebration for the new American citizen.

Senta and her seven surviving puppies were registered in the *American Field Stud Book* in 1926 as German Shorthairs, not German Shorthaired Pointers. They were all registered to Dr. Thornton, with Eduard Rindt listed as the breeder. The American Kennel Club did not recognize the German Shorthaired Pointer until 1930, and much controversy surrounded the name that would be finally conferred on the breed.

Dr. Thornton used several family names in registering his dogs throughout the tenure of his breeding activities. As a result, his contribution is not fully reached through the passing years until one looks at individual pedigrees. He called his first litter *Everyuse,* tying in with the German objective of developing a dog with many functions, all of which were useful to Dr. Thornton on his ranch. The term meant that the GSP could do it all: find, point and retrieve upland birds, track and find rabbits and other furred game, retrieve waterfowl and serve as a livestock protector. He also used *Brednight* as a kennel name. Puppies from his first litter were registered as Bob and King (both males) and Friskey, Pep, Queen and Smarty (females). In 1928, Dr. Thornton began registering dogs with the family name *Bitterwurzel,* a German version of bitterroot, for the Bitterroot Valley in which his ranch was situated.

Interestingly, Dr. Thornton registered another import in 1926 called Treu v. Saxony, bred by Ewald Manske of Kostritz Thur, Germany, and whelped March 21, 1923. The white and liver, ticked male was sired by Dewet Frankenstadt v. Kennitztal ex Emma v. Sperlingsberg. Dr. Thornton was not as fond of Treu as a stud as of some of his other imports because of his very large size. He used Treu sparingly until he could import another stud dog, and that next import was a good one whose name is in the background of many fine Shorthairs today.

Dr. Thornton was very satisfied both with his new male's field performance and his conformation. He was the great John Neuforsthaus, whelped May 9, 1926, by Taps Harrachstal v. der Burgewiese ex Helga Neuforsthaus. The breeder was Gilbert Carolath, Hammersmuehl, Germany. John Neuforsthaus was registered in 1927.

Senta v. Hohenbruch, the first recorded German Shorthaired Pointer in America, was imported from Austria by Dr. Charles Thornton and registered in 1925 in the *American Field Stud Book. Wayne Ward*

John Neuforsthaus, whelped in 1926, was heavily endowed with Altenau and May-lust bloodlines. Imported by Dr. Thornton, John was his second stud dog and was considered one of his best.

Dr. Thornton said he became interested in the German Shorthaired Pointer through an article he read in a January or February 1925 issue of the *National Sportsman.* "I saw an article with three pictures of Eduard Rindt's German Shorthaired Pointers," he later wrote. Within a matter of months he had made contact with Herr Rindt and bought Senta, along with a male that was killed in an auto accident the day he was to be shipped.

Dr. Thornton's romance with the German Shorthaired Pointer is described in an article he wrote in 1953 for a book called *German Shorthaired Pointer Activities,* edited by George J. Ruediger, himself a strong devotee of the GSP. The book was published by the National Breed Committee of the German Shorthaired Pointer Club of America, Inc., the forerunner of the current German Shorthaired Pointer Club of America. The article follows:

MY EXPERIENCE WITH THE
GERMAN SHORTHAIRED POINTER

by C. R. Thornton, M.D.

Rather than leave the high point for my closing sentence, I am going to wax bold and put it first. The German Shorthaired Pointer exceeds all that I had ever expected to find in one dog and then has some to spare. I was compelled by circumstances to be an all purpose dog man. I was born and raised on a farm in central Ohio where rats and chickens thieves were bad. My Dad, being a practical man, compelled me to have a dog that would kill rats with enthusiasm and serve as a watch dog besides. I always had a talent for getting anything out of a dog that he might have stored away in his latent brain cells. When a new dog came to our place, I went at the rat killing game with a vengeance. As soon as I had him ready for demonstration he was put on trial before my judge (Dad). In a very short time I had him barking at any stranger that got near the house. My dog's education at home was then complete. Next he was my hunting pal. He had to be able to handle rabbits and possum as that was my main source of pin money. Squirrel came in next which was always welcome on mother's table. My first hunting implements were . . . a special hickory club with a slight crook in it, rocks and a home-made bow and arrow. With these mastered I got away with a lot of rats and small game. I finally graduated to an old 20 gauge shotgun bored out from an old rifle. This I had to stand on a stump to reload, but I did the work. When Mr. Rabbit got up he had to get into the brush pretty fast, or I put it on him. So you will see why I early became an all purpose dog lover. I had two setters that graced my ownership before I went away to college. They were genuine all purpose dogs, but it took a lot of work and patience to develop them. It was in the January or February issue of the National Sportsman, I saw an article with three pictures of Eduard Rindt's German Shorthaired Pointers. I read and reread this article, looked at the pictures, and looked again and again. Finally I said to my wife, "If those dogs don't cost a million dollars, I am going to buy a pair." I got

Mr. Rindt's ad from the National Sportsmen, and in the next mail I had a letter on its way to him. On the second letter out I had bought a pair of dogs, the bitch to be bred before shipping. One day in early August here came the bitch but no dog. He was killed by automobile the day they were supposed to be shipped. I met Senta at the train and hurried up to her crate. I said, "Hello, Senta." Twenty-four days in a crate and she wanted out. She almost tore the crate up. "There is the man I am looking for," she seemed to say, and we were pals from that minute on. In due time she whelped seven puppies sired by Treff v. Hohenbruck. Three of them I kept as a foundation breeding stock and the rest were soon sold. I had at this time seven good setters. I hunted them together the first season. Before the next year rolled around I had sold all my setters but two and I loaned them out and have never had any desire to go back to the setters again. The facts were when the setters had finished their work, the German Shorthaired Pointer was ready for any and all kinds of other duty that might come his way.

Senta was as near human as a dog could be, did most unpredictable things. As a retriever she could have competed in a class of retrievers taking all breeds as they come. I have never yet seen her equal. On all upland birds she was equally good and on ducks she would sneak, crawl or do everything she could to get to point them for you. Saw her one time work a winged mallard for thirty minutes in slush ice during a blizzard until the duck died. On another occasion she trailed a winged cock pheasant over a mile through wild roses, brier brush and everything he could find trying to shake her. This bird had a thirty-minute start on her. I could lay my gun and hunting coat down and tell her to watch them, and that is what she did. She had a kind and gentle disposition, but I tried her out with a stranger on the gun and coat guarding. The minute a stranger attempted to touch any guarded belongings she became vicious as a lion, and I'm sure she would have fought to her death to defend the article or killed the offender if he had insisted. Just leave them alone was all she wanted. I could write a book on this one dog alone. Senta died at the age of four years just two weeks before she was due to whelp from that great dog, John Neuforsthaus. Blood poisoning due to a barbed wire cut on one of her teats was the cause. Money could not have bought her.

John Neuforsthaus was the fourth dog I imported. By this time I began to get wiser on the importing game and from now on I did not order a dog that had not had winnings on the bench and in the field. John had both and was capable of winning either on the bench or in the field in stiffest competition. Brains like a man and he used them. He saved the life of my kennel man or at least saved him from a bad goring by a stray bull. The bull was charging the man and was almost on him when John came into the picture. The first bite from his powerful jaws changed the bull's mind and before he got out of the pasture old John showed him a lot of tricks that the average cow dog had never read about. One day we had a young mule down that would not get up. I said, "bite his rear, John." He ran in and all he got the first round was a mouthful of hair. I said, "Oh, bite him." That time when he ran and shut down on the mule, the mule got up so fast it looked like the ground had fallen out from under him.

He knew we did not allow kennel fights, and he always stopped them like a well-trained policeman.

I mentioned these facts to show the great versatility of this breed. Every hunt I had with him was filled with new thrills. He knew that I killed all hunting cats I found in the field, so he did it for me if he ran onto one. If he got one up a tree he barked until I came and shot it out and then went on with his hunting. You know there is no closed season for a hunting cat. He never killed a cat at home or in the barn. This fellow sired many fine litters of pups but was hung by a careless attendant being tied with a chain long enough to let him jump over a partition. He had many years ahead of him at the time of his death. A $1500 offer did not even tempt me. In training young dogs he was worth more than any two men I ever had. Young Fritz v. Bitterwurzel was a pup out of John and one of his own daughters. He was an exact duplicate of his illustrious sire, with the exception of his light tiger color. An outstanding young dog. I have pictures of him retrieving wild geese out of the Snake River when he was nine months old and the river was full of slush ice. After siring a few fine litters of pups he was poisoned by hired help whom I had caught stealing from me. Fritz knew we did not kill hen birds and soon learned when he was pointing hens to back off and go on with his hunting. If a hen flushed wild on him he paid no attention to it but if a cock bird flushed he would stop, look back at you and bark and bawl like a hound telling you that it was no fault of his, that the bird must have been a coward.

Now one may say he is just telling about his good ones. No, that is not the fact in this case. I have many more than I would love to tell you about just as thrilling and as outstanding as any I have described but time and space forbid me to tell more. Dianna v. Otterstein, Jero v. Buchwald, Montana Bell, Nancy v. Hohenbruck, Seiger Holla Second, and many more should have their names on the honor roll but they will stay by me until death erases my memory.

I was once asked what we could do to improve the German Shorthaired Pointer. That is a good question. It is a crime the way this breed was abused in their early history in the United States. There was one man in a nearby state that crossed them with the German Wirehaired Pointer and gave out papers as pure bred GSPs on them. I have pictures in my desk of one especially that I remember that was sent to me—"a registered GSP," with a letter asking me if I thought he would make a good stud dog. A blind man could feel around with a stick and tell he was half Springer. Also had pictures of some beautiful pups sent me by one of the early officers of the breed here in the U. S. that were half Springer. Fact is they registered them falsely from Chesapeake to every traveling hound that happened along.

Breeding, itself, alone is an art that few men ever conquer.

My hot pen was constructed out of welded non-climbable wire six feet high with a wire top over it and wire buried in the ground 18 inches deep, well tamped in with rock. I had a special boarded breeding pen to the side so I knew what I was breeeding and when. I had at one time 23 brood matrons and four imported stud dogs. Raised over 200 litters of this breed and never made a false paper in the lot. Remember in the Irish Setter they went to breeding for champions. You all will admit they developed a beautiful dog but ruined him for bird work. Don't tell me no. I have owned them, broken them and they are away down the list when it comes to fine bird dogs.

Personally I would like to see any German Shorthaired Pointer be compelled to have so much field winning before he could become a bench champion and I love a good looking dog. Be honest in your making papers, honest in your dealings with your fellow men, do not cater to bench alone and the German Shorthaired Pointer will be out in front for many years to come. I believe I was the first man to register them in the U.S. I had a time getting by with them. Over a year and then they insisted on registering them as German Shorthair. I still contend that this means any German Shorthaired dog, as many German dogs are dressed in short hair. The terminal name should be Pointer, or as it is in German—Vostehund, meaning pointing dog.

Between the two Wars I subscribed to two of the leading German hunting journals and was a member of the German Shorthaired Pointer Club. In this way I kept a close tab on what was doing in German Sporting dogs. During my close watch about 80 percent of all registered gun dogs were German Shorthair Pointers. Some of the breeds that are now trying to be rejuvenated here in the U.S. were popular in the early 16th Century in Germany and at that time were controlled by the Royalty of Germany. If my memory serves me right, there were only about 250 to 300 of them registered each year in Germany according to the published records. The point is this, don't be led astray by catchy high-priced ads. The German Shorthaired Pointer is still the choice of German sportsmen today, and if you were to order a Gebrauchshund from Germany today you would get a German Shorthaired Pointer.

In closing it is my opinion to a careful buyer, you can get a better dog in U. S. today than you can get in Germany. The GSP suffered the same as the German people did. Guns were taken away from them, etc. You can't develop a good dog without birds or guns. Col. Herbert Zemke, of German cleavage, American born and an enthusiastic German Shorthaired Pointer owner, told me that it was pitiable the condition, and the way this breed and all others had suffered during the war. Left to rustle for themselves, stolen and carried away by U. S. soldiers. That it would take a long time for them to build up to where they were before the war. If I am fortunate enough to win a home in that Everlasting Kingdom, I am going to have Old Senta and some of my other faithful German Shorthaired Pointers as eternal companions.

Now that my shooting days will soon be over I can sit beside my fireplace and reminisce from memory's halls many pleasant hours spent with the greatest gun dog ever produced—the German Shorthaired Pointer.

Apparently, the article in the *National Sportman* did not go unnoticed by others. Two other imported GSPs were registered in the *Field Dog Stud Book* in 1926 following Dr. Thornton's registrations: Lord v. Ingeburgsruh and Treu. Lord v. Ingeburgsruh were owned by George Rittman, Trenton, New Jersey, and bred by Paul Knopf, Germany. Whelped October 10, 1921, he was by Ruben II Eichsfeld ex Cora Augustenburg. Treu, owned by A. H. Schmidt, Detroit, Michigan, and bred by Stadforster Dohs, New Zippendorf, Germany, was whelped December 29, 1922. He was sired by Blitz Mullingen v.d. Reichstadt ex Heidi New Zippendorf.

By 1927, Dr. Thornton was producing his own puppies from his imported stock and the bitches from Senta's breeding before she left Austria. Doctor Phil, by Treu v. Saxony ex Queen of Everyuse, went to P. S. Gaharan, Jr., Jena, Louisiana; Hund v. Saxony by Treu ex Senta went to R. T. Lamb and L. C. Spring, Neesinville, Ohio.

H. L. Clough of Parrish, Florida, bought Belle of Montana, by Treu ex Senta. A full sister, Fraulein v. Senta, went to Ray and Kathryn Russ of Oklahoma City, while her littermate, Queen of Helena, was shipped to W. M. Copenhaver of Helena, Montana.

Also registered in 1927 was Chief v. Saxony, by Treu v. Saxony ex Queen of Everyuse, sold by Dr. Thornton to Harry Craig, Canaseraga, New York.

In a very short period of time, Thornton dogs were all over the United States as other individuals began to import dogs directly from Germany to form a breeding pool of the best Germany and Austria had to offer. In a breeding career that lasted twenty-six years, the last litter whelped in 1951, Dr. Thornton imported at least thirty dogs from Austria and Germany. Six of the bitches were in whelp when they arrived. They came from the finest bloodlines in Europe. Thus, America started with an exceptional base of breeding stock, supplemented by good imports by other breeders throughout the country.

Dr. Thornton said that of all the Shorthairs he owned, the sires that did the most to establish the Shorthair's reputation in this country were Kamerad v. Waldhausen, Pal v. Waldhausen, John Neuforsthaus, Artist v.d. Forst Brickwedde and Fritz Bitterwurzel. Perhaps the greatest dog he bred out of his great imports was Tim v. Altenau, sire of fifteen champions, a remarkable feat at the time.

Dr. Thornton's contribution to the GSP in America is legendary, but his work in medicine is even more remarkable. I am indebted to Fred Singer of Kansas for sending me information about Dr. Thornton's background in Montana. Fred made a trip to the Bitterroot and Flathead Valley ranches of Dr. Thornton and brought back a lot of information about this period in his life. Details of his background are contained in the following obituary that appeared in the Missoula newspaper after his death in 1966:

Death of Dr. Charles R. Thornton, 87, early Saturday in a Loma Linda, Calif., hospital wrote "finis" to the history of two physicians who had important roles in the development of medicine in Missoula from 1918 through the late forties. He had been ill since early January.

His brother, Dr. William T. Thornton, died in April, 1943 at the age of 65 from a lingering illness. Dr. Charles and Dr. Will, as they were known to practitioners and patients alike, operated what is now Missoula Community Hospital under their name.

Dr. Charles was born on a farm in Fayette County, Ohio, Aug. 23, 1879. He spent all of his time there until he began preparation for a medical career.

His pre-medical training was done at Mount Vernon, Ohio, and he was graduated from American Medical Missionary College at Battle Creek, Michigan, about 1903. Most of his internship was in Chicago at Cook County Clinic. He also received training at St. Mary's Hospital, South Hallstead Free Clinic and other clinics in Chicago. He spent almost two years in the Battle Creek Sanitarium and Hospital.

Dr. Charles began practicing medicine in 1905 at Corvallis and Hamilton. At that time spotted fever had a mortality rate of about 90 percent. His success in treating it helped to establish his reputation. Subsequently he did considerable research on the disease, investigated insects and their larvae, and studied burns.

In 1917 Dr. Will established a hospital at 508 S. 3d St., W., now the Thornton Apartments. Two years later he was joined by his brother, Dr. Charles.

About 1920 the two brothers bought the property on which the home of the late C.H. McLeod was located at 324 E. Front St. In June 1922 the doctors and Ehel Martin incorporated the Missoula Clinic and the brothers let a contract to build the present Community Hospital building which was opened as the Thornton Hospital April 12, 1923. The McLeod home was remodeled as a residence for nurses.

The brothers operated the hospital as partners until Dr. Will's death when Dr. Charles took over his brother's interest. Later, Dr. R.E. Wirth purchased a half interest and he and Dr. Charles operated it until Jan. 1, 1947, when it was acquired by the Memoral Hospital Association.

At that point Dr. Charles retired. Subsequently, he lived about two years in Weslaco, Texas, and about three years in Siloam Springs, Ark. Returning to Montana he resumed practice at Ronan, where he resided two or three years. He retired again on moving to College Place, Washington, outside Walla Walla, residing there about seven years. Next he moved to Loma Linda.

Dr. Charles was an ardent sportsman, always interested in improving hunting and fishing. He worked with Thomas Marlowe to plant Chinese and Hungarian pheasants and other birds. Long ago he advocated planting wild turkeys in certain areas of Montana.

Most of the time Dr. Charles owned one or more farms in the Bittter Root and Flathead valleys. On them he experimented with various plants and grasses.

The physician introduced the German Shorthaired Pointer breed of dog to this country, importing more than thirty from Europe. Today they are one of the leading gun dogs in the United States. He also raised Belgian horses and registered dairy cattle.

Funeral services will be in Loma Linda Tuesday or Wednesday and burial will be there. The family asks that tributes be in the form of memorials to Community Hospital.

Survivors are: widow, Agnes M., Loma Linda; daughter, Mrs. William (Doris) Ellison, Loma Linda; son, Pfc. C. Robert, Ft. Lewis, Washington; three brothers, Dr. Harry, Kansas City, Missouri; Noah, Versailles, Indiana, and Dr. Fred, LaCrosse, Wisconsin; one sister, Mrs. Grace Cobban, Worthington, Ohio.

Many of today's leading Shorthairs trace back only a few generations to the great Thornton imports and the dogs he bred out in the Big Sky country. Dr. Charles Thornton truly is a legend.

chapter 7

Events and Titles

The German Shorthaired Pointer is fortunate to have so many different events in which to participate in America. In subsequent chapters you will read about many of the great Shorthairs that achieved these honors. Many competitive and performance events are administered by the American Kennel Club, but other organizations also offer a variety of competitive events.

The Shorthair is used in the United States primarily for upland bird hunting and occasionally for waterfowl. Some Shorthairs are trained for trailing furred game, as the bird finder in falconry, and for sled racing, among other uses. Although the breed was developed for versatility in Germany and still retains much of that ability, the GSP is used mostly for bird hunting.

The AKC events open to the breed include field trials, hunting tests, conformation shows, Agility and Obedience Trials. The largest entries are in shows, field trials and hunting tests.

FIELD TRIALS

In field trials the GSP can earn titles as a Field Champion (FC), Amateur Field Champion (AFC) and National Field Champion (NFC). To acquire a Field Champion title, a dog must have wins in open competition with only four amateur points counting toward the ten points required for the title. A three-point major in a retrieving stake is required for Shorthairs. Points are based on the number of dogs entered in the stake. Only amateurs may compete for the AFC title.

Clubs may hold three trials a year, all approved first by the parent club and then the AKC, but one of the three must be an all-walking stake. The stakes include open and amateur puppy for dogs up to 15 months, open and amateur derby for dogs up to 24 months; open all age and limited all age, Amateur all age and limited amateur all age, open gun dog and limited open gun dog, and amateur gun dog and limited amateur gun dog. Limited means that the dog must qualify through previous wins.

In the all age and gun dog stakes, the dogs must be steady to wing and shot and retrieve to hand where retrieving is required. They must also honor another dog's point when the occasion arises. The dogs are judged on their ground coverage and range, hunting style, bird-finding ability, style on point, steadiness, manners and retrieving. There are four places. The dog that puts it all together best earns first place. Placements are determined by two judges. If they do not feel any dog has met the requirements of the stake, they may withhold any or all placements. Handlers may be on horseback, except in walking stakes, and the two judges always ride except under unusual conditions.

A handler may use a scout to help find the dog if it disappears on the course, but the scout's only function is to locate the dog and signal whether it is on point or moving. The scout may not help handle the dog, although this rule is not always honored. In Shorthair trials, dogs may not be collared when moving off point after a bird has been flushed or retrieved except under American Field Rules. The GSPCA holds National All Age, Open Gun Dog, amateur Gun Dog and a National futurity.

American Field–licensed field trials for Shorthairs are conducted under the authority of the National German Shorthaired Pointer Association (NGSPA). The NGSPCA holds many regional championships, the National Chukar championship and the NGSPCA National championship. American Field championships are gained by winning a championship stake rather than through an accumulation of points as in AKC formats. Shorthairs are the backbone of the National German Pointing Dog Association (NGPDA), which holds an all-German breed national championship annually. Shorthairs may also compete in American Field Pointer/Setter trials and in the National Shoot To Retrieve Association (NSTRA) for championships.

TITLING TESTS

The AKC Hunting Test program is the leader in field testing. The requirements measure the natural and trained abilities of the dogs. They are similar to actual hunting conditions and are not too different from field trials, except that dogs do not compete against each other.

The nice thing about all the testing programs is that they reward good performance without involving worry about placing the dogs. Every dog that meets the minimum requirements is rewarded. AKC offers Junior Hunter for the introductory level. Dogs do not have to be steady to wing and shot. At the Senior Hunter level, dogs can be commanded to stay on point and to honor. They can move on the shot and may be collared on honor. At the Master Hunter level the dogs must be steady on point, flush and shot. They cannot be commanded to honor, but may be cautioned quietly after honoring on their own when they come into sight of the bracemate on point. When sent to retrieve, they must do it promptly and tenderly to hand. They are expected to demonstrate a finished performance in all aspects.

Dogs are judged in various categories, from pointing to retrieving, on a scale of ten points for each category. They must average seven points and may not be scored below five in any category. Juniors receive a JH degree for four qualificaitons. Seniors must have five passing scores but need only four if they have a JH title. They earn an SH title. Master Hunters (MH) must have six qualifying scores unless they have an SH title, and then need only two.

All handlers must handle on foot. No horses are allowed except those used by judges. Clubs are authorized to hold up to four hunting tests annually.

NAVHDA

The most difficult testing title to achieve is Versatile Champion (VC), offered by the North American Versatile Hunting Dog Association (NAVHDA). The test is even more demanding than that for the German KS title. It requires an intelligent dog with a lot of natural ability and trainability. At the 1996 NAVHDA International Invitational in Wisconsin, two German Shorthaired Pointers received perfect scores to earn the title of Versatile Hunter: Hoss v. Emil, bred and owned by Neil N. Nacchio, of Virginia Beach, Virginia, and handled by Bob West of Iowa, and Shooting Starr's Sharp Shooter, owned by Clyde and Marilyn Veter of Crystal Lake, Illinois. Hoss was sired by a German dog named Kim v. Uphuser Kolk out of Nacchio's Satin Sadie. Both sire and dam have some of the best German lines behind them.

There are various tests leading up to qualifying for the International Invitational. Only dogs that earn prize I in the qualifying tests make it to the Invitational, where the requirements are rigorous.

During the upland field portion of the International test, dogs are braced for an hour and expected to show a strong forward and productive search throughout, and to be aware of and cooperate with each other. When birds are located, dogs should point well off and stand intently. They are required to be steady to wing, shot and fall, then retrieve promptly and gently to hand on command.

Backing of a bracemate's point is also mandatory and once backed, a dog has to stand steady during the shot, fall and retrieve on its bracemate's bird, without command or contact from the handler.

The water test has three primary segments. One involves an honor during a short retrieve of a bye dog. The test dog is positioned behind and to the side of a bye dog and is expected to remain steady and quiet during the sequence. Once ready, shots are fired and a duck is thrown close to shore; the bye dog then retrieves to hand while the test dog sets without command.

Next is a water retrieve with a slight twist. The test dog is again expected to remain steady while a shot is fired and a duck is thrown approximately seventy yards from shore in a marsh area. At that point the dog is commanded to retrieve a live duck with one wing shackled and able to swim freely, which it quickly does. The test dog has to swim to the area of the marked fall for a water track and follow it to complete the retrieve and deliver to hand, which is mandatory to qualify.

The third segment is a 100-yard blind retrieve. In this test, a duck is thrown to the water's edge on an opposite bank at approximately 100 yards across open water from the starting line, then dragged ten yards up the bank into cover. The test dog, who has not seen any of the setup, is brought to line after all is ready. Once at the line, the handler fires a shot and sends his or her dog for the retrieve. To complete the retrieve, the test dog should stay to the handler's line all the way across to the other shore, then follow the drag to locate and retrieve the duck to hand. If not, it can be handled to the area and complete the retrieve, but either way, a retrieve is mandatory to qualify.

At NAVHDA's International Invitational, only those dogs successfully completing all phases of testing in the Prize I Category achieve the title of VC, Versatile Champion. NAVHDA holds a number of tests around the country annually where dogs try to earn titles designated Prize I, Prize II and Prize III.

NATIONAL SHOOT TO RETRIEVE ASSOCIATION (NSTRA)

As the name indicates, this is a test of finding, pointing and retrieving shot game. Emphasis is placed more on accomplishment than steadiness. A total of eighteen points and three wins are required for each title.

One of the most, if not the most, successful German Shorthaired Pointers to compete in NSTRA trials is Snips Chick v. Wildburg, MD, SH, owned by Brenda Roe of Rossville, Georgia. Snips has won five NSTRA championships.

Snips won one regional championship and placed in three others in 1991. She was second runner-up in the 1990 National Dog-of-the-Year Trial against 128 competitors, including Pointers, setters and Brittanies. She earned a Utility Dog degree in AKC Obedience Trials and a Senior Hunter title in five straight hunting tests. Snips was sired by Dual Ch. Esser's Duke v.d. Wildburg (Esser's Chick and Kay v. der Wildberg lineage) ex Birdacres Snip of Snow, SH, UD (Ch. Adam v. Fuehrerheim lineage in the background on both sides).

In two outstanding matings to Dual Ch. Timberdoodle Lancer's Answer and Dual Ch. Hillhaven's Hustler, Snips has produced several titled sons and daughers, including the first AKC show champion to obtain a NSTRA field championship, Ch. Snips Rajun Cajun v. Wildburg, SH, CDX.

DUAL AND TRIPLE CHAMPIONSHIPS

Shorthairs may earn dual champion and triple champion titles. A dual champion title is awarded for dogs earning both show and field trial championships. Adding an Obedience Champion title (OTCH) gives them a triple champion title. I do not think any GSP has yet earned a triple champion title, but there are many dual champions in the breed.

OBEDIENCE

The American Kennel Club records more than 100,000 entries in Obedience Trials every year, and Shorthairs earn their fair share of titles. Several have the coveted OTCH title. The basic degree is Companion Dog (CD). They advance to Companion Dog Excellent (CDX), Utility Dog (UD), Utility Dog Tracking (UDT) and Obedience Trial Champion (OTCH). Tracking Dog (TD), Tracking Dog Excellent (TDX) and Variable Surface Tracking (VST) titles are also available.

In Obedience exercises, the dogs walk at heel and change pace at the judge's direction, retrieve over obstacles and maintain long sits and downs. Obedience, as the name suggests, demonstrates the dog's willingness to follow commands and serve as a useful companion.

Snips Chick v.Wildburg, UD, SH, (Axel von Wasserschling ex Birdacres Snip of Snow, UD, SH), owned by Brenda Roe, won five National Shoot To Retrieve Championships.

Dual Ch. Timberdoodle's Lancer's Answer, owned by Dot and Dick Kern, going Winners Dog at the Shawnee KC under judge Bob McKowen. Dot Kern served as secretary of the GSPCA and the Eastern GSPC and was secretary of the 1997 AKC Gun Dog Championships. *William Gilbert*

AGILITY

Agility tests the dog's ability to master a series of obstacles such as high jumps and broad jumps, tunnels, in and out of weave polls and jumps through obstacles such as hanging tires. Dogs are scored on faults and time. In this competition, the dog and handler act as a team, going through the course together, with the handler indicating the obstacles the dog is supposed to master throughout the course. They receive suffix titles (at the end of the dog's name) indicating what level of accomplishment they have achieved.

In addition to AKC trials, they may also compete in trials sanctioned by several other Agility organizations.

chapter 8

Into the Thirties

In 1929, the stock market crash triggered a worldwide depression that went well into the 1930s until the buildup for World War II. Yet, amazingly, the breeding and importation of Shorthairs continued to increase. Wild game hunting was at its zenith in America, and with the Great Depression, there was more time for hunting. Those who could afford to buy one of the new breed did so because it suited the most basic kind of hunting in the United States. Pointers and Setters still held sway in the Southeast and in sports throughout the United States, but the Shorthair gained ground quickly in the grouse woods of the Northeast and upper Midwest and throughout all of the great pheasant and prairie chicken country of the central Midwest and the agricultural belts of the Far West.

In researching American Field Studbook registrations, I came across an entry that was slightly startling to me. Two Shorthairs—Kimmel's Fritz and Kimmel's Heiney—were registered by Dr. H. F. Kimmel of Derry, Pennsylvania. I was born and reared in Derry, which is a small railroad town in the coal-mining and farming country between the ridges in southwestern Pennsylvania. It is a working man's town and there were plenty of grouse, pheasants and rabbits in the fields and woods. But if anyone could afford a dog in those late Depression years, that dog most likely would have been a Beagle. Yet thirteen years from the first imports to America, a doctor in my remote hometown had registered two GSPs, and both were bred in nearby West Newton and Wilkinsburg. Dr. Kimmel was one of two doctors in Derry, but I never had an inkling then or now that two GSPs lived in my hometown. In 1938, I was 11 years old. Decades later, I would be literally and figuratively up to my neck in Shorthairs.

THE IMPACT OF THE 1930S

The American Kennel Club recognized the German Shorthaired Pointer in March 1930. The first registration in the AKC stud book was Greif v.d.

Fliegerhalde, by Panther Furstenfeld ex Miss Schnaitberg. Greif was a German import bred by Herr Muller, whelped June 25, 1928, and owned by H. S. Rochschild. The registration was published in the March 1930 issue of the AKC Studbook.

AKC recognition was the springboard for increased breeding and importation of outstanding dogs from the finest bloodlines of Germany, Austria and Denmark. Shorthairs could now enter shows where they could be more readily seen, and they could enter field trials more suited to the breed than those in which they were competing against wide-ranging Pointers and Setters. Six years after recognition, two Shorthairs earned the first AKC show championships. In the fall of 1936, Becky v. Hohenbruck and Baron v.d. Brickwedde, both from Thornton breeding, earned their championships. Becky's sire was Trill v. Hohenbruck ex Lotte v. Hoellenthor. Baron was by Artist v.d. Brickwedde, imp., ex Dixie Queen Buckswald.

In 1939, the Minnesota Club was granted AKC parent club status and the German Shorthaired Pointer Club of America, Inc., was born. In 1946, the breed Standard was approved by the AKC. It was based on the German Standard for the most part. Presumably, the dogs were judged against the German Standard until the American Standard was approved.

Once AKC status was achieved, the Shorthair began concentrating heavily in the Midwest and upward to Minnesota and Wisconsin, fueled by a new infusion of Shorthair breeding in Bennington, Nebraska, a small town a few miles northwest of Omaha. Two World War I veterans who had fought on opposite sides, Walter Mangold of the United States and Ernest Rojem of Germany, who had immigrated to Nebraska, became good friends through hunting.

They pooled their resources, and Rojem had his brother in Germany send them two German Shorthaired Pointers. The first to arrive was Claus v. Schlesweg-Konigsweg, whelped in 1931. Bred by Georg Greve, Claus was sired by Golo v. Got Torp, an Artus Sand son ex Karin Furstenmoor ex Arna v. Altenburg (Sepp v. Interlaken ex Pepita v. Interlaken).

The second to arrive was Jane v. Grunen Adler (in whelp, by Horst Furstenmoor ex Toni v. Grunen Adler). Rojem's brother had chosen well and in the next ten years, puppies from these great imports were distributed all over the United States and Canada. Jane's breeding was heavy on the outstanding Goldenen line in Germany. Another of their famous imports was Dora v. Heisenstein by Jager's Isgo ex Hertana Papinghausen, who arrived in June 1934. These strong family lines joined the Thornton dogs in breeding all over the country, leading to many of today's outstanding dogs.

Mangold said, "Claus was a great dog for us. He had the rugged constitution needed here, summers over 100, winters to 30 below, snow drifting to 12 feet and more quite often. We sent him through floating ice after duck. And he was a fireball on land, not even sand burrs stopped him. He was a gentle dog, too. As a Postmaster, I had him with me at the office. Children coming in for mail rode around on his back. But, he was a good guard, too, and no stray dogs ever bothered him twice. He got us lots of good dogs that were widely distributed and lived to be very old."

The next center of great imports and significant breeding leading to dogs that founded the great kennels was in St. Croix Falls, Wisconsin. A one-time German gamekeeper named Joseph Burkhart knew his German breeding and selected truly outstanding stock for his breeding kennel. Around this time, you must remember, the GSP was accepted in AKC shows and would soon have its own field trials for testing of both conformation and performance in actual competition. GSPs could compete in Pointer/Setter field trials under American Field sanction, but they had to run according to rules more suited to the bigger running dogs and also give up the advantages such as retrieving, stylish bird work and ease of handling. So, while many Shorthairs continued to be enrolled in the American Field and still are as we approach the twenty-first century, they were becoming more widely known because of their AKC activities.

While Thornton and Mangold/Rojem influences remained strong, Burkhart gave the breed its final shot toward widespread recognition and acceptance in America by importing some of the best specimens yet to come from Europe and placing them in the hands of people who would do something significant with them. Then as now, however, the preponderance of Shorthairs went to hunters, and many potentially great ones never achieved widespread recognition.

Three of Burkhart's earliest imports had a profound effect on the future of the breed in America, and they established the Minnesota/Wisconsin area as the hotbed for superior-quality Shorthairs.

St. Croix Falls is located on the Wisconsin/Minnesota border about thirty-five miles northeast of Saint Paul, Minnesota. This is one of the lushest farmland areas in the United States and a game hunter's paradise, with pheasants and grouse within easy distance. It is not surprising that the GSP became so popular in this area, as it set the exact requirements for the upland hunter.

In 1932, Burkhart imported Bob v. Schwarenberg and two bitches, Arta v. Hohreusch and Feldjagers Grisette, from Germany. Burkhart's brother, who lived in Germany, had firsthand knowledge of the dogs. Joseph Burkhart, himself, was well acquainted with the German pedigrees and the high esteem that Germans held for certain lines. The three closely linebred dogs he imported carried the Winterhauch-Schlossgarten family lines of the famous Mars Altenau-Artus Sand bloodlines. The great K.S. Benno v. Schlossgarten was the sire of Bob v. Schwarenbereg out of Wandadora, and of Arta v. Hohreusch out of Afra v. Schwarenberg.

The third key import, Feldjagers Grisette, was by Bob v. Winterhauch ex Edith v. Karlbach. Bob v. Winterhauch was a Mars Altenau grandson through Heidi Esterhof and the sire of K.S. Benno v. Schlossgarten. Within the direct background of Burkhart's three imports was the great Bob. The combination of these impressive bloodlines built a strong foundation that established Burkhart as one of the all-time great breeders. He later moved from Wisconsin to Alexandria, Minnesota, where he ran a resort, but he kept up his breeding activities for many years.

Burkhart sold Arta v. Hohreusch to Robert Donner of Buffalo, New York, in 1936 with the stipulation that she be bred to the import Hallo Mannheimia, sired by Frei Suedwest, who was by Artus Sand. His dam was Cita Mannheimia. From this mating, Burkhart got Treu v. Waldwinkel, who he considered his greatest sire even though he never earned a title. In addition to being an outstanding sire of ten champions, Treu was Burkhart's personal hunting dog, and he praised him highly. In addition to becoming Burkhart's leading sire, Treu also fathered dogs that helped establish other well-known kennels throughout the upper Midwest.

Another famous Burkhart producer that helped make his Thalberg Waldwinkel Kennels famous was the bitch Maida v. Thalberg, whelped in 1943. She was by Ozzie Schwarenberg ex Bibi Winterhauch. Her grandsire was Treu v. Waldwinkel and her granddam was Bessie v. Winterhauch. Burkhart obtained Maida from breeder Gerald T. Baskerville. Maida was the dam of four champions: Ch. Thalbach Waldwinkel Hans, Int. Ch. Searching Wind Bob (by Treu v. Waldwinkel), Ch. Thalbach Waldwinkel Heidi and Ch. Thalbach Waldwinkel Mark.

Burkhart's kennel also produced the dog that was to do the most, up to then, to popularize the breed across the country in Ch. Fritz v. Schwarenberg, the first Shorthair bought by Jack Shattuck, who established the Schwarenberg Kennels in America. Fritz, whelped in 1934, was by Bob v. Schwarenberg ex Arta v. Hohreusch. Shattuck campaigned Fritz all over the country. Among his wins was Best of Breed at Morris & Essex in New Jersey in 1940 and four years in a row at Chicago International. He was also Best of Breed at Westminister in 1940. Fritz sired seven champions.

With the handsome Fritz as his calling card, Shattuck promoted the breed with many articles and appearances at shows and field trials from the Midwest to the Atlantic coast.

Shattuck's next big star was Rusty v. Schwarenberg (Mars v. Ammertal, an import, ex Vicki v. Schwarenberg), who became a legend after gaining the first GSP Dual Championship in 1947. While Fritz was white, liver and ticked, Rusty was a solid liver. He competed against all comers in the field and the best in the dog show world. The day after winning the Shorthair Specialty Show, Rusty won the Open All-Age Stake at a Field Trial. In becoming the first dual, he won the first AKC Field Trial Championship.

Among other champions from Schwarenberg Kennels was Ch. Helga v. Schwarenberg (Ernst Bismark ex Katrina Schwarenberg), dam of two champions, one of which was Schatz v. Schwarenberg, who became the second dual champion in America and the first bitch to earn a field championship. Schatz was owned by Dr. and Mrs. H. J. Zahalka of Searching Wind Kennels, Minneapolis. The Zahalkas also owned Dual Ch. Searching Wind

Topper (Searching Wind Bob ex Fieldborn Katzie Karlwald), who finished his dual in 1951. Schatz finished her dual title in 1949, at the age of seven years.

Two other breeders appearing in the 1930s were Al Sause of Ellicott City, Maryland, and Harold Fuehrer of Carlisle Springs, Pennsylvania. Sause gained fame through ownership of several outstanding dogs, while Fuehrer established Fuehrerheim Kennels, where he bred outstanding Shorthairs with strong Thornton/Schwarenberg bloodlines to supply hunters in the Middle Atlantic and military officers who attended the war college in Carlisle. It was out of one of his bitches sold to a sporting goods store owner in Midlothian, Virginia, that Ch. Adam v. Fuehrerheim was whelped in 1962 to become the leading sire in the history of the breed.

Sause is known primarily for three great dogs. The most prominent was Ch. Dallo v.d. Forst Brickwedde, the first German import to gain an AKC show title and Bests of Breed at Westminster and Morris & Essex, the two most prestigious shows in the United States at the time. The others were Pheasant Lane's Schnapps and Pheasant Lane's Tomahawk.

Dallo was by Artus v. Hasetal (Furst ex Cora v.d. Brickwedde, an Artus Sand granddaughter) ex Artus was grandsire, through his daughter Gerda

Ch. Fritz v. Schwarenberg, owned by Jack Shattuck, helped popularize the German Shorthaired Pointer in America through his many wins at major shows all over the country.

Dual Ch. Rusty v. Schwarenberg, the first dual for the breed, shown with owner-handler Jack Shattuck.

v.d. Forst Brickwedde, of Berta Spiessinger v. Pfaffenhofen/Ilm, dam of the dog that was to become America's top-producing sire at the time, FC Greif v. Hundscheimerkogel. Dallo was killed early in a hunting accident but not before he had sired some of the important progenitors of today's leading Shorthairs. His daughter, Ch. Katinka of Sycamore Brook, owned by Dick and Bob Johns of Benton, Pennsylvania, produced two dual champions by the Johns' Dual Ch. Blick v. Grabenbruch, who finished in 1951 to become the first dual on the East Coast.

One of the early importers of Shorthairs from the Western part of the country was Rudolph Hirschnitz, who lived for a while in Cheyenne, Wyoming, before moving to Redwood City, California. His imports ultimately resulted in the first Shorthair to win a Best in Show in the United States, Ch. Sportsman's Dream.

Hirschnitz was a Forest Ranger apprentice in his native Germany. He said that since the duties of the Ranger required the use of a hunting dog, he naturally selected a German Shorthaired Pointer. In a letter describing the GSP in Germany, he wrote: "At this point I would like to bring out the fact that although the nobles were the owners of these dogs, the Forest Rangers who were employed by the noblemen needed an all-purpose dog to meet the varying situations encountered on their daily rounds through the forest. This enabled them to develop the sterling qualities now found in the German

Shorthair Club by selective breeding. Thus the noblemen, Forest Rangers, land owners and in later years the sportsmen, all worked together in developing the modern German Shorthaired Pointer."

This simple but profound statement sums up nicely how the German Shorthaired Pointer came to be without all of the "begats" of jawbreaking-named sires and dams. Shirley Warren used excerpts from this letter in describing the GSP in America for the aforementioned *German Shorthaired Pointer Activities,* prepared by the National Breed Committee of the GSPCA and published in 1953.

Hirschnitz's first import from breeder Wilhelm Masch of Germany was Astor v. Fischtal, born on May 8, 1935. Astor sired Ch. Sportsman's Dream out of Sieglinde v. Meishen, whom Hirschnitz bought from J. T. Rader, of Platte City, Missouri.

Sportsman's Dream was owned by V. E. Lantow of Denver, Colorado. In addition to winning the first all-breed BIS, in San Diego in 1940, he won four Sporting Groups, as well as BB at Westminster, Morris & Essex in New Jersey and Chicago International.

Ch. Sportsman's Dream and Ch. Fritz v. Schwarenberg were the first nationally campaigned Shorthairs, and they helped gain recognition for the breed through their successful, widespread exposure. Keep in mind that World War II was underway at this time and travel was much more difficult than it is today, with some top dogs shown on opposite coasts on successive days thanks to modern airlines. Ch. Sportsman's Dream also was an excellent field dog, and he had an act that helped secure blood donations for the Denver Red Cross for servicemen in World War II.

Another Western dog, Ch. Flash v. Windhausen, won the second all-breed BIS in Salt Lake City, Utah, in October 1950. Flash was owned by Carl Nussbaum, Salt Lake City. Bred by Charles E. Fielden, Flash was by Ch. Rex v. Windhausen ex Lady Waldwinkel.

The third dog to win an all-breed BIS, Ch. Sir Michael of Hanson Manor, also was from the West. Owned by L. V. Linville, Denver, Sir Michael won his BIS at Fort Collins, Colorado, April 29, 1951. Bred by Leo Hansen, he was sired by Ch. Sportsman's Dream ex Bugle Ann Waldwinkel.

The fourth dog to win an all-breed BIS did it in the East, in Brooklyn, New York, December 1, 1951. This was the famous Pheasant Lane's Storm Cloud, bred by Mr. and Mrs. Walter H. Warren and owned by Mrs. John Worth Gordon. Storm Cloud, sired by Ch. Pheasant Lane's Stormalong ex Ch. Pheasant Lane's Deborah, was whelped in 1949. The Eastern German Shorthaired Pointer Club awarded Storm Cloud a special rosette as the Best Show Dog of 1951.

Vance McGilbrey, who founded Columbia River Kennels, bought his first Shorthair from Mangold while living in Nebraska before moving to Washington state. Ch. Pheasant Lane's Stormalong was the foundation of Vance McGilbrey's Columbia River Kennel in Washington. When bred to

Ch. Pheasant Lane's Deborah and Columbia River Tillie, he sired fifteen show champions and one field champion. The get included three BIS winners: Chs. Pheasant Lane Storm Cloud, Columbia River Cochise and Columbia River Lightning. With Stormalong's mating to Columbia River Princess and Helga v. Crawford, there emerged three more BIS champions: Chs. Columbia River Ranger, Jeepers and Vagabond.

A son of Lightning, Ch. Columbia River Thundercloud, was bred to Columbia River Jill to produce Ch. Gretchenhof Moonshine, who became the greatest ambassador of the breed in America at that time. Owned and handled by Walt and Joyce Shellenbarger, Moonshine won fifteen BIS and fifty Sporting Group firsts. Her winning brought national recognition to the Shellenbargers' Gretchenhof Kennels, which were based on Columbia River breeding.

Moonshine's record stood until broken by another Gretchenhof dog, Ch. Gretchenhof Columbia River, who was bred by McGilbrey and acquired by the Shallenbargers for Dr. Richard P. Smith and handled by the Shellenbargers. He won the coveted Best in Show award at Westminster in 1974.

Columbia River breeding also figures prominently in the creation of Dual Ch. NMK's Brittania v. Silbelstein, who became the all-time show-winning Shorthair as well as taking the Sporting Group at Westminster in 1987 and 1988 and BB at the GSPCA National Specialty in 1987. A factor that gave Britt even greater distinction is her field championship, which made this all-time top-winning bitch a dual champion. She has produced a number of outstanding champions, including duals.

Brittania was sired by Ch. NMK's Placer Country Snowbird ex Rani v. Silbelstein on May 30, 1984, bred by Kathy Sibley. She was owned by Dr. Gary Stone and Carol Chadwick of Citrus Heights, California. The show handler was Bruce Shultz of California and the field trial handler and trainer was Terry Chandler of Ruggerheim Kennels in Las Cruces, New Mexico. In addition to the Gretchenhof/Columbia breeding on the sire's side, Brittania carried Ch. Adam v. Fuehrerheim on both sire and dam sides along with v. Bess and v. Greif bloodlines.

Another highly recognized kennel name stemming from the early 1950s is Kaposia, owned by Don and Betty Sandberg, formerly of Eagan, Minnesota, near Saint Paul, and now in retirement at Barnum on Hanging Horn Lake in Minnesota, about 100 miles north of Saint Paul. Their kennel is largely based on the Burkhart dogs through Oakcrest Kennels, owned by Mr. and Mrs. Joe Deiss, and the Schwarenberg Kennels of Jack Shattuck. Joe and Magdaline Deiss purchased their first GSP, Lady v. Treuberg, from John Areod of Mankato, Minnesota, in 1937. Lady was sired by Esser's Pike (by St. Croix Fritz ex Berg's Choice) ex Treu's Bitterwurzel (by Blitz Bitterwurzel ex Treu's Jill). Oakcrest also owned Ch. Cora, a littermate of Dual Ch. Rusty v. Schwarenberg, the first bitch in the Northwest to complete her championship. Cora was bred to Ch. Glantz v. Winterhauch (Treu v. Waldwinkel ex Bessie

v. Winterhauch) to produce Ch. Cora's Penny of Oakcrest, who finished her championship in 1949. Oakcrest Kennels also owned Ch. Oakcrest's Rick v. Winterhauch, who was by Ch. Glanz v. Winterhauch ex Chimes Girl, a daughter of Mars v. Ammertal and Berg's Choice, from Burkhart breeding. Rick sired eleven champions, including Dual Ch. Captain v. Winterhauch and Ch. Oakcrest Cora v. Winderhauch, the first BIS-winning GSP bitch in America and the dam of six champions.

The Sandbergs lived not too far from Joe Deiss, and Don talked with him often. So it was not surprising that the first Shorthair owned by the Sandbergs came from the Deisses' Oakcrest Kennels. He was FC Kaposia's Chief of Oakcrest, CD, by Chip v. Winterhauch ex Ch. Cora's Penny of Oakcrest. Don handled him to his field championship.

The next Kaposia dog was Dual Ch. Kaposia's Firebird, sired by Ch. Count Snooper v. Dusseldorf ex Dual Ch. Lucky Lady v. Winterhauch and owned by Al and Sis Thrush of Minnesota. When "Birdy" was bred to Chief, they produced Am., Can. Ch. Kaposia's Wildfire. Wildfire bred back to his granddam Dual Ch. Lucky Lady v. Winterhauch and produced Ch. Fire Hawk of Kaposia, another famous sire. Wildfire sired sixteen show champions.

Out of this famous line came hundreds of champions, including Ch. Kaposia's Waupun II (Ch. Kaposia's Otsego ex Ch. Kaposia's Blue Chinook), who won three National Specialty Bests of Breed, an all-breed BIS and 151 BBs before retiring at age five, after winning his last GSPCA Specialty and the Minnesota GSPC Specialty Show the following day. He sired Ch. Kaposia's Tucumcari, owned by Don and Betty Sandberg, who was BB at the 1973 National Specialty. Another famous Kaposia sire was Ch. Kaposia's Oconto, an all-breed BIS winner, Winners Dog and Best of Winners at the 1966 GSPCA National Specialty.

The Sandbergs remain active in Shorthairs. During a June 1997 visit to their home, they were preparing to place another litter of puppies while the older Shorthairs had the run of the house and the property above Hanging Horn Lake. Don and Betty are both Honorary Life Members of the GSPCA. Don has served as secretary of the early GSPCA and as president in the 1970s. They have judged around the world and have shipped dogs to the four corners of the earth. Their dogs figure prominently in many of today's kennels and are a link to the great foundation dogs of America.

We are indebted today also to two men who arrived on the scene in the upper Midwest in 1936 with like-sounding names: W. A. (Bill) Olson, founder of Waldwinkel Kennels, Minneapolis, and Hjalmar Olsen, of Fieldborn Kennels in Michigan. Later, Hjalmar moved to Cordele, Georgia, to manage a four-thousand-acre plantation. Cordele also happens to be one of the greatest centers for quail and bird dogs in the nation. A number of dog men are concentrated in the town, and among them today is Phil Morris, former trainer of Fieldacre Kennels.

Bill Olson's foundation bitch was Lady v. Waldwinkel. He followed with Ch. Hans v. Waldwinkel, who finished his championship by going WD at the first GSP Specialty Show in America, held in conjunction with the Chicago International All-Breed Show March 29–30, 1941. Whelped in 1937, Hans was bred by Dr. Elmer Berg and sired by Treu v. Waldwinkel ex Berg's Choice. But his most famous dog was Ch. Rex v. Krawford, who was bred by John Crawford and whelped March 1, 1947. Rex was by Schnapps v. Waldwinkel ex Katrinka. Rex shows up in a number of pedigrees featuring handsome offspring, and he is the sire of Ch. Baron v. Fuehrerheim, the father of Tessa v. Fuehrerheim, who is the mother of Ch. Adam v. Fuehrerheim. Olson was one of the founders of the parent club and became its second president, after Jack Shattuck.

Hjalmar had a long string of champions and trained many field champions in the 1940s and 1950s, but he is best remembered for Timm v. Altenau, which he obtained as a puppy from Charles Thornton. He placed nine points on Timm before selling him to William Erler. As noted earlier, Timm sired fifteen champions to become the all-time leading sire of champions at the time. Olsen immigrated to Canada in 1928 and then moved to the United States. He imported fifty or sixty dogs from Denmark in addition to Germany to provide a strong Danish influence on the GSP in America.

Olsen helped Dean Kerl of Sioux City, Iowa, import a number of Danish dogs, including FC Tell, who produced two dual, two show and eight field

Hjalmar Olsen with five champions of his breeding: (from left) Ch. Prince v. Waldwinkel, Ch. Madchen Karlbach, Ch. Dreaming Sweetheart, Ch. Waldo v.d. Golden Mark and Ch. Fritz Schlossgarten.

champions. Tell, an almost all-white dog with a liver head, appears in many pedigrees of top-winning field champions.

Kerl, who had several field champions from his Danish breeding, served as president of the GSPCA in 1978 and 1979. He initiated a number of businesslike innovations that proved to be of definite benefit to the association.

chapter 9

The German Shorthaired Pointer After World War II

Although some of the outstanding dogs that appeared in the 1950s and into the 1960s were discussed in the preceding chapters, for the most part discussion was limited to the early pillars of the breed through the second World War. As might be assumed, imports from Germany and just about everywhere else ceased during the war years. However, GSP activities did not cease during and immediately after the war.

The 1940s, with no imports coming out of Europe, was a time for consolidation of clubs in the United States. Because there was such a concentration of outstanding Shorthairs, breeders and energetic owners in the Minneapolis/St. Paul area, it was only logical that the Minnesota German Shorthaired Pointer Club would apply to the AKC to be chartered as the German Shorthaired Pointer Club of America, Inc. AKC approved the request in 1939 after rejecting a request to name the club "The German Shorthaired Pointer and Retriever Club," which the founders believed more adequately distinguished the Shorthair from other pointing breeds.

Shortly after the Minnesota Club applied to be chartered as the parent club for the breed, the Eastern German Shorthaired Pointer Club, founded in 1940, also applied for this status. As a concession to the Eastern Club's not being approved as the parent club, it was permitted to be a member club of the AKC, the only single breed club in history to be so designated. An AKC member club has voting privileges in the AKC.

The GSPCA underwent a revision in 1947, but the Minneapolis Club was the parent club until 1953, when the AKC mandated that the parent club be a separate organization. The GSPCA was reorganized into its present structure in 1962.

The Minneapolis GSP Club reverted to its original regional club status while the new GSPCA assumed parental responsibility for all AKC Shorthair activities, including the Conformation Standard and approval of field trials and Specialty Shows, all of which continue to require official approval by the AKC. The first secretary of the revised GSPCA was Don Sandberg, who had entered the Shorthair world with the dog he had obtained from Joe Deiss.

The first Shorthair Conformation Standard was approved in 1946, and it has undergone few changes since then. The most sweeping occurred in 1962 and 1992, when changes were made to clarify ambiguous descriptions and to use a format similar to most other AKC breed Standards. For the most part, however, it remains similar to the German Standard. The GSPCA has never adopted a field Standard, using the requirements and procedures approved by the AKC.

With a strong parent club in place, a number of regional clubs emerging all over the country—mostly in the Midwest, Far West, East Coast and Rocky Mountains—and a clear Standard, there was now form and substance for guiding the German Shorthaired Pointer in a common direction. It would take two more decades before the regional characteristics began to blend with the cross-fertilization of the outstanding dogs across the country. Size, color and field performance all began to blend into a Standard that could be assessed.

chapter 10

Significant Post-War Imports and American-breds and Their Impact on the German Shorthair

Imports from the late 1940s, 1950s and 1960s were to have a great impact on the German Shorthaired Pointer in the show ring and in the field in the closing decades of the twentieth century, with a history of almost seventy-five years of recorded GSPs in America. The dogs described as the early imports provided a strong base on which to build with the good imports that came in after the war. It is slightly short of miraculous that there were any dogs left in war-torn Europe, but a few dedicated breeders managed to hold on to some of the very good ones and somehow managed to keep them fed when it probably meant foregoing some of their own meals to do it.

I served in the U.S. Army of Occupation in Europe, stationed for most of the time in Austria, and I can attest to the terrible conditions that existed in almost all of Europe during the immediate years after World War II. Interestingly, I never saw a GSP in Germany or Austria, and I saw very few dogs of any kind during my time in Europe. Millions of displaced persons were being relocated and food was rationed by calories. How could a dog survive when the humans were barely making it? But they did, and the United States managed to get some of the best. I imagine the U.S. dollars looked pretty good to people devastated by war.

Today, one must go beyond the fourth, fifth and sixth generations to get to the original stock in America, and even some of the most recent leading producers require research to the fifth generations to find their links to the breed's foundation stock. Almost without exception, however, today's leading show and field dogs owe their quality to those early imports.

It is also interesting to observe that, although most imports were selected because of their proven field ability, conformation was not forfeited in the process, as attested to by the number of dual champions. The Shorthair was not brought into this country at any time strictly for show, but the old German goal of breeding first for performance proved old Prince Solms' philosophy that type would follow form. If they weren't made right, they could not perform right. Thus, the Shorthair continues to provide good performance in a handsome package in spite of some clandestine breedings designed to gain an edge in field trial competition.

There are many good dogs in America today and their names appear regularly in the win columns for trials, shows, obedience and hunting tests. A great majority trace their roots to those dogs that came into this country after World War II and the influential ones before them.

Inevitably, some good dogs will slip between the cracks when setting forth absolutes, but observation of pedigrees of today's winners will show that many trace their ancestry to a handful of truly outstanding dogs that landed in America in the second half of the century and one native-bred that does not appear to have much recognizable ancestry behind him. Most, but not all, of these dogs that so greatly influenced today's breeding are in the GSPCA Hall of Fame. Some have been passed over because they did not meet the criteria established for selecting dogs for the Hall of Fame; nevertheless, their influence was highly significant.

In naming some of these great post–World War II dogs, I am not minimizing the good kennel lines of current significance nor am I unmindful of the contributions made by great dams, a number of whom shall be singled out. But these latter-day winners and producers trace their ancestry to a relatively small number of dogs that went before. They proliferate in the generations of breeding.

These dogs (and certainly they aren't the only great ones of the period) are K.S. Sepp v. Grabenbruch, Essers' Chick, Dual Ch. Kay v.d. Wildburg, FC Greif v. Hundscheimerkogel, Int. Dual Ch. Adam, FC Tip Top Timmy, Int. FC Moesgaard's IB and FC Windy Hill Prince James.

When I first began field trialing in the fall of 1962 and the spring of 1963, only Tip Top Timmy was still competing regularly, but the offspring of all were dominant in field trials and they were producing dual champions. Naturally, I didn't know much of what was going on in those early trials, but Timmy and Kay seemed to be well known by the field trial fraternity, and some of them were curious about my first dog, Adam v. Fuehrerheim. I realized later that they wanted to see an offspring of the Swedish import Int. Dual Ch. Adam. Two of the prominent members of the Eastern German Shorthaired Pointer Club, Dick and Ruth Eitel, were more than curious because they were among the few who had bred to the import Adam and had kept a male and female. The bitch, Ch. Warrenwood's Kandy Kane, produced fourteen champions out of half-brother, Adam v. Fuehrerheim, only a few years later.

Dogs of that era were not well broken and with only a few exceptions, like Kay and Timmy, did not run especially big. Dual Ch. Fritz of Sleepy Hollow, owned by Fred Z. Palmer of the Hudson Valley GSP Club and handled by Tom Getler, the breeder and handler of Timmy, was retired. But Palmer would bring Fritz along when he came to see his dog Timmy run.

Kay had won the American Field National GSP Championship a short while before and Dick Johns had more or less retired him. Dick would bring him along when he came to some of the trials so that people could see him. Some promotional pictures and movies were made of Kay during some of these visits, and I gathered from all the attention that he was held in some awe by my fellow, more experienced, field trialers. Timmy, like Kay, gained great respect in both Shorthair and Pointer ranks by winning the well-known Jockey Hollow field trial in New Jersey, a predominantly Pointer/Setter stake of great prestige.

All AKC trials were on foot then; only judges and gallery followed on horseback. There was a lot of talk about letting handlers ride, and there was great emphasis being placed on range. There was not a lot of uniformity in either field performance or type, and the color of the dogs for the most part was sun-bleached brown. Another reason for the curiosity aroused by Adam was his color: white and liver ticked with large, dark liver patches.

In those short two seasons of my entry into field trials, I also ran into Dual Ch. and NFC Moesgaards Dandy, Fieldacres Ib, the Hall of Fame son of the Danish imported Hall of Famer Moesgaards IB, a small white dog with a solid liver head who was winning many field trials and would sire thirty-one field champions along the way.

There was great respect for the name Grabenbruch, and the name Sepp cropped up occasionally in conversations along with names like Greif (who most mispronounced to sound like *Greef*) and Radbach, but the latter were way off somewhere in the West. There was a dog that came up occasionally with the jawbreaker name of Hundscheimerkogel, doing great things and siring many champions in California. Most couldn't pronounce the name of old FC Greif v. Hundscheimerkogel, and seeing it in print didn't help either. In fact, I'm not sure anyone ever figured out what the name meant in English. But people had heard that he was a gifted producer even if they couldn't pronounce his name.

I saw Esser's Chick on a cold spring morning at the Mason-Dixon GSP field trial at Dr. Gailey's farm south of York, Pennsylvania, in the early 1960s. Col. Darwin Brock, who had served in the U.S. Army in Germany, had brought him back to America. He was an agile-looking, solid liver dog and a little light in bone, as most of the German imports were that came in at the time and afterwards. He was being handled by Dick Johns.

Of course, none of us knew then that these dogs for several generations would mix and match to develop most of the biggest winners with both field ability and type in America. Some of these winners even returned to the original countries of origin or beyond.

K.S. SEPP V. GRABENBRUCH

K.S. Sepp v. Grabenbruch was the first German Seiger brought to the United States at the end of the war. At the same time his new owner, Dick

K.S. Sepp v. Grabenbruch (Odin v. Weinbach ex Leda v. Grabenbruch), owned by Richard S. Johns, was the first K.S. titled German Shorthaired Pointer imported to the United States after World War II. Sepp was a strong influence on later generations of outstanding Shorthairs.

Nanny v. Luckseck, owned by Richard S. Johns, was whelped in Germany in 1940 and was imported to the United States after World War II. She was an outstanding dam and proved a great asset to the American gene pool.

Johns, acquired Nanny v. Luckseck, and the two would eventually make breed history.

Sepp and Nanny's story is extremely interesting, because they were among the quality of what was left in the aftermath of war. Through their son Dual Ch. Blick v. Grabenbruch they have left a lasting impression on the breed.

Dick Johns grew up in the Wilkes-Barre, Pennsylvania, area in a family of doctors and bird dogs, mostly Setters attuned to the grouse woods in the Pocono Mountains. Dick said he brought in one of the first Pointers to the area and was treated with disdain, because his contemporaries believed there was no other bird dog worthy of the name than the English Setter. But he made believers of them. "It was an awful thing to have that Pointer in the Wyoming Valley," Dick laughed.

When he was in his teens, he and some companions got to arguing over the impact of the .22-caliber birdshot cartridge. Dick said it was not very effective beyond fifty yards and was immediately challenged to prove it with a five-dollar bet in the offing, a considerable amount at the time. So, he walked off fifty yards, dropped his trousers and bent over and told them to take a shot. He said he heard a bang and immediately felt a tremendous burning sensation in his buttocks. He ran directly into a creek and went immediately to his doctor uncle at a nearby hospital. As the doctor was picking out what shot he could from his nephew's stinging posterior, he told Dick: "I think you are going to make a good man if you ever reach the age of twenty, but I don't think you will." Dick did reach the age of twenty and then some, and he became the "Squire" of Fishing Creek on a hillside farm above the little village of Benton, in northeastern Pennsylvania. He was establishing his reputation as a dog trainer and was also riding show horses when he went into the Army in World War II.

Sgt. Gen. Dick Johns went to Europe with the 63rd Infantry Division and was looking forward to returning home after the war when Gen. Terry Allen, an old cavalry officer in charge of a tank division in a military district in Germany, decided to establish a cavalry unit. He also wanted to get some dogs for hunting, because the area was saturated with game birds that had not been hunted since the beginning of the war.

I went up to see Dick at his home in Benton in late spring of 1997 to get some firsthand information about his breeding. I had known Dick for some thirty years and, as mentioned earlier, it was in a small book he had written on the Shorthair that I first learned what they were. At eighty-two, Dick was still as sharp as a young man, and he was still training dogs, mostly for hunters, and running his farm.

"I received word that a Col. Budolf from Gen. Terry's command wanted to see me," Dick reminisced. "They had learned that I had experience training both dogs and horses and wanted me to take charge of horses for his new cavalry unit at Baden in the Rhineland and also to find some dogs for hunting."

They located a pre-war breeder of German Shorthaired Pointers named Peter Kraft, of Hof Grabenbruch, Rhine-Hesson, who was living in a burned-out house and who was reported to have the finest bitch in Germany.

"When I first saw Nanny v. Luckseck, I knew she was going home with me," Dick said. "She had a rich blanket down her back, and it was the richest chestnut I had ever seen. She had a lot of speed and went very wide in the sugar beet fields but was under control. She would stand on birds and drop on hare. She was the only all-around Shorthair I ever saw."

He said Herr Kraft told him, "I can't feed her and you can; I'll sell her to you." Herr Kraft had been feeding her on bread, milk and some fat.

"I paid 250 Reichmarks for her, about twenty-five dollars in U.S. money," Dick said. "She was a wonderful bitch. I also hunted over Sepp v. Grabenbruch, and I tried to buy him but Kraft wouldn't sell him at first. I eventually talked him into it."

Dick recalled, "We had a wonderful time hunting and riding horses all over southwestern Germany's great, flat sugar beet fields. There had been no hunting in Germany for five years or more and there was a lot of game on the big flat land of the Rhine district. Nanny would run out of sight and come back with a hare. She once disappeared, and we kept walking in the direction she was going. After some distance, we ran across a one-legged former German soldier, and he told us the hare had run into a drain pipe and the dog was standing on one end of it. When we caught up, we looked down the pipe and there was the hare. We gave it to the soldier, who tied a piece of string around it and hung it around his neck. It would make a great meal for his family."

Nanny and Sepp became great companions, and she looked after him all the time. "One time," Dick recounted, "We were down at the house when we heard Sepp screaming. Nanny took off like a shot to the edge of the barn-yard where some cows had Sepp cornered. She bit one of the cows on the leg and nipped another on the nose, and they scattered. A greatly relieved Sepp emerged."

Dick described Sepp as a "smallish dog with great desire." He had earned his K.S. in Germany. Sepp was sired by Reichs-Sieger Odin v. Winbach ex Leda v. Grabenbruch. Leda was sired by a K.S. Frei Sudwest son out of a daughter of K.S. Benno v. Schlossgarten.

Sepp died of a viral infection after a few short years, but when bred to Nanny they produced, among other good dogs, Bob John's Dual Ch. Blick v. Grabenbruch, whose name permeates the pedigrees of many of today's top winners, including three dual champions among his immediate get. Blick finished his dual in 1951, becoming the first GSP dual on the East Coast.

A daughter of Al Sause's short-lived Ch. Dallo v.d. Forst Brickwedde (which traces back to the German family that produced FC Greif v. Hundscheimerkogel) was obtained by Dick and Bob Johns to breed to Blick. This mating produced two dual champions, Valkyrie and Junker v. Grabenbruch.

Dual Ch. Blick v. Grabenbruch (K.S. Sepp v. Grabenbruch ex Nanny v. Luckseck), owned by Richard and Robert Johns, was a strong early influence on the breed throughout the United States and the first dual champion Shorthair in the East.

Dual Ch. Valkyrie v. Grabenbruch (Dual Ch. Blick v. Grabenbruch ex Ch. Katrinka of Sycamore Road), owned by Richard Johns.

Valkyrie, an outstanding field trial winner among all comers, was bred to Ch. Tell v. Grabenbruch (Int, Ch. Franco Beckum, imp. ex Adda v. Assegrund, imp.) to produce Kenwick's Diana Beckum, dam of the 1957 NFC Bobo Grabenbruch Beckum, owned by Dr. William Schimmel of California. Bobo became a distinguished producer in his own right, siring the 1961 AKC NFC V. Saalfield's Kash, owned by Walter Seagraves of California, and Dual Ch. Bee's Gabby v. Beckum, owned by D. Briggs of California and handled by veteran Jake Huizenga. Seagraves was a neighbor of Don Miner, owner of the 1968 NFC Thalberg's Seagraves Chayne. Chayne was sired by FC v. Thalberg's Fritz II, an FC Greif v. Hundscheimerkogel son ex FC Patsy Grabenbruch Beckum. Patsy is by Bobo, and the lineage goes back to Valkyrie. Bobo also sired the top-producing bitch FC Mitzi Grabenbruch Beckum out of Becky v. Lueven. This trail can be traced to the present.

Dick's brother, Bob, died at the age of seventy-two in 1992. He was an ardent hunter of grouse and woodcock and kept a kennel of dogs for that purpose. During World War II, Bob was in the Army Air Force and was at Hickam Field during the attack on Pearl Harbor.

Dick, who went to the war in Germany, made an interesting observation about the diversity of type both in Germany and in the United States at the end of the war and into the 1950s and 1960s. "There was a hodge-podge of type," he said. "They wondered why they couldn't breed true."

In Germany, GSPs seldom intermixed with other Shorthairs out of their native territories, both because of lack of knowledge of the dogs and difficulties in transportation—and, of course, the war. Dick said Sepp and Nanny were from the same territory and were very similar in type.

That the Germans usually bred for the breed's main purpose was another factor. For shows, they wanted small dogs. For big game such as wild boar and roe deer, they wanted big dogs. For bird hunting, they wanted medium-size dogs. Shorthairs of all sizes came to the United States, and, in the 1960s, the big ones were often referred to as the old German type. This gave rise among the uninitiated to the mistaken assumption that the dogs from Germany were big and blocky. Actually, as pointed out earlier, handsome, medium-size dogs were the rule rather than the exception among early imports. There were, however, some big GSPs appearing here and there. I saw one of the original Fieldacres dogs in Ohio in the 1960s that weighed 120 pounds, while most of her kennelmates were about the size of Fox Terriers. They used her to train young dogs on point. When this dog went on point, it never broke. Most likely it didn't have the inertia to break.

Dick said the dogs that came from the Rhine Hessen Palatine regions of Germany were medium-size with big run because, speaking of the hunters that shot over these dogs, "they were rather portly men and didn't want to take one more step than necessary; they wanted the dogs to do the hunting and all the work. In those big fields, the Germans didn't want to do any more walking than they had to."

Dick made arrangements with the Army officials to ship the dogs Nanny and Sepp to America when he returned home.

"The government had wonderful arrangements. They had kennels set up at the port and did everything once you turned them over. Ten days after I got home, here came Nanny and Sepp to Wilkes-Barre. They came over on the boat after me and were shipped by rail from New York. They took wonderful care of them, and they were in great shape."

Noting the difference between then and now, Dick said, "I believe they were better dogs than today. They were easy to train."

DUAL CH., NFC KAY V.D. WILDBURG

Kay v.d. Wildburg was another of Dick Johns' imports to cast a large shadow on American GSP breeding. Kay was co-owned by Joe Eusepi of New York state and was by K.S. Pol v. Blitzdorf ex Cora v. Wesertor. Whelped in Germany in 1956, Kay was first imported to Canada and resold to Johns and Eusepi. Dick had judged a derby and knew that the owners had trouble handling him. He made an offer, and after paying for the dog and waiting a long time for the registration transfer to be delivered by the owner, he finally took possession and completed Kay's championships. Kay sired four dual champions, which tied him with Greif for the most duals for all time through 1979, thirteen show champions, twelve field champions and one amateur field champion.

Among Kay's notable get was Dual Ch. Frei of Klarbruk, UDT (ex Ch. Gretchenhof Cinnabar), who from 1966 to 1970 earned every title AKC had to offer, becoming the only triple title holder in show, field and obedience at the time. With the Obedience Trial championship today we now have triple champion titles. Frei was owned and bred by Joseph France of Maryland. Cinnabar was a sister of Gretchenof Tallyho, and both were full sisters of Ch. Gretchenhof Moonshine from another litter. All three made the GSPCA Hall of Fame.

Dual Ch. Kay v.d. Wildburg, owned by Richard Johns, was a national field champion and outstanding sire.

Kay won the 1959 National German Shorthaired Pointer Association Championship (American Field sanctioned) and was runner-up in 1961 and 1963. He also won some big American Field Pointer trials to help enhance his reputation as an outstanding performer.

Kay lived a long and productive life at the Johns' Kennels in Benton, Pennsylvania. He sired his last litter at the age of fifteen (with special dispensation from AKC) and reached the age of seventeen years before he died. His legend lives on through the long line of champions coming from him down through the generations. And he lives on in the mind of his owner and trainer up in the hill above Benton.

FC GREIF V. HUNDSCHEIMERKOGEL

FC Greif v. Hundscheimerkogel was an Austrian import that came into the possession of Dave Hopkins of Watsonville, California, from the Hundscheimerkogel Kennels of Viktor Rohringer of Vienna. Whelped in 1947, Greif was brought to America by a soldier stationed at Fort Ord, who sold him to Hopkins. Greif was by Alf Gindl ex Berta Spiesinger v. Pfaffenhofen. Four generations back in his pedigree we find recognizable ancestors: K.S. Kobold Mauderode-Westerhold, K.S. Kascha v. Schlossgarten, K.S. Furst v. Fuchpass, Cora v.d. Forst Brickwsedde and K.S. Hummel Sudwest.

FC Greif v. Hundsheimerkogel, a GSPCA Hall of Fame member, was imported from Austria and eventually owned by David Hopkins of California. His influence through his get still remains strong.

Greif (pronounced *Grife*) was shipped to the United States in 1949. The story goes that Hopkins was not much interested in the dog and kept him at home, where he amused himself chasing chickens and entertaining Mrs. Hopkins. Hopkins had other dogs for hunting and did not offer much opportunity to Greif. He sent Greif at the age of six to J. Stanley Head for field training and to cure him of chasing chickens, according to C. Bede Maxwell, who visited Mr. Head at a later date.

Head saw the dog's potential as a field trial prospect and told his owner, but according to reports Hopkins was not interested. One day, Hopkins took Greif hunting and returned greatly excited. He gave Head the green light to trial Greif, and at the age of eight years, in 1955, Greif finished his field championship. Those who saw him run were great in their praise of his performances. Before, during and after his brief field trial life, he was bred to some of the most outstanding bitches in California and produced remarkable progeny. It is Greif's progeny that distinguishes him from other outstanding Shorthairs.

Greif sired four duals, eight show champions and thirteen field champions, to hold the title of top sire of dual champions into the 1970s, when he was tied by Dual Ch. Kay v.d. Wildburg and FC Lutz v. dem Radbach. All three would be surpassed in the 1990s by Dual Ch. Hillhaven's Hustler and Dual Ch. Rugerheim's Bit Of Bourbon. Greif died in 1958 at the age of twelve.

Greif's four duals came out of two litters from Ch. Yunga War Bride, owned by Jake Huizenga of Salinas, California. Yunga, from one of Dr. Thornton's last breedings, was by Major v.s. ex Lassie v. Man O'War. She was bought as a puppy by Bob Holcomb, who sold her to Huizenga.

Three sisters from the matings went to Gene and Ercia Harden in Salinas, California, and they made dual champions of them all. Huizenga kept the fourth dog to become a dual, a male he named Dual Ch. Oxton's Bride's Brunz v. Greif. The sisters are Dual Ch. Oxton's Leislotte v. Greif, Dual Ch. Madchen Braut v. Greif and Dual Ch. Schoene Brant v. Greif.

While Greif's record for four dual champion get has now been surpassed, Yunga's four duals kept her the number-one top-producing dam of duals into the mid-1990s.

Huizenga's Dual Ch. Oxton's Bride Brunz v. Greif sired three dual champions, fourteen show champions and five field champions to tie for fourth place in all-time top sires of dual champions through 1996. Among his get was Dual Ch. Oxton's Minado v. Brunz, out of Ch. Sorgeville's Happy Holiday, a Canadian import. The breeders of the litter were Happy Holiday's owners, John and Gertrude Dapper. The owners of Minado were Ken and Inge Clody of California, whose Minado affix graced the names of many subsequent champions.

Dual Ch. Greif v. Hundscheimerkogel also sired FC Yunga v. Hundscheimerkogel in a mating to Bettina v. Schwarenberg, a daughter of Dual Ch. Rusty v. Schwarenberg. Greif also sired FC Karin v. Greif from a

Ch. Yunga War Bride, dam of four dual champions and owned by Jake Huizenga.

Bob v. Schwarenberg, imported from Germany by Joseph Burkhart.

mating with Ch. Freida v. Schoenweide. FC Yunga v. Hundscheimerkogel was bred to FC Karin v. Greif to produce American and Canadian Dual Ch. Gretchen v. Greif, who was bred and owned by Ralph and Francis Park of Seattle, Washington. Gretchen whelped in 1953 and was the first Am., Can. dual champion bred by the Parks, all from the same family. Among her titled get, Gretchen produced three duals to become the second all-time leading dam of dual champions.

The Parks also owned Dual Ch. Arrak v. Heisterholz, who was imported from Germany by Sgt. Bob Holcomb after his second tour of duty. Holcomb was stationed off and on at Fort Ord, Fort Lewis and other Western military bases before retiring from the Army to a small ranch near Yakima, Washington. His Army career allowed him to become heavily involved in Shorthair training and field trialing in the western United States and in Germany. His strong contacts in Germany, notably with the Radbach Kennels, enabled him to obtain some of the finest German dogs for America. In addition to Arrak, Holcomb imported, among others, FC Gert v.d. Radbach and Am., Can. FC Lutz v.d. Radbach, all of whom have had strong influence on American breeding even until the time of this book through the succeeding generations of quality get.

Arrak, who was acquired by Ralph Park, may be best known through his siring Am., Can. Dual Ch. Janie Greif v. Heisterholz, out of Am., Can Dual Ch. Gretchen v. Greif. Janie was owned by Elaine Stout of Colorado. Arrak, as with the other Radbach imports, was elected into the GSPCA Hall of Fame. Lutz v.d. Radbach sired four dual champions, eleven field champions, two amateur field champions and six show champions among his thirteen titled offspring. From Lulubelle v. Greif, a daughter of Gretchen, came Am., Can. Dual Ch. Ricki Radbach v. Greif, the fifth Am., Can. Dual Champion in the family-related line of duals owned by the Parks. Ralph Parks was the first president of the reformed GSPCA.

FC Gert v.d. Radbach, with a strong Blitzdorf background, will be remembered not only for siring two Am., Can. Dual Champions out of Gretchen but for being the grandsire of three-time national field trial champion Patricia v. Frulord. Her sire was the Gert son FC, Can. Dual Ch. Gert's Duro v. Greif and her dam was Juliana v. Frulord, with strong Greif lines on both sides. Patricia was bred and owned by Gladys and Dr. Fred Laird. She was the granddam of the 1976 NFC Frulord's Tim, who, at the age of twenty-nine months, was the youngest to become a national field trial champion. Dave McGinnis did most of the training and handling of Patricia and Tim.

Another great son of Greif was Don Miner's FC v. Thalberg's Fritz II out of v. Thalberg's Kaytydid, who was by Greif's son FC Yunga v. Hundscheimerkogel. Fritz II sired NFC v. Thalberg's Seagraves Chayne out of FC Patsy Grabenbruch Beckum. Under the handling of John Merrel, Chayne won the 1968 GSPA National Championship at Watertown, New York. I competed in that championship with Ch. Adam v. Fuehrerheim and witnessed

FC v. Thalberg's Fritz II, by FC Greif v. Hundsheimerkogel, is a Hall of Fame member, owned by Donald Miner.

NFC v. Thalberg's Seagraves Chayne, owned by Donald Miner, won the 1968 GSPCA National Field Championship.

Chayne's great performance through three all-walking series in heavy cover. His owner, Don Miner, was as gracious in victory as he was as a person. Runner-up was Cle and Shirley Carlson's Dual Ch. Richlu's Dan Oranian. Third was Dual Ch. Bo Diddley v. Hohentan, and fourth was Dual Ch. Tip Top Timber, a son of the famous Tip Top Timmy. It was a remarkable finish, with three duals placing second, third and fourth in strong national competition.

Fritz II also sired another great champion in national field competition, Rip Traf v. Bess ex FC Mitzi Grabenbruch Beckum. Bred by Jack Bess and owned by Gene Harden of Salinas, California, Rip Traf v. Bess was the sire of four show champions, fourteen field champions and seven amateur field champions. Among his get was a son, Ch. Schatzie's Greif der Ripper ex FC Schatzie's Grilla v. Greif, who sired Ch. Ripper v. Greif, who won back-to-back Bests of Breed at the GSPCA's National Specialties in 1984 under the author and in 1985 under Helen Case. Owned by Gene Ellis, a close friend of the Hardens, Ripper was shown only sparingly, mostly at Specialty shows. In the Minneapolis show, he was one of three dogs I kept in the ring for final judging, and it was a close contest between Ripper and a dog that was to become the all-time leading sire of dual champions, Dual Ch. Hillhaven's Hustler, a magnificent dog owned by David and Jan Hill of Wisconsin.

Rip's field performance is described in the following article by Art McDole that appeared at the time. McDole was Captain of the Guns at the GSCPA National for fourteen years.

THE GREATEST GERMAN SHORTHAIRED POINTER I HAVE EVER KNOWN

(Reprinted from the German Shorthaired Pointer News)

... The snow was falling gently on the white fields when through the trees a brown dog appeared running like the wind. "It's Rip", I cried with the other gunners waiting with me at the edge of the bird field.

... The scene was the Rocky Mountain Arsenal in Denver, Colorado, at the GSP Open National Championship Stake in October 1975. It was early in the morning and Ercia and Gene Harden of Salinas, California, had entered their NFC Rip Traf V. Bess in his ninth consecutive national. At the age of twelve when most Shorthairs have been retired, Rip was still a serious contender. This particular morning, Rip preceded the handlers and judges into the bird field by several hundred yards and locked into solid point on a cock pheasant, buried in the snow. With head and tail held high he stood intensly as his handler, Jack Bess approached and produced the bird. When the bird was down, he went eagerly on command and retrieved tenderly to hand. A second similar sparkling performance on another find and Rip was assured of a call back to the next series.

. . . How many times I have been thrilled by this sight! I've had the privilage and pleasure of the great dogs in the country, including fourteen National Champions. I have many wonderful memories of these big running, stylish and well-trained animals. Without detracting from these in any way, I can truthfully say that Rip has a very special place in my heart.

. . . I remember him as a wild running derby dog—of waiting for him at the bird field and seeing him tear through and a half mile out the other side before any of the handlers or judges were in sight. I told Jack then, "If you ever get him on a bird long enough for the judges to see him you've got a winner." He did, and went on to collect his derby points.

. . . And then he was broke—or almost so. As I waited at the bird field one day, Rip came tearing in far ahead as usual and slammed into a rock solid point. He stood for two or three minutes and no one came to help him. He cocked his head, raised both front feet and stomped! The pheasant flushed and Rip stood and watched until it was out of sight, turned and raced back over the hills in the direction from which he had come some five minutes before.

. . . And one of the greatest moments of all, when in 1967, I came back to shoot after the third series while Rip was called back for an honor and then declared the National Champion, and while he has never again won, he has often been in the finals, and placed both third and fourth.

. . . He was whelped April 6, 1963. His almost unbelievable record stands at 141 placements and 148 points, plus a National, in AKC trials enough to make him a Champion fifteen times over! I'm sure this is a record which will never be seriously challenged.

. . . Rip has sired a great number of field trial champions, and his daughter won the national in 1971. You cannot go to a field trial on the West Coast without seeing first, second and third generation offspring competing against each other, and even against Rip himself.

. . . Rip is characterized by a sweeping, effortless style of running with head held high. He points in the same manner, with erect tail, and a head held so high you think the bird must be many yards in front. He has always demonstrated a natural back with the same high style, without command, and as far away as he can see the pointing dog.

. . . His gentle disposition is in sharp contrast to his driving style in the field. It always gives me a warm feeling when I speak to him after the trial. He greets me with a wag of his tail and grasps my arm in his mouth and proudly "retrieves" me.

. . . Thanks Rip for the countless thrills, and for helping me to know and appreciate how a great All Age Shorthaired Pointer can perform. You're the greatest of them all!

The Greif name and the combinations of Greif and Radbach still appear high in many pedigrees of winning dogs toward the end of the twentieth century. The great influence of Greif in the West while he was active is wonderfully described in an article printed about 1960 providing the history of the German Shorthaired Pointer Club of Central California, one of the earliest clubs in the West. It is printed here intact, along with a list of field champions and owners of the time.

HISTORY: THE GERMAN SHORTHAIRED POINTER CLUB OF CENTRAL CALIFORNIA, INC.

The club was formed in 1954 after the late Geo. Richardson, Stan Head and Jake Huizenga had attended a Southern California Field Trial that March. After talking with some of the Shorthair owners in this area, they felt the need for a central club more convenient to them than the Northern and Southern California clubs operating at that time. They secured thirty-four names of prospective members and forwarded the necessary papers to the AKC. The Club's first Licensed Trial was held in March 1955 and the first Licensed Specialty took place in May of the the same year.

Geo. Richardson had, in the meantime, finished the first Western AKC Field Trial Champion, Karen v. Greif, shortly after which Sgt. Robert Holcomb finished the second Western Field Trial Champion, Yunga v. Hundsheimerkogel. Feeling great pride in Mr. Richardson's achievement with Karen, and sharing his bereavement in his loss of her, the club used Field Trial Champion Karen v. Greif as its symbol and goal toward better Shorthairs.

The members worked hard, giving much of their time and effort in trying to make this the outstanding German Shorthaired Pointer club in California. Mr. and Mrs. Ralph Parks, members of our club at this time, finished their Gretchen v. Greif's field trial championship at the tender age of twenty-two months. Close on her heels a little sister, Kristen v. Greif— "Tiska," as she is affectionately called by her owners, Donna and Andy Christensen—finished her field trial championship at twenty-six months.

Greif v. Hundsheimerkogel by this time was beginning to make himself known with his breedings. His owner, Dave Hopkins, a valuable member and devoted friend, was doing some research into the welding of the efforts of the California clubs into a unified group with his and Jake's idea of an Inter-Club Council. Greif finished his field trial championship, and we began to see his offspring making history in the Western field trials. One of his fine grandsons, FC Rex v. Hundsheimerkogel, owned by Col. Bartlett, one of our members, placed second in the 1955 National held in Michigan. He was trained and handled by Stan Head.

Stan Head, who had given so much of his valuable time in helping to organize the club, trained most of the dogs and, even with those he had not trained, was willing and ready to lend a helping hand to an owner with a problem concerning his dog. Our club and members, plus the all-important dogs, have greatly benefited by having the help of so fine a person as Stan.

Nineteen-fifty-seven saw the culmination of the club's dream of bringing the National German Shorthaired Pointer Field Trial to California. Unfortunately, we lost that year our valued friend and member, Mr. Dave

Hopkins, who had wanted so much to see the National held on the West Coast, and to make it a part of our progressive program; his passing was a great loss to all of us and to the club. The National Field Trial was a tremendous success, with Ivan Brower as President, Stan Head as Secretary and Jake Huizenga as Field Trial Chairman supported by the hard-working Central California club members. The other California GSP clubs co-hosted the event, but the lion's share of its success can be credited to the committees from this club.

In the short span of five years our club has held eight successful field trials, and five specialty shows. Our members have finished sixteen field trial champions—Harold Christensen has contributed three of these of which we are very proud: Konrad Christensen v. Greif, Della v. Hundsheimerkogel and Katy v. Hundsheimerkogel. The members have also finished eight bench champions, with three of them attaining the coveted Dual title: Ralph Parks' Gretchen v. Greif, Gene Harden's Oxton's Lieselotte v. Greif and Jake Huizenga's Oxton Bridge's Brunz v. Greif. There were also two bench champions with CDX titles in Obedience. Ch. Liza v. Greif has contributed a nice record for our club by finishing her bench championship at the age of fourteen months, and with her win of Best of Opposite Sex at the Westminster show in New York this Spring. These impressive wins total up a terrific record for our club and its members.

There are other potential champions on their way up, such as Dr. and Mrs. Benoit's Big Sky, who is really knocking at the door of success. He is a consistent winner at bench shows and has four points towards his field championship. There is also Ercia Harden's Schoene Braut v. Greif who, like Sky, has been winning regularly on the bench and needs only one more major to complete her bench championship. She, too, has Field Trial points. Ed Francis with his nice string of dogs is coming right along, as well as the very fine young dogs shown this past year in the puppy and derby stakes.

One of our club's greatest losses was the passing of Mr. Geo. Richardson, whom we all dearly loved. We will always remember him for his sportsmanship, loyalty, love for his fellow man, and devotion to his dogs.

Our officers are to be commended for their superb work in guiding our club so successfully. Jake Huizenga as Secretary had the hard and tedious task of organization. Harold Christensen as the second President with Margot Nelson as Secretary did a very fine and commendable job. Gordon Nelson, the third President and Margot Nelson staying on as Secretary and Field Trial Secretary for the second year, did a grand job, although they had to battle very bad weather for both of their Field Trials. Our hardest working member, Dell Gard, was our fourth President, and Ercia Arden was a very competent Secretary. They gave us a full and active year with all our events well done, leaving us with a sense of warm and pleasant accomplishment. The club is very happy to have as President for the coming year and hard-working Vice President and Field Trial Chairman, Dr. Arthur Benoit. He will have as Secretary his very charming wife, Myrtis. Our Treasurer will be Paul Brown. Paul replaced Geo. Richardson, who had been our Treasurer for four of our five years. We are sure Paul will continue to keep our finances in order as he has so ably done this past year.

Indeed, our club members have much to be proud of. Their very fine membership, their cooperation, sportsmanship and pure determination to make this the best possible club, and to foster the interests of the German Shorthaired Pointer breed.

GSPCC FIELD CHAMPIONS AND THEIR OWNERS

FC Karen v. Greif (George Richardson)

FC Yunga v. Hundsheimerkogel (Sgt. Robert Holcomb)

Dual Ch. Gretchen v. Greif (Ralph Parks)

FC Kristen v. Greif (Andy Christensen)

FC Moesgaard's IB (Ivan Brower)

FC Greif v. Hundsheimerkogel (Dave Hopkins)

FC Doktor Gaardens' Lucky (Ivan Brower)

FC Rex v. Hundsheimer (Col. Frank Bartlett)

FC Bobo Grabenbruck Beckum (Dr. Wm. Schimmel)

FC Konrad Christensen v. Greif (Harold Christensen)

FC Della v. Hundsheimerkogel (Julia Christensen)

Dual Ch. Oxton's Lieselotte v. Greif (E. E. Harden)

FC Fritzel v. Greif (George Richardson)

FC Katy v. Hundsheimerkogel (Harold Christensen)

FC Feld Jager v. Greif (Leta B. Swanson)

Dual Ch. Oxton Bride's Brunz v. Greif (Jake Huizenga)

GSPCC BENCH CHAMPIONS AND THEIR OWNERS

Ch. High Schatzi v. Schoenweide (Ercia Harden)

Ch. Yunga War Bride (Jake Huizenga)

Dual Ch. Gretchen v. Greif (Ralph Park)

Dual Ch. Oxton's Lieselotte v. Greif (E. E. Harden)

Ch. Liza v. Greif (Betty Eschen)

Dual Ch. Oxton Bride's Brunz v. Greif (Jake Huizenga)

Ch. Nee Rolf v. Hagen, CDX (Marie and Archie Nee)

Ch. Big Boy v. Hagen, CDX (Marie and Archie Nee)

Int. FC Moesgaard's IB, Danish import, foundation sire of Moesgaard and Fieldacres Kennels, owned by Jim Karns.

INT. FC MOESGAARD'S IB

Int. FC Moesgaard's IB (Pronounced *eeb*) was one of the first of the many Danish imports to America and, amazingly, his influence on American Short-hair development is just as vital today as it was when he was active. His production record in terms of numbers is not particularly impressive, but in terms of quality he left a lasting impression. He sired one dual champion, seven field champions and two show champions in America.

IB was sired by Danish Ch. Holevgaard's Kipp out of Nybjergs Rit—two names that mean little in America, but in Denmark they were backed up by a number of respected Danish champions such as Ch. Casper Koge, Ch. Moesgaard's Leddy, and Ch. Bob Koge several times on both sides.

He was bred by Niels Hykkelbjerg and imported by Hjalmar Olsen, who understood the strange names with extra letters in the pedigree since he was born and grew up in Denmark. During his frequent return trips, Olsen brought back an estimated fifty to sixty Danish dogs. IB was sold to Ivan Brower of Washington state; after Brower's death, he was sold to Jim Karns, who owned Fieldacres Kennel in Ohio, where Phil Morris was the trainer and handler. Fieldacres Kennels is no longer operating, but at one time it had many big-winning field trial dogs whose offspring were dispersed all over the country.

Jim Karns with Int. FC Skovmarken's Sep, imported from Denmark in 1955.

Fieldacres Kennels trainer Phil Morris shown with five field champions (from left): Int. FC Skovmarken's Sep, NFC Gunmaster's Jenta, FC Fieldacres Ib, FC Fieldacres Ammy and FC Moesgaard's Doktor.

IB was a brown ticked dog with liver patches, and his most famous son was similarly marked. That was Dual Ch. and NFC Moesgaard's Dandy, owned by Dr. Lewis Kline of Florida, a former president of the GSPCA, and trained by Don Spreadbury. Karns had another Moesgaard dog, FC Moesgaard's Doktor, who was also ticked with liver patches. Interestingly, almost all the other dogs coming out of Karn's breeding were small and solid white with liver heads, including the prepotent FC Fieldacres Ib. During the heyday of the Moesgaard era, run was the name of the game, and these dogs had a lot of run. They are still running into the twenty-first century through several dogs carrying heavy concentrations of Moesgaard inheritance, including FC Dixieland's Rusty, the greatest field trial sire in history in the number of both field champions produced and major wins.

They were off and running in the 1960s, and their speed and distance accelerated as the years rolled by once the AKC authorized horseback handling in the mid-'60s. That changed the color of the game both literally and figuratively. Range and speed became the catchword, and a lot of it came from the Moesgaard line and other Danish imports. Why Denmark? What was it about the Shorthairs of Danish breeding that made them so desirable for field trials? Because Denmark was not a belligerent in the war, and the Danes continued breeding Shorthairs while Germany and the rest of Europe could not? Many imported Danish dogs are pure white with some liver patches. Several dual champions have come out of the Danish dogs, although structurally many vary in appearance from the German and Austrian dogs. Or was it because breeders like Olsen, who came from Denmark, had many contacts in the United States and brought so many dogs there? Whatever the reason, there is a proliferation of Danish breeding in the United States and, inbred, linebred and outcrossed, they have a decided influence on the field trial game today.

When I was looking for a Shorthair in the early 1960s, one kennel I visited was Fieldacres. It was a large operation with several buildings, including kennels and stables. The owner, Jim Karns, was also interested in Arabians. His kennel was doing considerable winning in those days, especially by Fieldacres Ib and Ammy, who were sired by his import IB. I saw the Danish import Int. FC Skovmarken's Sep, who earned his American FC under Karns' ownership. Sep was not field trialed much after completing his field title. Unlike many of the other Fieldacres dogs, he was beautifully marked with ticking and liver patches.

When I was running my newly acquired Adam v. Fuehrerheim in puppy and derby stakes in the spring of 1963, I went to one of the first field trials held by the Pittsburgh GSP Club, where I found a large entry of Fieldacres dogs handled by Phil Morris. Adam won the puppy stake to become the only dog to win a first place that wasn't from Fieldacres. Adam was also sired by a dog from Scandinavia, Sweden to be exact, but he was solidly ticked against a white background with large liver patches. One of the puppy judges was

Dr. Clark Lemley, of Detroit, owner of Dual Ch. Dandy Jim v. Feldstrom, who won the first GSPCA National Field Trial Championship in 1953.

Two of the most famous Shorthair lines in the United States beginning in the late 1950s and flourishing in the 1960s came from Int. FC Moesgaard's IB: Karns' Fieldacres and Dr. Kline's Moesgaard breeding. Before their get began moving to the West and East, where they had much influence, the Fieldacres and Moesgaard dogs were a dominant force in the Midwest. Other lines, as mentioned earlier, were winning in the East, West, and upper Midwest as the Moesgaard and Fieldacres dogs were gaining dominance in their area. When breeders began mating dogs from these two lines, their names began to show up in pedigrees of big-winning dogs all over the country. A look back into the pedigrees of the top-winning dogs of today show many generations of Fieldacres and Moesgaard Shorthairs.

Dr. Kline's Dual Ch. and NFC Moesgaard's Dandy was one of IB's first big winners in America, and Dandy became the keystone of Moesgaard Kennels. Even though the import Moesgaard's IB was owned by Dr. Karns, Kline used the prefix Moesgaard's on his line of dogs. He was influenced, no doubt, by his handler and trainer Don Spreadbury, who had his own kennels near Fieldacres Kennels on the outskirts of Akron, Ohio. Dr. Kline lived in Florida, where he did winter training at Spreadbury Kennel.

Dr. Kline, who served as president of the GSPCA for several years in the 1970s, had a strong interest in dual champions, so conformation was an important aspect of his breeding. Dr. Kline was interning at a hospital in Detroit when he met Dr. Clark Lemley, who introduced him to Shorthairs.

Dandy was a solidly built dog with attractive ticking, a liver head and a large liver patch across his shoulders. He brought in run that was sought by field trialers as the number of trials increased. Whelped in 1957 out of FC Doktorgaarden's Lucky, a Danish import, Dandy earned his field championship in 1961 and his show title in 1964. His sire, Moesgaard's IB, was also his grandsire on his dam's side.

Dandy gained broad recognition by winning the 1962 GSPCA National Championship. He sired two dual champions, sixteen field champions and four show champions. Both Dandy and his sire are in the GSPCA Hall of Fame. Dandy's two duals are Dual Ch. Moesgaard's Dandy's Lucy Ball ex Pearl of Wetzler and Dual Ch. Gruenweg's Dandy ex Ch. Tessa v. Abendstern. Lucy was bred by the Estate of Paul Pfaff and owned by Dr. Kline. Her mother's line includes Dual Ch. Rusty v. Schwarenberg. Gruenweg's Dandy was bred and owned by Ralph Neff of North Canton, Ohio, and is the sire of two dual champions himself.

Another outstanding dog owned by Dr. Kline sired by Int. FC Moesgaard's IB is FC Moesgaards Ruffy ex Moesgaard's Arta. Ruffy is behind many of the top field dogs today, through his eleven field trial champions.

Two more Moesgaard top producers are FC/AFC Moesgaard's Dee Dee's Jackson and FC Moesgaard's Coco, both important in numbers and impact

Don Spreadbury, trainer and handler for Dr. Lewis Kline's Moesgaard Kennel.

1962 National Field Champion and Dual Ch. Moesgaard's Dandy, owned by Dr. Lewis Kline.

Dual Ch./NFC Dandy Jim v. Feldstrom, first GSPCA National Field Champion, owned by Dr. Clark Lemley.

on the breed. Jackson, owned by Dr. H. A. Reynolds and Linda Attig of Mahomet, Illinois, was by FC Moesgaard's Dandy Jac (Moesgaard's Ruffy ex FC Fieldacres Cindy Lou of Barcar) ex Moesgaard's Deejay's Dee Dee (Dual Ch. Tip Top Timmy ex FC Moesgaard's Angel's Deejay). She is from an early mix of Fieldacres, Moesgaard and Tip Top Timmy, another of our most influential sires, who will be discussed next. Jackson is sixth in the all-time list of producers of field-titled dogs with thirty-two.

FC and 1967 Amateur NFC Moesgaard's Coco is another deeply infused Moesgaard's IB champion that figures so prominently in modern GSPs as a prolific producer. Coco was whelped in 1959, bred by M. L. Saunders and owned and handled by Lloyd Sanders. Coco was sired by FC Moesgaard's Ruffy ex Moesgaard's Six (FC Moesgaard's IB ex FC Doktorgaarden's Lucky). Coco sired twenty-one field-titled dogs and nine show champions to tie for fourteenth place in the all-time production of field champions. He was tied with Don Miner's great champion, FC v. Thalberg's Fritz.

The Moesgaard's line also includes FC and 1963 NFC Moesgaard's Angel, a Hall of Fame selection, and tied with Angel's Queen of Points for fourth place in all-time production of field trial champions, with thirteen, through 1994.

Other outstanding Moesgaard dams are AFC Moesgaard's Dandy's Cindy Lu and FC Moesgaard's Dandy's Dora II, tied for tenth in the all-time production of field trial champions with seven, and Hall of Fame member Moesgaard's Angel's Deejay, tied for eleventh with six field champions. Bred

Fieldacres Kennels' leading sire and dam were FC Fieldacres Ib (left) and FC Fieldacres Ammy (right).

NAFC Moesgaard's Coco, owned by Lloyd Sanders, a leading sire of field champions.

Dual Ch. Lucy Ball, a winning field champion and strong producer, was owned by Dr. Lewis Kline. Dr. Kline, GSPCA president for many years, was a strong proponent of the dual champion.

NFC Moesgaard's Dee Dee's Jackson, handled by John Rabidou, is the breed's seventh leading sire of field trial champions.

by Alice Phaegen and owned by Dr. H. H. Reynolds of Savoy, Illinois, Deejay counts among her get Hall of Fame member FC Checkmate's Dandy Dude, who is third in all-time production of Field titles with forty-two. His get also includes a dual and three show champions. His sire was FC Moesgaard's Ruffy. Deejay's four grandsires are Int. FC Moesgaard's IB.

Int. FC Moesgaard's IB also provided the foundation for the successful Fieldacres Kennels. It is rather ironic that the owner of Moesgaard's IB would name his kennel Fieldacres when he owned the foundation dog, while Dr. Kline, who only bred to the dog, named his kennel Moesgaard and most of the succeeding dogs coming out of his kennel carry the Moesgaard's prefix. But Fieldacres became a highly recognizable name that remains prominent in big-winning dogs to this day even though the kennel has not been active for many years. The dogs that put the name on the map were Fieldacres Ib, who was out of Moesgaard's Girl, who was by Moesgaard's IB out of FC Doktorgaarden's Lucky Jujens Tommi. Through 1994, Ib was tied for seventh place in the all-time production of field-titled offspring, with thirty-one.

FC Fieldacres Ib sired the 1966 GSPCA National Field Trial Champion, FC Fieldacres Bananza, out of Fieldacres Lesa. Int. FC Moesgaard's IB was the grandfather on both sire and dam sides, and he appears six times in four generations. Bananza was bred by Jim Karns and was owned by Harold and Jean Dowler of Union City, Pennsylvania. His handler, Ralph Terrel, was one of the leading handlers in the Midwest.

The pedigree of 1983 NAFC October's Punkin shows Mooesgaards IB, Fieldacres Ib, Moesgaard's Ruffy, Fieldacres Ammy and NFC Moesgaard's. Punkin, owned by Dr. John Baillie of Minneapolis, was sired by FC Brown L (Fieldacres Ib's Dek ex, who is by Fieldacres Ib) out of FC October's Frost, by Fieldacres Ib's Dek ex Callmac's Heidi v. Moesgaard, who was sired by Coco.

FC Tip Top Timmy, shown with breeder-handler Tom Getler (left) and owner Fred Palmer, was a GSPCA Hall of Fame sire.

FC Fieldacres Ammy was sired by the Danish import Int. FC Skovmarkens Sepp out of Fieldacres Sheen (FC Gunmaster's Pacer ex 1955 NFC Gunmaster's Jenta, also owned by Karns). Ammy is tied for sixth place in the all-time production of field-titled champions through compilations of 1994 with Ib. When mated to her half-brother Fieldacres Ib, Ammy produced many field champions with major wins all over the United States. Among their offspring were NFC Fieldacres Sir Jac, FC Fieldacres Ib's Dek (owned by Dean Kerl), who sired FC Brown L (important in the chain of producers with field-titled champions) out of Moesgaard's Dandy Star, who was sired by Dual Ch. and NFC Moesgaard's Dandy.

Although both lines came from the same sire, they differed in running style, structure and color. The Moesgaard line produced medium-size solid dogs that covered ground smoothly without much up-and-down movement. They were ticked with brown patches, with some pure white that came along with certain matings. For the most part, with the exception of Skovemarken's Sepp, Moesgaard's Doktor and one or two other dogs, Fieldacres Shorthairs were almost solid white with liver heads and an occasional liver spot. They were smallish dogs, rather light in structure, and ran with great animation. Although wedded to a common sire, it was as if they had come from two entirely different branches. But singly, through pure Fieldacres dogs or Moesgaard dogs, they produced a long bloodline that continues today. When dogs from the two lines were mated to each other, the results were equally successful. Strong linebreeding and inbreeding of these families consistently produced winners.

FC TIP TOP TIMMY

FC Tip Top Timmy appeared almost out of nowhere in New Jersey in 1958, about four years before I acquired my first Shorthair. He was already a household word in Shorthairs in the East when I started field trialing in the fall of 1962. Dual Ch. Fritz of Sleepy Hollow's days of campaigning in the Northeast were at a close, and all the talk was about FC Tip Top Timmy and FC/NFC Kay v.d. Wildburg.

Timmy was bred by Tom Getler, a genial young professional who was gaining a reputation as an outstanding trainer. The only other major field trial trainer in the East at the time was the inestimable Dick Johns. Owned by Fred Palmer, Timmy was sired by Duke v. Jager ex Rexann v. Stolzhafen. The most recognizable dog in the background was FC Scott's Pride.

Timmy had the run and pointing style much in demand in the mid-1960s, when handlers got the green light by the AKC to handle off horseback. Timmy had won the prestigious English Setter Club Championship and Jockey Hollow championship in New Jersey that were mainstays of Pointers and Setters. Why he caught the national attention he did was largely because of his reputation as a consistently big-going, purposeful dog. He was distinguished by his long distance, high-headed pointing style.

Timmy was a medium-size dog with solid brown ticking and a brown head. He is tied for the seventeenth all-time top producer of field-titled dogs, counting among his get seventeen field champions, seven show champions and one dual champion. Through such famous dogs as his son Dual Ch. Tip Top Timber and his grandson FC Tip Top Savage Sam, tenth on the list of all-time producers of field-type champions, Timmy's lines went into the development of generations of outstanding dogs that make up the big winners through the mid-1990s. Dual Ch. Tip Top Timber sired eight field and amateur field champions and four show champions.

Tip Top Savage Sam (Timber-sired FC Checkmate's Dandy Duke ex Hurckes Choice of Navaho by FC Windy Hill Prince James) sired three dual champions, three show champions and twenty-eight field and amateur field champions. Field champion sire of the year in 1986 and 1987, Sam sired Dual Ch. and AFC Checkmate's August Dog, Dual Ch. Wilkenson's Yue-He and Dual Ch. and 1987 NFC Leipchen Buddendorf among his famous get. Dual Ch. August Dog was whelped in 1978 out of Uodibar's Sister Brown, bred by Leon Sienkowski, Sr., and owned by Kimberly and Glenn Isaacson of Antioch, Illinois.

Yue-He, bred by James Claire and owned by Harry Wilkinson of Pentwater, Michigan, was out of Claire's Gouldren v. Stratin, who was sired

Dual Ch. Tip Top Timber was a famous son of FC Tip Top Timmy, owned by Harold Brunke.

FC Hugo v. Bergeskante was a national-champion son of FC Tip Top Timmy, owned by John Ullman.

by FC/NFC Checkmate's White Smoke, by Checkmate's Dandy Dude, by Dual Ch. Tip Tip Timber, by Tip Top Timmy.

Dual Ch./NFC Leipchen Buddendorf was bred by Ronald Herman in 1980 and is owned by Mary Finley of Encinal, Texas. Liebchen's dam was Leighton's Ace Mona (FC Moesgaard's Ace ex Jimmy's Fieldacres Joy). Ace is by FC Moesgaard's Ruffy, and Joy's grandsire is FC Fieldacres Ib. She combines the bloodlines of FC Tip Top Timmy through Dual Ch. Tip Top Timber, FC Checkmate's Dandy Dude and FC Tip Top Savage Sam and FC Windy Hill Prince James on the sire's side and Moesgaard's Ruffy and Fieldacres Ib on the dam's side.

Leipchen's dam, Leighton's Ace Mona, also produced the dam of the all-time leading sire of field-titled champions, FC Dixieland's Rusty, also bred and owned by Ronald Herman, of El Dorado, Arkansas.

Leipchen had an illustrious field trial career handled by Ed Husser of Louisiana. She was the first American dog ever to win Germany's Hubertus Hannover award, in 1987, and the Gulf Coast GSP Club awarded her its first Field Trial Dog of the Year in 1986 and 1987. Her field trial record, in addition to the 1987 GSPCA National Championship, includes the National

Dual Ch./NFC Leibchen Budden-dorff, owned by Mary Finley, won the 1987 National Championship. She was bred by Ron Herman, who also bred a half-brother, FC Dixie-land's Rusty, the all-time leading sire of field champions. She is shown here with her trainer, Ed Husser.

Leighton's Ace Mona, shown at ten years old, dam of FC Dixieland's Rusty, the breed's all-time leading sire of field champions and Dual Ch./NFC Leipchen Buddendorff.

German Pointing Dog Championships in 1982, 1985, 1986 and 1987. She also won the 1985 GSPA Shooting Dog Championship and the 1986 and 1987 NGSPCA Chukar National Shooting Dog Championships—all American Field titles.

A member of the GSPCA Hall of Fame, Leipchen produced several field and show champions, with the final count still to be determined. Mary Finley and her husband, Joe, own the famous 90,000-acre Callaghan Ranch between San Antonio and Laredo, Texas, where Leipchen spent her time when not with her handlers.

Mary also owns the famous Pointer Brush Country Spectre. Also trained by Husser, Spectre won the National Derby Championship, the National Free For All three-hour championship and the National Championship, a spectacular feat that should place him in the American Field Hall of Fame someday.

FC Uodibar's Boss Man was the most prolific sire to come from Timmy. His dam, NFC Heidi v. Ufenwald, was the daughter of FC Windy Hill Prince James, which combined two of the biggest-winning bloodlines of that time. Boss Man is the second leading sire of field-titled get through 1994, with forty-three field and amateur field champions, two duals and four show champions. Boss Man was bred by Henry Meyer and Ree Le Beau Meyer and owned by John Rabidou of Hondo, Texas. He became the backbone of Uodibar breeding, which produced many nationally renowned trial winners.

Boss Man was named to the GSPCA Hall of Fame in 1985; he was an outstanding field dog who finished second in the 1975 GSPCA National Championship in Denver from an entry of 105. The winner was Ronald Rainey's FC Mark V's One Spot. Boss Man's get included two GSPCA National Gun Dog Champions, three GSPCA National Amateur Champions and one GSPCA All-Age National Field Champion. Additionally, his get won numerous National and Regional Field Trial Championships in American Field Competition.

Bossman's AKC National Champion (All-Age) was FC Ammertal's Boss Ranger out of FC/AFC Ammertal's Kitt v. Shinback, a daughter of the German import Esser's Chick, a son of Germany's all-time leading sire of German field champions. Ranger was bred by Gary Stevens and owned and handled by Gary Nehring of Edina, Minnesota. I was privileged to marshal that trial in 1980 near Clarksburg, New Jersey. He put on a wonderful performance from start to finish to leave no doubt that he was the winner. Ranger also sired eleven field and amateur field champions to rank in a tie for twenty-second on the all-time list. Bossman's two GSPCA National Gun Dog Champions were Dual Ch. and AFC Bosslady Jodi v. Greif, who also won two National Amateur Field Trial Championships, and FC/AFC Uodibar's Mouse. His other National Amateur Field Champion was FC and AFC Fleeta v. Boss Man, and his other American dual champion was Dual Ch. Uodinbar's PDQ v. Waldtaler.

FC Uodibar's Iron John, handled by John Rabidou.

FC Uodibar's Boss Man, second leading sire of field champions, owned and handled by John Rabidou.

NFC Ammertal's Boss Ranger, winner of the 1980 National Field Trial Championship, owned and handled by Gary Nehring.

The owners of Dual Ch./AFC Bosslady Jodi v. Greif, Gary and Harriet Short of Independence, Iowa, are the only winners of all four AKC National Championships. Bosslady's dam was Dual Ch./AFC Dee Tee's Baschen v. Greif (by Dual Ch. Oxton's Minado v. Brunz ex Dual Ch. Cede Mein Dolly der Orrian, the second-top-producing dam of dual champions with three duals, twenty-one show champions and four field champions). She was bred, owned and handled by Gary Short. Bosslady won the 1979 and 1981 National Amateur Championships and the 1980 National Open Gun Dog Championship. The Shorts also owned and Gary handled the 1979 National Field Champion Dual Ch. Lika Buckskin, sired by FC Buckskin ex Albrecht's Cora's Miss.

The winner of the 1979 National Gun Dog Championship was FC/AFC Uodibar's Mouse, sired by Bossman out of Fieldacres Candoit, who was sired by FC Fieldacres Ib out of an Ib granddaughter. Mouse was bred by John Rabidou, owned by Dr. John and Sandi Burk of Aledo, Texas, and handled by Dave McGinnis.

The 1982 National Amateur Championship was won by FC/AFC Fleeta Bossman, by Bossman ex Cindy v. Wasserschling, an Esser's Chick granddaughter. She was bred and handled by Chuck Mayor and owned by Marie Mayo of Kent, Washington.

Dual Ch. Uodibar's v. Waldtaler was owned by Patricia Toner of Ocala, Florida. Bred by David Hill, she was out of Ch. Whiskey Creek Whirlwind, who was by Dual Ch. Baron Fritz v. Hohen Tann ex Ch. Becky v. Hesselbach.

By now, in case the reader has not figured it out, Uodibar is Rabidou spelled backward, which is only one of many clever names coined by John Rabidou's fertile mind. John is not only a breeder, trainer and handler of outstanding dogs, he is also a horse trader and farrier. He has a Master's Degree in Sociology and taught at the University of Wisconsin before turning professional. He was elected president of the German Shorthaired Pointer

NFC Uodibar's Mouse, winner of the 1979 National Open Gun Dog Championship. Owned by Dr. John and Sandy Burk and handled by John Rabidou.

Club of America in 1997. In a December 1994 letter to me from his home in Hondo, Texas, he passed on some of his thoughts on the important breed influences, with high marks for FC Tip Top Timmy:

My trek with GSPs began with a great one—Windy Hill Prince James—when I accidentally moved next to Don Thomack in Sun Prairie, Wisconsin, while attending graduate school at the University of Wisconsin. [*Author's Note:* Thomack was a trainer and handler of James.]

James was a great bird dog—would run himself to death to find another bird. But his legacy isn't winning but producing winners for several generations. Simultaneously, Tip Top Timmy was producing well in the East and when we mated three-time NFC Heidi v. Uferwald, a James daughter, to Tip Top Timmy, we got Bossman. In this same era came Checkmate's Dandy Dude who was a Timmy grandson by Dual Ch. Tip Top Timber who was bred to FC Moesgaard's Angel's Deejay, a Moesgaard's Ruffy granddaughter by Coco.

Of the Moesgaards, two were clearly superior producers—Fieldacres Ib and Moesgaard's Ruffy—in terms of their production and continuing genetic impact. Timmy and Bossman both crossed very well on the Ib daughters and granddaughters.

Rabidou's 1986 National Field Champion Uodibar's Koonas is the result of a Timmy granddaughter, Uodibar's Dirty Girty, bred to all-time top field champion FC Dixieland's Rusty. Rusty has a Moesgaard's/Fieldacres background, with Danish import Dual Ch. Tell added to the mix.

John Rabidou is the breeder and owner of Koonas, who through 1994 sired one dual champion, one show champion and nineteen field and amateur field champions.

Koonas' dual is Dual Ch. Vogelein's Billy of Sundance (Koonas ex FC Sundance Gypsy Lee), bred and owned by John Voglein. Voglein also owned Gypsy Lee, a member of the Hall of Fame, who is by NFC Tip Top Savage Sam, a Timmy grandson, out of NFC Burr Oaks Dora, a Prince James daughter.

FC Checkmate's Dandy Dude, the third leading sire of field champion get, combines Timmy, Moesgaard and Kay v.d. Wildburg bloodlines. Whelped in 1969, Dude was sired by Dual Ch. Tip Top Timber, a son of FC Tip Top Timmy, out of FC Moesgaard's Angel's Deejay (FC/NFC Moesgaard's Coco ex FC/FC Moesgaard's Angel). He was bred by Dr. H. A. Reynolds and was owned by Edward Arkema of Chicago. His get through 1994 included one dual, three show champions, and forty-two field and amateur field champions. His dual is Dual Ch. Checkmate's Challenger.

FC Checkmate's Dandy Dude sired the 1980 National Amateur Field Trial Champion FC/AFC P.J. Wildfire, out of Wyoming's Gretchen, the daughter of FC Windy Hill Prince James ex Her Nibbs of Navajo. Wildfire, who was bred by Lynn Sommer and owned by Pat Vicari of Medinnah, Illinois, is the

NFC Uodibar's Koonas, sired by the all-time leading sire of field champions, FC Dixieland's Rusty, was also a National Field Champion and leading sire of field champions in turn.

NFC Uodibar's Stub A Dub, winner of the 1991 National Open Gun Dog Championship, owned by Kent Kislingbury and handled by John Rabidou.

A gathering of celebrated Shorthairs and their handlers at the 1975 National Championship in Denver, Colorado (from left): John Merrell with NFC Mark Five's One Spot, the winner; John Rabidou with FC Uodibar's Boss Man; Eric Erickson with Tip Top Teddy and Jack Bess with FC Golden West Chucko.

This group of famous dogs and handlers includes (front row, from left): John Merrell with Wyatt's v. Shinback, Walter Epps with Big Island Sassafrass, Donna McGinnis with Frulord's Tim and Dave McGinnis with Patricia von Frulord. Patricia and her son Tim von Frulord are both National Field Champions. Those in the back row are (from left): John Rabidou, Mary Finley, Gary Stevens and Phil Morris.

ninth leading sire of field champions, with seventeen field champions, twelve amateur field trial champions and two show champions through 1994.

Dude was also the grandsire of 1985 National Gun Dog Champion Moesgaard Deejay's Sin, bred by Dr. Kay Lindsay and Dr. H. A. Reynolds and owned by John Rabidou. Sin was sired by FC Checkmate's Savage Sam (FC Checkmate's Dandy Dude ex Hurke's Choice of Nava by Windy Hill Prince James). His dam was FC Moesgaard's Deejay's Vixen by NFC Hugo v. Bergeskante, a Timmy son, out of FC and AFC Moesgaard's Deejay's April Love, who was sired by Dual Ch. Tip Top Timber.

A number of the top field trial champions based on Checkmate's Dandy Dude and Uodibar's Boss Man have been owned and handled by Lynn Hadlock of Cary, Illinois. Except for some assistance in training and occasional handling by professionals, the Hadlocks have trained and handled their Shorthairs themselves.

Lynn said in a letter to me in July 1997, "We decided a long time ago the fun of field trialing is training and handling your Shorthairs yourself—you may not have as many ribbons at the end of the year, but the ones you have are more meaningful." The record shows the Hadlocks have been very successful with that philosophy, campaigning twenty-two dogs to field championships since 1977, with several national champions along the way. Among the best were Checkmate's Dude's Big Foot, Hadlock's Torrid Todd, Uodibar's Rachel and Cappy II.

FC Checkmate's Dude's Big Foot was sired by Dandy Dude out of Wyoming's Gretchen (FC Windy Hill Prince James ex Her Nibbs of Navaho). Big Foot (a.k.a. Casey) won an all-age regional and was runner-up in three other regional all-age championships and the 1985 Quail All Age Championships. Through 1997, Casey sired three national champions holding six national championship titles, three runner-up national champions holding four runner-up titles and seventeen field and amateur field champions. He is the grandsire of the dam of NFC Rawhide's Clown, the only dog to win three GSPCA National All Age Championships in a row.

Big Foot's son FC Hadlock's Torrid ex Heide Creek Dandy (FC Quail Creek's Dandy ex K's Triple T—with Tip Top Timmy, Moesgaard, Kay v.d. Wildburg and Big Island in the background) was the 1985 GSPCA All Age Dog of the Year. He won the 1983 NGSPCA National Futurity and National Derby Classic and the 1988 Region 5 Amateur All Age Championship. He was runner-up for the 1986 NGSPCA National Championship.

The Hadlock's FC Uodibar's Rachel was an FC Uodibar's Boss Man daughter out of Wyoming's Gretchen. Rachel won the 1978 NGSPCA All Age Championship and the 1980 Region 5 All Age Championship and was the 1978 GSPCA All Age Dog of the Year. She produced seven field champions and is the granddam of two-time National Champion Sanjo's Sin City Slicker.

Timmy is the grandsire on his dam's side of 1977 NFC Jocko v. Stolzhafen, bred by Richard Johns and owned by Dr. Joseph Brown of

NFC Uodibar's Rachel, top-producing dam of field champions and #7 in 1992, owned by Lynn Hadlock.

FC Checkmate's Dude's Big Foot, a big-winning field trial dog and a leading sire, owned by Lynn Hadlock.

FC Hadlock's Torrid Todd, owned by Lynn Hadlock, was the 1985 GSPCA All-Age Dog of the Year.

Hall of Fame member and leading sire of field trial champions, FC Windy Hill Prince James, owned by John Urso.

Lewistown, Pennsylvania. Whelped in 1971, Jocko was sired by FC Doc v. Brot ex William's Ramblin Sue. Doc was sired by FC Fritz v. Smidt, also owned by Dr. Brown, and he was by Duke v. Jager ex Rexann v. Stolzhafen, making him the full brother of Timmy.

FC WINDY HILL PRINCE JAMES

FC Windy Hill Prince James, as has been shown in the various pedigrees of aforementioned winning dogs, was a major force in many of the top German Shorthair bloodlines in the United States through the 1960s, 1970s and 1980s and continues exerting his influence to this day.

James was sired by Tri State Trooper out of Windy Hill Whylimina in 1962. His breeder was Albert Dax and his owner was John Urso of McFarland, Wisconsin. His background gave no indication of his ability to produce. One must go back five generations to find Dual Ch. Baron v. Strauss, Waldheim, Brickwedde, Schnellberg and Winterhauch on the dam's side and Ch. Fritz v. Pepper and Ch. Otto v. Strauss on the sire's side. I have never met anyone who had ever seen Tri State Trooper or could describe him, yet his son became one of the most famous dogs in America. He showed up in the field trial hotbed of the Upper Midwest as handlers were getting on horse-back and run was increasing in importance and came to the attention of Don

Thomack and John Rabidou. Coupled with some of the best sires and dams in the game, James made a significant contribution.

James is the fifth-leading sire of field champions through 1994 with thirty-eight, along with one dual champion and three show champions. His production record is impressive in both numbers and quality. Many of the national champions, as has been shown already, carry his bloodlines. He was an early electee to the GSPCA Hall of Fame.

ESSER'S CHICK

Advertised in the GSPCA 1965 Yearbook as "A new shot of gunpowder from Germany," Esser's Chick arrived in the United States in June 1965 at the age of three.

Chick (Axel v. Wasserschling ex Jagers Nama) was imported by Col. Darwin A. Brock, USA-Ret, Temple Hills, Maryland. Col. Brock acquired Chick while stationed in Germany. His ad contained a photograph of the solid liver dog standing in a field and included vital statistics on his conformation, his breeding and his field and show record in Europe.

Col. Brock went on to say, "I purchased Chick for import after four years experience as a judge in German Derbies and all-breed trials. He was one of the greatest Shorthairs in Germany and was highly regarded by the breed fancy."

Esser's Chick, an Axel v. Wasserschling son, brought to America by Col. Darwin Brock of Maryland, appears frequently in the pedigrees of top-winning field trial dogs.

I saw Chick for the first time at the Mason-Dixon Field Trial near York, Pennsylvania. He was a light-boned, smallish liver dog very similar in appearance to some of the German dogs that were arriving in the United States at that time in the second wave of post–World War II imports.

Chick was entered in a few field trials but was unable to win a title because he was not steady to wing and shot. Apparently, he had been kept too long in unbroken stakes in Germany and could not be steadied. Dick Johns, his handler, said he was just about impossible to break. I don't know if he was ever shown. He was a busy gun dog with a lot of energy, but I never saw him show the all-age potential that emerged in the offspring of a number of his early breedings. His greatest attraction was his sire, Axel v. Wasserschling, who, like his son, was also untitled. Axel was the most prolific sire of field trial winners in Germany, and Chick made his bloodlines available in America. He found great favor in the Upper Midwest and on the East and West coasts. Early successes of his get placed him in brisk demand at stud.

Through 1994, Chick was tied for seventh place among all-time top sires for field trial champions with thirty-one field champions, nine amateur field champions, one dual champion and nine show champions. The quality of his get was exceptional.

Chick's get included one German Sieger, one Canadian Champion, one dual champion, the 1969 GSPCA National Field Trial Champion, the 1970 GSPCA National Amateur Field Trial Champion, the 1972 NGSPD Shooting Dog Champion, the 1975 NGSPD National Shooting Dog Quail Champion and the 1977 NGSPA National Amateur Champion. Chick's name is prominent in the pedigrees of many of the top-winning dogs of his era through the present.

The greatest dog sired by Chick was the 1969 NFC Blick v. Shinback out of Melissa v. Greif, a daughter of FC v. Thalberg's Fritz II. Blick was bred by John Hulcy and owned by Cal Rossie of San Francisco. Rossi is listed as his owner in the 1969 Yearbook, when he was voted into the Hall of Fame. His handler was John Merrell, an outstanding professional trainer who is still winning at the time of this writing.

Blick is fourth among all-time top sires of field champion get, with twenty-seven field champions, twelve amateur field champions, one dual and five show champions. Blick sired the 1972 GSPCA National Field Champion, the 1973 Dam of the Year for field-type champions and the 1973 Amateur Field Trial Dog of the Year. His 1972 NFC was FC Wyatt's Gip v. Shinbach, out of Onna v. Bess (FC v. Thalberg's Fritz II ex FC Mitzi Grabenbruch Beckum). John Merrell was the breeder and handler and Warren Palmer of Sherman Oaks, California, was the owner.

John Merrell, in a note to me in early 1997, said, "Blick was the best GSP that I have ever had. He had a good mind, very smart, lots of style and nose." Merrell has trained and finished more than seventy field champions.

NFC Patricia v. Frulord, owned by Mrs. Gladys Laird, won two AKC National Field Championships and one American National Field Championship.

NFC Blick v. Shinback, an Esser's Chick son and winner of the 1969 National Championship, was owned by Brad Calkins and handled by John Merrell.

He added: "He taught me a lot of things that a bird dog should do. He always ran in front and knew where to go to find birds. Dogs like Blick could make a young trainer look pretty good. He made his FTC in September and won the National in October before his third birthday in January, 1970.

"In those days we used pheasants in trials and sometimes they would leave a dog standing on point for a long time. When I sent Blick on to relocate, he never went straight in the wind. He would turn and make a quartering pattern and pin the bird. It was instinct; he was not taught. Another thing he would do, on a long retrieve, was run ten to fifteen feet down wind and turn into the bird."

Esser's Chick's dual champion is Dual Ch. Esser's Duke v.d. Wildburg, whose dam was De-Lors Brandie v.d. Wildburg (NFC/Dual Ch. Kay v.d. Wildburg ex Dual Ch. Fee v.d. Wildburg). Duke attained both his field and show championships in 1976 to become a dual champion. He was bred by Frank Critelli, owned by Joseph and Mary Avolio of Orland Park, Illinois, and handled in the field by Tom Schwartfeger.

Duke sired the 1984 GSPCA National Gun Dog Champion Esser Wendy v. Wildburg out of Duke's v. Patty (Huffers Duke of Earl ex Nicola Patti v. Babo). The breeder was Lowell Edwards and the owner was Robert Ryan, D.V.M., of Sycamore, Illinois. He was handled in the field by Dan Anderson.

Chick appears in many of the winning pedigrees to this day.

THE AXEL V. WASSERSCHLING INFLUENCE

A few other Axel v. Wasserschling sons and daughters came to America around the same time as Chick, but they did not make the same overall impact. Of the Axel imports, next to Chick in production were Am., Can. FC Radbach's Bimbo and Peron.

Axel was bred to Jessy v.d. Radbach in Germany, and the bitch was imported to Texas, where she whelped the litter that produced Bimbo. Listed as breeder was Col. W. L. Anthony. Bob Holcomb obtained Bimbo for William F. Peters, M.D., Seattle, and trained and handled him in the field. Bimbo won more than 100 first places in field trials, was named Northwest Field Trial Council's Shooting Dog of the Year for five consecutive years, from 1968 through 1972, and was elected to the GSPCA Hall of Fame.

Bimbo was tied for seventeenth among the all-time top sires of field trial champions through 1994, with seventeen field trial champions and one show champion. Among his get was the 1974 National Amateur Field Trial Champion Rex v.d. Hirschau out of FC Freya v.d. Hirschau. Freya was by Esser's Chick ex Dual Ch. Fee v.d. Wildburg, thus placing Axel v. Wasserschling on both the sire's and dam's side of the pedigree. Bimbo lived in the house with the Peters family when he was not field trialing until he died at the age of sixteen years.

Popular professional field trial handler John Merrell, handling from horseback.

Handlers at the 1977 National Futurity in Michigan. Front row (from left): Tom Schwertfeger, Mike Butler, C. B. Watts, Fred Dempsey and Ralph Terrell. Second row (from left): John Rabidou, Claude Butler, Dave McGinnis, Brad Frederickson, Dick Farr, John Merrell and Ernie Poor.

Am., Can. FC Radbach's Bimbo, owned by William E. Peters, is a Hall of Fame member and a leading sire of field champions.

Peron is best known for siring GSPCA Hall of Fame member Dual Ch. Erick v. Enzstrand, the great grandsire of the second all-time top sire of dual champions, Dual Ch. Hillhaven's Hustler.

Erick was bred by Robert Check of v. Enzstrand Kennels in Stevens Point, Wisconsin, in 1971 and was sold to David and Jan Hill of Beloit, Wisconsin, who also owned Hustler. He was handled in the field by Dave and in shows by Jan.

Erick's dam was Hope v. Luftnase by Dual Ch./NFC Kay v.d. Wildburg ex Ch. Wag-Ae's Sheba Bruner. Axel's influence in America through his son Peron primarily centers around Erick.

Erick is tied for fourteenth for all-time top sires of champions through 1994 with twenty-four show champions, one dual and four field champions. He was sire of the year for Obedience dogs in 1980, and his get has earned ten CDs, three CDXs and two TDs.

Axel v. Wasserschling has left a lasting impact on American Shorthairs through Esser's Chick, Bimbo and Peron, but the greatest single impact came from Chick. It was reported that Don Miner was negotiating to buy Axel and bring him to America when he died.

INT. DUAL CH. ADAM

If Esser's Chick brought a new shot of gunpowder from Germany, Int. Dual Ch. Adam brought a stick of dynamite from Sweden in the late 1950s.

Int. Dual Ch. Adam, with titles in Sweden, Denmark and Finland, was the sire of Ch. Adam v. Fuehrerheim, the breed's all-time leading sire of champions.

A significant number of dual and show champions and some of the biggest-winning field champions in America carry his name directly and through his son Ch. Adam v. Fuehrerheim, the greatest sire in the history of the breed.

Adam won dual championships in Sweden, Norway and Denmark and an international championship in Belgium. He is believed to have been the greatest Shorthair in Sweden at that time and possibly still is, as the twentieth century draws to its close.

Adam was sired by a dog simply named Jack out of a dam named Heidy. Jack was by Chipps Artemis ex Raya. In Jack's third generation, his grandsire is Ch. Eck Schoneflieth and his granddam is Orbyhem's Toppsy. Raya's sire is Ch. Kuna v. Schlossgarten and her dam is Frostorp's Bessie.

Adam was imported from Sweden by John Wilkins, who lived on an estate in Chestnut Lawn, Virginia, near Washington, D.C. I have been told that he bought the dog from the widow of the man who owned him for hunting quail on his farm, which covered about 1,000 acres. No one knows how Wilkins heard about him.

Adam was a beautifully marked dog with solid ticking and large dark liver patches and was an outstanding bird dog, with thousands of birds shot over him. Wilkins asked Dick Johns to retrain him to the American style of hunting and to respond to English words. Wilkins stocked his farm, the big sorghum fields, with flight-trainer's quail he raised on the farm. Johns said Wilkins didn't like "the business of springing birds into the air as Adam had been taught in Sweden."

Ch. Warrenwood's Kandy Kane, owned by Ruth Eitel. Sired by Int. Dual Ch. Adam, she produced eleven champions when mated to her half-brother Ch. Adam v. Fuehrerheim.

Veteran breeder and founder of Fuehrerheim Kennels, Harold Fuehrer is shown hunting over two of his Fuehrerheim champions, with lines going back to the Thornton imports.

"I shot hundreds of birds over Adam at the estate and at home," Johns said. "He would point the bird and stand until you walked up to him and got the gun ready, and then he would spring the birds into the air. Wilkins didn't like that, but I explained to him the dog was doing what he had been trained to do, and it would be wrong to try to change him at that stage in his life."

He noted, "Adam was one hell of a bird dog. He was a smart, well-built, big running dog. He always retrieved two birds at a time, every time."

Adam was not trialed or shown in the United States because, as Dick explained, he already was a dual in three countries; Wilkins wanted him for hunting.

Adam was used at stud only a few times, and not many people knew about his presence in America. But in those few breedings in the 1960s he produced nine champions, of which several would produce a rainbow of champions that would strongly influence breeding in the United States through the rest of the century.

The two most important breedings were to Cindy of Warrenwood, owned by Dick and Ruth Eitel, and Tessa v. Fuehrerheim, owned by Charles L. Jordan IV. From Cindy came Ch. Warrenwood's Kandy Kane, and from Tessa came Ch. Adam v. Fuehrerheim.

When Adam v. Fuehrerheim was mated to Kandy Kane, she produced twelve champions, becoming tied for ninth place for all-time top dam of show champions through 1994.

Adam also produced champions out of Traude v. Hackenschmidt, owned by John and Marge Schulte. Adam was mated to Ch. Xenia Oranien Nassau to get Ruth Johns Betti in Omaha, Nebraska. Bred to FC Fieldacres Buddy (FC Fieldacres Ib ex Fieldacres Sassy), Ruth Johns Betti produced six field champions including FC John Adam, the sire of FC Adam's Royal Raider. A daughter of Ruth Johns Betti, Ruth Johns April, was bred to Adam v. Fuehrerheim to produce more champions in Nebraska. FC Fieldacres Jake v. Ib and Smokey Ike's Snoopy Son, a son and grandson of Ruth Johns Betti, are in the fifth generation on the dam's side of the great three-time GSPCA National All Age Champion FC Rawhide's Clown, handled by Don Paltani of Omaha, in the 1990s.

CH. ADAM V. FUEHRERHEIM

Ch. Adam v. Fuehrerheim was Adam's greatest offspring. Int. Dual Ch. Adam was mated to Tessa v. Fuehrerheim at the suggestion of Harold Fuehrer, owner of Fuehrerheim Kennels, who had sold Tessa to the Jordans.

Tessa was sired by Ch. Baron v. Fuehrerheim (Ch. Rex v. Krawford ex Ch. Gretchen v. Fuehrerheim) out of Ch. Katrin v. Fuehrerheim (FC Zitt v.d. Sellweide, German import ex Ch. Kenda v. Fuehrerheim) and was whelped on April 24, 1962. The linebred Tessa, going back to the Thornton imports,

Tessa v. Fuehrerheim, dam of all-time leading sire of champions Ch. Adam v. Fuehrerheim. Owned by Charles L. Jordan IV.

Ch. Adam v. Fuehrerheim, all-time leading sire of champions with one dual and two field champions and an impressive tally of 115 show champions. He was owned by the author Robert H. McKowen.

Ch. Rex v. Krawford, a famous producer behind many winning lines today, owned by Bill Olson.

Ch. Adam's Diplomat, a son of Ch. Adam v. Fuehrerheim and grandson on his dam's side of NFC Kay v.d. Wildburg, owned by author Bob McKowen.

Ch. Adam v. Fuehrerheim shown winning Best of Breed at the Finger Lakes GSPC Specialty under the famous breeder Al Sause at Rochester, New York. Adam was handled by his owner Bob McKowen to this much-coveted win.

Ch. Adam's Happy Warrior (Ch. Adam v. Fuehrerheim ex Gretchenhof Tallyho) resulted from the first mating for both his parents. "Happy" is shown here with his owner-handler Bob McKowen.

crossed well with the complete outcross Adam. They had a large litter that produced three champions. Harold bought two of the puppies, Kreg and Crista, who earned championships before Adam. Harold had passed over Adam when he selected his two pups. I got Adam at four months and was totally thrilled with this gangling teenager. He was exactly what I wanted, but I had no idea of what he was to become. I wanted him for hunting, and I had a vague notion of showing and field trialing him even though I didn't know how to go about it. When I brought him home, he came right into the house and planted a big slurp on my wife when she bent down to pet him.

I hunted over Adam that fall of 1962 before he was six months old and entered a field trial right after he was eligible at six months. In his second trial, in the spring of 1963, he won the puppy stake at Pittsburgh under Dr. Clark Lemley, owner of the first National Field Trial Champion, and I was hooked. He was campaigned in both field and show to try for a dual championship. He finished his conformation title at thirteen months, with fourth, third, second and first placings in the Sporting Group in one month en route to his title. He had fifty-four field trial placements, including firsts in Puppy, All-Age, Amateur Gun Dog and Open Gun Dog and fourth in the big Pointer/ Setter Pennsylvania Bird Dog Championship, where he had more bird finds than all of the other dogs in the stake combined. He was the only German Shorthaired Pointer entered. He never finished his field championship because he needed one more win to become a dual. He earned twenty-seven seconds in major retrieving stakes and ran in the 1968 National Championship won by v. Thalberg's Seagraves Chayne, the same year he won the GSPCA National Specialty Show.

Adam was one of the biggest-running puppy and derby dogs I ever saw, but I had to cut him back because I couldn't handle him that far out without a horse. At home, I had to run to keep up with him to stop him from crossing highways. He was a great bird dog, and during his trialing years, we ate a lot of pheasant.

In addition to his fifty-four field trial placements, Adam won sixty Bests of Breed, twelve Specialty Bests, including the 1968 GSPCA National Specialty, and seven Sporting Group firsts, among many other placements.

People began asking me about breeding him, but I was not interested at the time. However, during the Westminster show in New York, a man named Rudy Jordan came up to me to say he would like to breed his bitch Gretchenhof Tallyho, a sister to the BIS-winning Ch. Gretchenhof Moonshine, to Adam. Rudy brought Tallyho to my home when she came into season, and that was the start of Adam's spectacular breeding career. Rudy said he asked Oscar Gobol to which dog he should breed; Oscar just marched him over to Adam's bench and pointed. Tallyho produced six champions in her first litter by Adam and a total of fourteen from successive breedings.

Adam was the breed's leading sire of champions for five years and the top Sporting Dog sire in 1970 and 1971. He was the top sire of all breeds in the United States in 1970 and is the all-time leading sire of Shorthair

Gretchenhof Tallyho, owned by Rudy Jordan, was the outstanding producer of four-teen champions and a member of the GSPCA Hall of Fame.

champions, with an official count of 115 show champions, two field champions and one dual. Unofficially, we believe he has more champions, because not all were published in the AKC records.

Two of Tally's get, Ch. Whispering Pines Tally Hi, owned by Mrs. S. Conroy, and Ch. Whispering Pines Ranger, owned by Bernard Ginsberg, won National Specialty Bests of Breed in 1967 and 1971. Several successful new kennels started with foundation stock from the Adam/Tallyho breedings and other Adam get from outstanding dams.

CH. WHISPERING PINES PATOS AND
CH. FIELDFINE'S COUNT RAMBARD

Ch. Whispering Pines Patos, owned by Angelo and Patricia Stefanatos, of Bohemia, New York, was a big-winning dog and a highly successful sire in his own right with twenty-three show champions to tie for fifteenth on the all-time list for show champions. He is best known for siring Am., Can. Ch. Fieldfine's Count Rambard, the all-time number-two leading producer of champions with ninety-one, second only to his grandsire Ch. Adam v. Fuehrerheim. Rambard is the backbone of Fieldfine Kennels, owned by Dot (formerly Voorhees) and Bill Simberlund, of North Carolina.

Whelped in 1973, out of Fieldfine's Tacha (twelfth on the all-time dams' list, with nine champions), Rambard won a number of Specialty shows and sired many champions. Among his famous get were Am., Can. Ch. Fieldfine's Lord Tanner and Ch. P.W.'s Challenger v. Fieldfine, who were Best of Breed at the 1980 and 1981 GSPCA National Specialty shows, respectively. Both were also all-breed BIS winners. Tanner was owned by Leonard and Mark Shulman, of Vermont, and Challenger was owned by Larry Berg, of New York.

Tanner was out of Cinnamon Dutchess, by Ch. Bruiser v. Fuehrerheim, an Adam v. Fuehrerheim son. In addition to winning the National Specialty, he also won the Eastern Canada GSP Club Specialty and went on to win Best in Show at the sponsoring all-breed show.

Challenger's dam was Ehrich's Jaeger Traum, which goes back four generations to find a champion, Ch. Tequilla v. Duke II on the sire's side. Challenger was the top-winning Shorthair in bench competition for 1980.

Two of Dot Simberlund's favorite Rambard daughters are Ch. Fieldfine's Happy Memories and Ch. Fieldfine's One and Only, both by Ch. Fieldfine's Rapscallion Luke (a Rambard son) ex Ch. Fieldfine's Dark Magic (a Rambard daughter). Both are multiple Group and Specialty winners. Happy Memories is tied for eighth on the all-time dam's list for champion get, with thirteen.

Rambard was also the grandsire of another important show dog, Ch. Fieldfine's Ribbons, owned by Joyce Oesch and Kathleen Plotts of Lancaster, Pennsylvania. Bred by Dot Voorhees' son and daughter, Allen and Debra, Ribbons racked up impressive victories in 1982, the year she finished her championship. She was top show Shorthair of the year and Best of Opposite Sex at the GSPCA National Specialty for the second successive year. She was also BB at the 1982 Westminster KC show. By Am., Can. Ch. Fieldfine's Rocky Run (Ch. Rocky Run's Stoney ex Fieldfine's Tascha) ex Ch. Fieldfine's River Shannon (FC Fieldfine's Count Rambard ex Shaas River Risque), Ribbons reigned supreme in the show ring throughout the early 1980s.

Another outstanding champion by Rambard was Ch. Sheridan's Brandy v. Fieldfine ex Fieldfine's Jill. Owned by Michael Coniglio of Seaford, New York, Brandy was Best of Opposite Sex at the 1985 National Specialty and BOS at the 1985 Westminster show, among many outstanding awards.

When Rambard offspring were bred back to Columbia River bloodlines, another whole family of winners emerged to continue producing outstanding champions into the present. Since Gretchenhof Tallyho was so instrumental in the development of this line, it is appropriate to explain her never achieving a title. Tallyho was an attractive bitch who, I felt, was a better specimen than her sister, Ch. Gretchenhof Moonshine, but titles didn't really mean much to her owner, Rudy Jordan. Tallyho had fourteen points, needing only one point to finish. At the time, I was showing an outstanding Adam daughter, Adam's Sweet 'N Sassy. Rudy would bring Tallyho to nearby

Ch. Fieldfine's Count Rambard, the breed's top show dog and #2 all-time leading sire with eighty-nine champion get, owned by Bill and Dot (handling) Simberlund. *John Ashbey*

Am., Can. Ch. Fieldfine's Lord Tanner, winner of the 1980 National Specialty. Tanner was owned by Len and Mark Schulman, and sired by Am., Can. Ch. Fieldfine's Count Rambard. *Ashbey*

shows, turn her over to Jack Horan to handle and then take her home. I did not enter any shows that I thought he might enter for about a month, when "Sweety" was really ready to finish. Rudy did not enter any of those shows, so I began showing again. Sure enough, just after going into the ring, at the next show, here came Rudy with Tallyho. I won, and Rudy never showed

Ch. Fieldfine's One and Only, owned by Bill (handling) and Dot Simberlund. *John Ashbey*

Am., Can. Ch. Fieldfine's Happy Memories, owned by Bill and Dot (handling) Simberlund. *Dave Ashbey*

Tallyho again. We were always friends, but he simply stopped showing her. In the right hands, there is no telling what kind of a record she could have had. But she did leave a legacy as a dam of influential champions. Tallyho was tied for seventh place for all-time top dam of show champions with fourteen, all by Adam. She is a distinguished member of the GSPCA Hall of Fame.

ROCKY RUN KENNELS

The only direct line breeding to Adam—except one by Harold Fuehrer—that went back to the Fuehrerheim line was that of Bob Arnold, who owned Rocky Run Kennels in Boothwyn, Pennsylvania. Bob explained his line this way:

> My dogs are primarily from Harold Fuehrer's Fuehrerheim bloodline. I tried to breed close to his Ch. Baron v. Fuehrerheim and it ended up where I had more Fuehrerheim bloodlines than Harold, and he has bought dogs from me to get his own bloodlines back. He used to call me *Fuehrerheim East.* He had been in the breed a long time and he had a definite type. It's what I liked and my dogs are primarily Fuehrerheim.
>
> I had three litters by Ch. Adam v. Fuehrerheim out of Ch. Rocky Run's Poldi (Ch. Rocky Run's Rascal ex Deda v. Fuehrerheim) and they were probably the best dogs we've ever bred. Out of one of those litters came Stoney, our BIS/Hall of Fame dog. His registered name is Ch. Rocky Run's Stoney. I had been in Shorthairs for fifteen years, I guess, before I saw Adam. I had seen him as a puppy, and I remembered him from the first time I saw him. I followed him and decided that was the dog I wanted to breed to. I guess we had about ten champions by Adam.
>
> Stoney was my biggest winner. He had 105 Bests of Breed and won the Eastern Specialty in 1962, the largest Specialty in the country that year with 160 entries. He went Best in Show that day. I hunted him until the week before he died. He was a good hunting dog.

I believe Stoney was one of the two best dogs Adam ever sired. The other was Ch. Hungerhausen's Dreiemal Adam. Both were of excellent type, and both were wonderful bird dogs. There were other bigger-winning dogs that may have left a larger imprint on the breed, but Stoney and "Pache" were textbook examples of the Standard.

I met Bob Arnold at a show when I was exhibiting Adam as a puppy, and he stopped me one day and told me to put Adam on the tailgate of his station wagon. He pulled out a pair of scissors and trimmed his whiskers and the feathers on the back of his legs. He then told me how to set him up for showing. I always remembered this because I was in competition with his dogs at the time, and he helped me. We used to hunt and drive to shows together. Another good dog out of his breeding was a pick of litter I kept named Ch. Adam's Rib of Rocky Run, who finished in four straight shows. He had half of his field trial points when I sold him to a family that had its own private hunting preserve.

GSPCA Hall of Fame member Ch. Rocky Run's Stoney, a BIS winner, was owned by Robert L. Arnold. Stoney was one of the most famous sons of Ch. Adam v. Fuehrerheim. *Stephen Klein*

Ch. Rocky Run's Poldi was a foundation bitch for Robert L. Arnold's Rocky Run Kennels. Bred to Ch. Adam v. Fuehrerheim, she produced seven champions and one Hall of Fame dog. *William Brown*

Bob bred the Adam/Fuehrerheim line of dogs for many years, producing numerous champions before branching out to tie in with Fieldfine lines, which brought in Columbia River for modern-day winners.

CH. WINDSONG'S MISTY MEMORIES

The 1979 GSPCA Specialty Best of Breed was Ch. Windsong's Misty Memories, a Hall of Fame member traced back to Rocky Run and Tallyho on her sire's side out of a daughter of the big-winning, prepotent Ch. Happy Go Lucky, another Hall of Fame member. Bred by John Herring and handled by Susan Harrison of Fort Lauderdale, Florida, Misty Memories was one of the most beautiful females to come from this breeding, and she produced eight champions to pass along her quality. In the first sixteen national specialty shows, she was one of only three females to win a BB. Her sire was Ch. Windsong's Whispering Pines (Adam ex Tallyho). Her dam was Serakraut's Lucky Charm (Ch. Strauss's Happy Go Lucky ex Strauss's Dandy Candy, dam of nine champions, with both sides going back to Dual Ch. Esso v. Enzstrand).

Some fifteen years later, Susan Harrison again had Best of Breed at the 1994 GSPCA National Specialty, this time with Ch. Wyndbourne's Keepsake, a lovely bitch by Ch. Wyndbourne's Bustin' Loose ex Ch. Wyndbourne's Remembrance, dogs with family relationships to her foundation dogs based on the two Hall of Fame and National Specialty winners Ch. Mighty Memories and Ch. Jillard of Whispering Pines, CD. Keepsake was BOS at the 1992 and 1996 GSPCA Nationals, was twice BB at Westminster and had seventy-five Group wins and other placements.

The first bitch to win the National Specialty was Ch. Whispering Pines Tally Hi, the Adam/Tallyho daughter mentioned earlier. The second bitch to win the National Specialty, Ch. Jillard of Whispering Pines, CD, also had strong connections to Adam and Tallyho. She was by Bruha's Whispering Pines Fury (Bruha's Heisterholz Era ex Ch. Gretchenof Snowflake) ex Tama of Whispering Pines (Ch. Adam v. Fuehrerheim ex Gretchenhof Tallyho). The BIS and multi-group winning bitch was bred by J. R. Potash and owned and handled by Salleyann Meier Nannola.

Another outstanding producer of champions sired by Adam was Fieldfine's Lady of Adam, tied for sixth among All-Time Top Dams of show champions with fifteen to her credit. Her dam was Ch. Avonderrays My Fair Lady, who traces back to Dual Ch. Robin Crest Chip on both the sire's and dam's sides.

CH. NMK'S PLACER COUNTRY SNOWBIRD

My Fair Lady is the dam of Ch. NMK's Placer Country Snowbird, a Hall of Fame member who, through 1994, was tied for sixth among the All-Time Top Sires of show champions with forty-three titlists, two duals and two

National Specialty Show BOB Ch. Windsong's Misty Memories, owned and handled by Susan Harrison, was Best of Breed at the 1978 GSPCA National Specialty under Robert Arnold. *Anderson*

field champions, including the all-time top-winning show dog in German Shorthaired Pointer history. He was bred by David Miller and owned by Carol Chadwick, Citrus Heights, California. His sire was Ch. Wing King v. Brandenburg (Am., Can. Ch. Gretchenhof Columbia River ex Ch. Heidi v. Brandenburg, CDX).

DUAL CH. NMK'S BRITTANIA V. SILBELSTEIN

Snowbird sired Dual Ch. NMK's Brittania v. Silbelstein out of Rani v. Silbelstein. Bred by Kathy Sibley, Britt was whelped May 30, 1984. She finished her show title in 1985 and her FC on February 16, 1992, after setting a new world record for show wins. Britt won 49 all-breed BIS; 149 Group firsts; 12 Specialty Bests, including the 1987 National, with 901 entries; and in Canada, 4 BIS in all-breed shows and 7 Group firsts. She is the only BIS dual champion bitch. She won the Westminster Sporting Group in 1987 and again in 1988.

Britt was handled in the show ring by Bruce Shultz of California, who kept her happy with occasional forays into the fields while traveling, and in field trials by Terry Chandler of Las Cruces, New Mexico, who, along with his wife, Janet, has written his own chapter on dual champions.

Dual Ch./Can. Ch. NMK's Brittania v. Sibelstein, owned by Carol Chadwick and bred by Kathy Sibley, was the all-time top-winning GSP in history. Britt won the Sporting Group at Westminster two years in a row and was BB at the GSPCA National Specialty.

Am., Can. Ch. NMK's Placer Country Snowbird, owned by Carol Chadwick. A Hall of Fame member, Snowbird has produced two duals and more than forty-two show champions, including the top winning Dual Ch. Brittania v. Sibelstein. *Fox & Cook*

Dual Ch. NMK's Brittania v. Sibelstein

                    Gretchenhof Moonfrost
        Am., Can. Gretchenhof Columbia River
                    Columbia River Della
    Wing King v. Brandenburg
                    Chayne's Bobo v. One Spot
        Ch. Heidi v. Brandenburg, CDX
                    Hidie v. Muller

Am., Can. Ch. NMK'S Placer Country Snowbird

                    Int. Dual Ch. Adam
        Ch. Adam v. Fuehrerheim
                    Tessa v. Fuehrerheim
    Ch. Fieldfine's Lady of Adam
                    Am., Can. Ch. Robin Crest Ringo Riant
        Ch. Avonderry's My Fair Lady
                    Ch. v. Der Rays Gingerbread
                    FC v. Thalberg's Fritz II
        FC Rip Traf
                    FC Mitzi Grabenbruch Beckum
    FC Rex v. Bess
                    Herr Gunnar v. Blitz
        Fieldmaster's Anna v. Bess
                    FC/AFC Craig's Magnum v. Bess

Rani v. Sibelstein

                    Ch. Adam v. Fuehrerheim
        Dual Ch. Schatzi's Eric v. Greif
                    FC Schatzi Dem Balder v. Greif
    Schau Speiler's Amy v. Greif
                    FC v. Thalberg's Wurtze v. Greif
        FC v. Dante's
                    VC Geisterholz's Helga v. Greif

In addition to her spectacular career in both field and bench competition, Britt was also a strong producer of dual-type champions. She is fourth All-Time Top Dam, with twenty-one champions, two duals and four field champions.

A number of Britt's offspring were still being campaigned at the time of this writing, and it is likely that she will advance to the top of the list in the production of both show and dual champions within a couple of years.

She is well on the way with two dual champions already. Bred to Dual Ch. Rugerheim's Bit of Bourdon, she produced daughters Dual Ch. NMK Irresistible v. Rugerheim, finishing her dual in 1994, and Dual Ch. NMK's Shining Star v. Rugerheim, finishing in 1995.

Britt earned her field championship after nearly dying of bloat in May 1991. However, an operation saved her life and late that summer, Terry Chandler began the campaign to get her back in shape to win the one remaining point she needed for her dual championship. Following her win in February, she won first in the Open Limited Gun Dog at a trial the next weekend—just for good measure.

Following is Britt's pedigree, which shows strong maternal influence on both sire and dam sides along with NFC Rip Traf v. Bess and FC v. Thalberg's Fritz II. Of interest is her dam's grandsire, Dual Ch. Schatzi's Eric v. Greif, who was by Adam ex FC Schatzi dem Balder v. Greif. Eric is the sire of Starlite's Greif v. Kazia (nicknamed Hank the Yank), the first American-born German Shorthaired Pointer exported to Australia. More on this will appear later.

CH. PAWMARC'S SIERRA MTN SONG

Snowbird also produced the big-winning Ch. Pawmarc's Sierra MTN Song out of Ch. Abiqua Pawmarc's Alpenglow in 1987 for breeders Paul Williams and Pat Wilaby and owners Benny L. Conboy and Margaret Sylvester of Santa Fe, Texas. Ch. Pawmarc's Sierra MTN Song was BB at the 1996 GSPCA Specialty after going BOS at the 1994 National. He was BB or BOS at many other Specialty shows, was a BIS winner and had more than fifty Sporting Group firsts.

chapter 11

The German Shorthaired Pointer After Mid-Century

LIEBLINGHAUS

Few kennel names carry more distinction for producing top-winning champions than Lieblinghaus Reg. of Philadelphia, Pennsylvania, owned by Ruth Ann Freer, who did most of her own handling in both the show and field. Lieblinghaus is another kennel based largely on the Ch. Adam v. Fuehrerheim/ Whispering Pines Tally Ho lines, with the addition of some good outcrosses blended in at various times.

The 1997 GSPCA National Specialty BB, Ruth Ann's Ch. Lieblinghaus Chief Executive, CD, JH (Ch. Pawmarc's Sierra Mtn Song ex Ch. Lieblinghaus Here's to Freedom, JH), established a new kind of record. Never before has a son, his sire and dam all won BB at the National Specialty. Chief's dam, Flair, won in 1988 in Portland, Oregon, and his sire, Freckles, won in 1996 in El Paso, Texas.

The Lieblinghaus story, as written by Ruth Ann Freer, is worth recounting here:

Lieblinghaus, Reg. was established in 1969 with the purchase of Ch. Mein Liebchen v. Werner, CD, as a seven-week-old puppy from Joan Harkins of Holland, Pennsylvania. "Lovey" as she was known, was a daughter of Ch. Grouse Manor Windstorm and Ch. Harkins' Hi-Dee-Ho (GSPCA 1968 Show Dam of the Year by Am., Can. Ch. Fliegen Meister's Gunner ex Vic Van Princess) and is behind all of the fifty-six champions, dual champion, field champions, obedience and hunting titlists produced by Lieblinghaus over almost thirty years.

In 1971, Lovey was bred to a litter brother of her sire—Ch. Whispering Pines Ranger (1971 GSPCA National Specialty BB) giving a strong

Ch. Pawmarc's Sierra Mtn Song, was BB at the 1996 GSPCA national Specialty under Ruth Ann Freer, and sired Ch. Lieblinghaus Chief Executive, CD, JH, the 1997 national Specialty BB. "Freckles", owned by Margaret Sylvester and Benny Conboy was an all-breed BIS winner, had 10 Specialty BBs, 298 BBs at all-breed shows, 41 Group 1sts, 39 2nds, 33 3rds and 23 4ths. *Allen*

Ch. Lieblinghaus Chief Executive, CD, JH, bred, co-owned and shown by Ruth Ann Freer (handling) with Jolene Whitfield, was BB at the 1997 GSPCA national Specialty under judge Patricia Mowbray. His sire was the 1996 NSS BB and his dam, "Flair," was BB at the 1988 national. *Lee Meadows*

Am., Can. Ch. Hungerhausen's Dreimal Adam, a prominent winner from the 1970s owned by Ruth Ann Freer and bred by Wolfgang Hunger of Canada. *Dreimal* means "three times" and "Pache" was so named because of the three crossings to Ch. Adam v. Fuehrerheim in his pedigree. He was the GSPCA Show Dog of the Year for 1974 and 1975.

Dual Ch./AFC Lieblinghaus Hunter's Moon, SH, bred and owned by Ruth Ann Freer, was the first dual champion for Lieblinghaus Kennels and was handled in the field by Greg Nicholson.

foundation based on the Ch. Adam v. Fuehrerheim/Gretchenhof Tally Ho combination known as "Whispering Pines." From this breeding came Ch. Lieblinghaus Snowstorm, an electee into the GSPCA Hall of Fame in 1985. Snowstorm was a multiple Group winner and placer, a Top Ten bitch and was BB at Westminster in 1975. She became a GSPCA All Time Top Producing Dam of fourteen champions and was the 1982 GSPCA Show Dam of the Year.

Also in 1974, another great German Shorthaired Pointer was added to the Lieblinghaus gang. Am., Can. Ch. Hungerhausen's Dreimal Adam was brought in from Canada. "Pache," as he was known, was an outstanding breed representative and was the #1 GSP in 1975 and the GSPCA Show Dog of the Year in 1974 and 1975. He was a multiple Group and Specialty winner and was Best of Breed at Westminster in 1976. Pache was a son, grandson and great grandson of Ch. Adam v. Fuehrerheim, thus the name Dreimal (three times) Adam!!!

His dam was Hungerhausen's Debe, owned by Wolfgang Hunter Montreat. Pache was an unbelievable "bird dog" with tremendous bird-finding ability and pointing style. Unfortunately, he died early in a 1980 hunting accident. The only comfort from this tragic episode is that at the time Pache was doing what he loved best—finding birds!!

Snowstorm was bred to another litter brother of her sire and grandsire—Ch. Whispering Pines Patos, producing Ch Lieblinghaus

Ch. Lieblinghaus Here's to Freedom, JH, owned, bred and handled by Ruth Ann Freer was BB at the 1988 national, was an all-breed BIS winner and the dam of the 1997 GSPCA Specialty BB. *Stephen Klein*

Starshine and Ch. Lieblinghaus Storm Trooper (Winners Dog—1977 GSPCA National Specialty). Stormy was also bred to Ch. Gretchenhof Columbia River (#1 GSP and #1 Sporting Dog in 1974), producing Ch. Lieblinghaus Storm Hawk, CD (youngest Shorthair to ever finish a championship; Hawk was 8½ months old finishing in seven shows) and Ch. Lieblinghaus April Snow (a GSPCA All Time Top Producing Dam of twelve champions). Stormy's third mate was Ch. Gretchenhof Westminster (by Ch. Gretchenhof Columbia River) and this combination produced ten champions.

Her most famous progeny and subsequent descendants have been:

Ch. Lieblinghaus April Snow, who was bred to Ch. Columbia River Superstar and produced Ch. Liebmeister Lieblinghaus Riker who was the #1 GSP (all systems) in 1984 and a GSPCA All Time Top Producer of eighteen champions. April was then bred to Ch. Indian Country Columbia Moon and this combination produced ten champions. The most famous of these are Ch. L'bmeister Lieblinghaus Abagab (a GSPCA Top Producing Dam) and Ch. Lieblinghaus Flagstaff, CD. "Flag" produced twenty-seven champions including two BIS daughters—Ch. Lieblinghaus Here's To Freedom, JH and Ch. Shannon's Riverside Ruffian.

Now going back to the basics, Ch. Lieblinghaus Starshine was also bred to Ch. Gretchenhof Westminster, who in turn produced the Group winner Ch. Lieblinghaus Miss Liberty. Miss Liberty, a Top Producer of six champions, was bred to Ch. Lieblinghaus Flagstaff, C.D. This breeding produced the greatest winning German Shorthaired Pointer for Lieblinghaus in the person of Ch. Lieblinghaus Here's To Freedom, JH. "Flair" was the #1 GSP all systems and GSPCA 1990 Show Dog of the Year. She was a multiple BIS winner, BB at the GSPCA 1988 National Specialty. Known for her outstanding movement and showmanship, plus exemplary breed type, she was handled to all her wins by her owner-breeder Ruth Ann Freer. Flair was the GSPCA Show Dam of the Year in 1993 and a GSPCA All Time Top Producer.

Flair was only bred once, to Ch. Pawmarc's Sierra MTN Song (a GSPCA Top Producer and the #1 GSP in 1991, 1992 and a 1993 BIS winner), and produced an all-champion litter of eight. The most notable of these are:

C. Lieblinghaus Flirtatious, JH—BW at the 1992 GSPCA National Specialty from the Bred-by-Exhibitor class, multiple Group Specialty BB winner, and Ch. Lieblinghaus Chief Executive, CD, JH—#3 GSP in 1996, Multiple Group and Specialty winner and 1997 GSPCA National Specialty BB. Chief was in the Top Ten for 1997 when these notes were written and was on his way to Top Producer status with six champions and many more major pointed get.

With the advent of Hunting Tests in 1984, Ruth Ann felt here was an avenue to display her Shorthairs' hunting abilities. Ch. Freedom's Thriller, JH (Ch. Lieblinghaus Flagstaff, CD ex Ch. Lieblinghaus Miss Liberty), was the first show champion of all pointing breeds to earn a hunting title. She was trained and handled by Ruth Ann.

Finding the enjoyment of competing with her dogs in the field, Ruth Ann decided to get involved in field work even more seriously. "It truly is wonderful to watch the dogs running through the windblown fields, slamming into a staunch point, their nostrils flaring, bodies rigid with bird scent. Only then can you truly understand what the breed was bred to do and the excitement of watching a beautiful GSP working in the field," she said.

With a special goal in mind, Ruth Ann Freer then outcrossed her birdiest bitch, Ch. Lieblinghaus Snowstorm, to Dual Ch. Moesgaard's Deejay's Derek in hopes of producing a Dual Champion. Dual Ch./AFC Lieblinghaus Hunter's Moon, SH, was produced. "Trek" finished as the 181st Dual Champion in German Shorthaired Pointer history on March 19, 1994. Trek was professionally trained by Daniel Burjan, but amateur-owner handled by Greg Nicholson and Ruth Ann Freer. Another litter brother, Ch./AFC Lieblinghaus Moesgaard's Erin, finished his Amateur title and needed one point to be a dual champion, but was not championed further.

All of the above was done with a minimal amount of breeding—about twenty litters in less than thirty years. Usually, no more than five to six dogs have been kept at any one time, and all have been house dogs and great family companions. In 1993, nine of the Top Ten German Shorthairs in the United States all went back to a Lieblinghaus sire or dam.

Ruth Ann Freer is currently an AKC-approved judge of eight Sporting breeds, is still showing on a small scale and competes in field trials and hunting tests. In 1996, she judged the GSPCA National Specialty in El Paso, Texas—the ultimate honor for a breeder-judge. Occasionally, a litter is bred or co-bred by Lieblinghaus and, fortunately, the current winner at this writing, Ch. Lieblinghaus Chief Executive, CD, JH, was being actively used at stud, thus keeping still more generations of Lieblinghaus German Shorthaired Pointers at the forefront.

KINGSWOOD KENNELS

Jim Burns and his wife, June, of Cuddebackville, New York, are people of quiet demeanor and few words. Their distinguished record as important breeders of top-winning dogs speaks eloquently for them.

"We acquired our first Shorthair in 1974 from Paul and Eleanor Fairfield and Kingswood Kennels was born," Jim said. That was Am., Can. Ch. Wentworth's Happy Wanderer, CD, a solid liver female who produced fifteen champions (tied for sixth in the All-Time Top Producing Dams list) and was elected to the GSPCA Hall of Fame. Wanderer was by Jaeger v. Langstadt (Esser's Chick ex Irving Lane Katrinka) out of Northview's Lady Hyacinth. Katrinka traces back to FC Moesgaard's Doktor, FC Moesgaard's IB and FC Doktorgaarden Lucky.

The Burnses used several different outcrosses, but their line was strongly anchored to the breeding of Ch. Adam v. Fuehrerheim. In reference to their

Ch. Kingswood's Miss Chiff, owned by Jim and June Burns, had a string of impressive national Specialty wins. She was Best In Futurity, Best in Sweepstakes and Winners Bitch at the 1982 GSPCA national Specialty, BB at the 1983 event and BOS there in 1984. *Stephen Klein*

Am., Can. Ch. Weinland's Matinee Idol, a GSPCA Hall of Fame member and a Best in Show dog bred and shown by Jim Burns. *Stephen Klein*

Ch. Kingswood's Maximilian, owned and handled by Jim Burns, is shown here winning under the legendary all-breed judge and Sporting dog authority Maxwell Riddle. Maximilian was a member of the GSPCA Hall of Fame.

John Ashbey

Dual Ch. Kingswood Glinkirk Zanzibar, co-owned by June and Jim Burns and Mary Beth Kirkland was the first dual champion for the Burns and Ms. Kirkland, former secretary of the GSPCA. Zanzibar was handled to her conformation title by June Burns.

John Ashbey

Ch. Kingswood's Buffy of Geremy, shown by June Burns of Kingswood Kennels.   *John Ashbey*

Am., Can Ch. Wentworth's Happy Wanderer, CD, foundation bitch for Jim and June Burns' Kingswood Kennels.
William Gilbert

foundation bitch, Am., Can. Ch. Wentworth's Happy Wanderer, Jim said, "Bred to the top sires of the time her get have done well, winning National Specialties, Sweepstakes and Futurities." They count in their line Adam, Esser's Chick, Columbia River, Ricky Run, Whispering Pines, Ashbrook's Papageno and Fieldfines.

Over the years the Burnses have bred or owned many Specialty winners, two Best in Show dogs, two GSPCA Hall of Fame dogs and several Top Ten Shorthairs, and, to quote Jim, "We still enjoy our GSPs for their hunting ability, good companionship, and the many friends we have made through them over the years."

Wanderer was bred to three different studs to produce her fifteen champions. Ch. Fieldfine's Rambard sired nine of her champions, Ch. Nock's Chocolate Chip (a Hall of Fame Kaposia linebred son) sired five and Am., Can. Ch. Kingswood's Windsong, the Burnses' first male, sired one.

The most famous of the Wanderer get was Ch. Kingswood's Miss Chiff. Her sire was by Ch. Windsong's Country Squire ex Windsong's Debbie, an Adam daughter. Squire was sired by DH Rocky Run's Jason, who goes back to Adam on both sire and dam side. His dam, Ch. Windsong's Whispering Pine, is a daughter of Adam and Gretchenhof Tallyho.

Miss Chiff is the only GSP in history to win everything at the National Specialty shows. She was the 1982 National Futurity and National Sweepstakes winner and Winners Bitch. She went Best of Breed at the 1983 National Specialty and won Best of Opposite Sex at the 1984 Specialty. I judged her at the 1984 National Specialty and liked her very much. She was of excellent type and moved true—a very pretty, feminine bitch. However, I had three dominant males that put on a spectacular show, and I had to go with a male that day, Gene Ellis' Ch. Schatzi's Ripper v. Greif, one of the very few GSPs in the country who moved perfectly true.

Ch. Kingswood's Maximillian, owned by Frank and Joan Nehrwien of Commack, New York, and bred by the Burnses, was a sound, beautiful, correct-sized dog with attractive, large liver patches. He was BW at the 1984 National, and two years later I gave him BB at the Westminster KC show. Maximillian was by Am., Can. Ch. Weinland's Matinee Idol (co-owned by Jim Burns and Lynda Bynum), a BIS-winning member of the Hall of Fame. Maximillian's dam was Ch. Kingswood Buffy of Geremy, CD, by Am., Can. Ch Kingswood's Windsong ex Ch Geremy's Farrah. Matinee Idol's sire, Ch. Hollyhof's Jason Kristoff, goes back to the breeding lines of Adam, Gretchenhof, Whispering Pines, Rocky Run and Ch. Machtolff's Flying Colors (Chukar Hill Pride) on the sire's side and to Gretchenhof, Rocky Run and Whispering Pines on the side of her dam, Ch. Windsong's Sweet as Candy.

Ch. Matinee Idol, who was bred by Lynda Bynum and Tim Baranski, produced forty-three champions to tie for sixth on the All-Time Sire's list, and his descendants are still going strong through the 1990s.

CH. MAEKENET'S FLYING PERSUASION

"Matty" is the grandsire of Ch. Weinland Mr. Peepers, who sired Ch. Maekenet's Flying Persuasion, the 1991 GSPCA National Specialty BB winner. Flying Persuasion, in turn, sired Ch. Minando's Parade Drum Major, the reigning top show dog in the late 1990s, with at least ten all-breed BIS at this writing. Let's take a look at Flying Persuasion's pedigree to see how he is backed up with quality antecedents, and then at the pedigree of Ch. Minado's Parade Drum Major to see the solid Minado background of his dam.

Pedigree of Ch. Maekenet's Flying Persuasion
Bred and Owned by Linda M. and Roger K. Armstrong

                                        Ch. Hollyof Jason v. Kristoff
                            Am., Can Ch. Weinland's Matinee Idol
                                        Ch. Windsong's Sweet As Candy
                        Ch. Weinland's Ode To Kingswood
                                        Am., Can. Ch. Kingswood's Windsong
                            Ch. Kingswood's Buffy of Geremy
                                        Ch. Geremy's Farrah
            Ch. Weinland Mr. Peepers
                                        Ch. Machtolff's Flying Colors
                            Ch. Hollyof Jason v. Kristoff
                                        Ch. Hollyof Charade
                        Ch. Weinland's Ms. Quito
                                        Ch. Gretchenhof Westminster
                            Ch. Windsong's Sweet As Candy
                                        Ch. Windsong's Holy Terror

                                        Ch. Ashbrooks Papageno
                            Birdacre's Magnum Force
                                        Birdacres' Kristi
                        Karasyl's True Grit
                                        Ch. Birdacre's Aruba
                            Birdacre's East Wind II
                                        Ch. Birdacre's East Wind
            Ch. Karasyl's Rainbow Connection
                                        Ch. Adam v. Fuehrerheim
                            Ch. Machtolffs Flying Colors
                                        Ch. Machtolff's Chukar Hill of Pride
                        Ch. Witt's Nakoma
                                        Ch. Hunger Liter's Jug O' Punch.
                            Swift's Pawnee of Kaposia
                                        Ch. Swift's Light N' Lively, CDX

Flying Persuasion's dam, Ch. Karasyl's Rainbow Connection, is owned by Linda and Roger Armstrong. The sire, Mr. Peepers, was bred by Lynda Bynum and Tim Baransky and was owned by Lynda Bynum and Libby de Mille.

Eleven of the sixteen dogs in the fifth generation are either from Adam v. Fuehrerheim or out of Adam breeding. The other contributors to the lineage that produced Flying Persuasion are Ch. Hollyof Charade, Ch. Gretchenhof Westminster, Ch. Windsong's Sweet as Candy and Ch. Swift's Light N' Lively, CDX.

Ch. Hollyof Charade is by Gretchenhof White Rain ex Gretchenhof Moondancer. Moondancer is by Dual Ch. Baron Fritz v. Hohentann ex Gretchenhof Blue Moon, a daughter of Ch. Gretchenhof Moonshine ex Ch. Columbia Thundercloud, from Moonshine's only litter.

Ch. Gretchenhof Westminster, as noted earlier, is by Ch. Gretchenhof Columbia River, fifth all-time top show champion producer and the second all-time top GSP show winner. His dam was Ch. Gretchenhof Moonbeam.

Ch. Windsong's Sweet As Candy is by Ch. Gretchenhof Westminster ex Ch. Windsong's Holy Terror, an Adam daughter.

Ch. Swift's Light N' Lively was by Ch. Firehawk of Kaposia ex Kaposia's Shoshone Maiden.

Ch. Flying Persuasion was bred and owned by Linda and Roger Armstrong of Altadena, California. Whelped in 1986, Persuasion is tied for thirteenth place on the all-time list of sires of show, champions with twenty-five through 1994. There have been many more champions finished since then.

CH. MINADO'S PARADE DRUM MAJOR

Ch. Minado's Parade Drum Major (Toby) was bred by Inge and Leann Clody of Minado's GSPs, is owned by Barbara and Robert Caron and is trained and handled by Valerie Nunes-Ewing, who has been showing GSPs for twenty-five years. All are from Southern California.

Toby was sired by Ch. Maekenet Flying Persuasion, whose pedigree appears earlier, out of Ch. Minado's IM Precious Crystal. The sire's side is strongly Adam and the dam's side is strongly Minado, with the great producer Oxton Minado Inga v. Greif appearing twice in the third generation and the Clodys' great foundation dog Dual Ch. Oxton's Minado v. Brunz appearing three times in the sixth generation. The sixth generation of the dam's side is a virtual *Who's Who* of the pillars of the breed. Among them are Dual Ch. Cede Mein Dolly Der Orrian, number-two All-Time Top Dam of field champions and number three All-Time Top Dam of show champions with three duals, twenty-one show champions and four field champions; Dual Ch. Zipper Der Orrian, who goes back to Ch. Baron v. Fuehrerheim; NFC Blick v. Shinback, another Hall of Fame member, and FC Greif v. Hundscheimerkogel. Six of Drum Major's ancestors are in the GSPCA Hall of Fame.

Toby was the number-one German Shorthair in the show ring for 1995 and 1996 and number-ten Sporting dog in 1996. Midway through 1997, he was well on his way to another banner year.

Pedigree of Ch. Minado's Parade Drum Major

                          Ch Weinland's Matinee Idol
                Ch. Weinland's Ode to Kingswood
                        Ch. Kingswood's Buffy of Geremy
        Am., Can. Ch. Weinland's Mr. Peepers
                        Ch. Hollyhof Jason v. Kristoff
                Am., Can. Ch. Weinland's Ms. Quito
                        Ch. Windsong's Sweet As Candy
Ch. Maekenet's Flying Persuasion
                        Birdacre's Magnum Force
                Karasyl's True Grit
                        Birdacre's East Wind II
        Ch. Karasyl's Rainbow Connection
                        Ch. Machtolff's Flying Colors
                Ch. Witt's Nakoma
                        Swift's Pawnee of Kaposia

                        Am., Can. Ch. Weinland's Mr. Peepers
                Ch. Maekenet's Flying Persuasion
                        Ch. Karasyl's Rainbow Connection
        Am., Can. Minado's Maekenet Mac
                        Minado's Jack Daniels
                Oxton Minado's Inga v. Greif
                        Minado's Flying Chips
Ch. Minado's I-M Precious Crystal
                        Marilee's Titan v. Greif
                Ch. Marilee's Ziel v. Jango
                        Valkyre v. Drake
        Ch. Minado's Izabo v. Greif SH
                        Minado's Jack Daniels
                Oxton Minado's Inga v. Greif
                        Minado Flying Chips

Continuing their successful breeding program into the mid-1990s, the Burnses produced yet another BIS winner, Ch. TRF Kingswood's Past Returns, JH (Ch. Huntabird's Belmar Main High ex Ch. Echelon's Kahlua and Cream), and Dual Ch. Kingswood Glinkirk Zanzibar (Ch. Crossing Creek's Homesteader, CD ex Ch. Kingswood's Candy Kiss, CD), co-owned with Mary Beth Kirkland of Maidens, Virginia, a former secretary of the GSPCA.

MINADO KENNELS

In the half-century since World War II and the wave of German and Danish importation, many noteworthy dogs, kennels and individuals have come, played their part and are now gone from the scene. Lines from the great ones have continued through some of the same breeders or through new kennels, and some have almost disappeared. But one of the greatest lines dating back to old FC Greif v. Hundscheimerkogel is not only alive and well but continuing its outstanding production of champions, including the top-winning German Shorthair in the country in the final decade of the twentieth century. One of the most familiar names in GSP history in the United States is Minado, and the kennel came into being because Ken Clody, of Lakeside, California, wanted a Labrador Retriever for hunting and got sidetracked. In the mid-1990s, most Minado breeding has been handled by Ken and Inge Clody's daughter Leanne Farrell, who has prepared the short history of the Minado Kennels that follows:

HISTORY OF MINADO
GERMAN SHORTHAIRED POINTERS
by Leanne Farrell

It all began in June 1966. My dad, Ken Clody, after dog sitting a friend's Labrador Retriever, and being a hunter, decided we should get a dog. We answered an ad for a trained Lab and went to look at him. At that kennel there was also a litter of German Shorthaired Pointers and, of course, we fell in love with them. We purchased a solid liver puppy bitch, who we named "Toni's Coffee of Be-Len."

The kennel owner was a hunting dog trainer and told us he would train Coffee for us but first we should obedience train her. My dad enrolled her in obedience class. Coffee not only attained her CD, but earned a *Dog World* Award in the process with all scores over 195 points. Since she was now obedience trained, Dad called the trainer/breeder to have Coffee field trained only to find he had passed away. My dad went on to get Coffee's CDX and joined the GSPC of Southern California. Dad went to Gene Shultz's field training class, as well as reading some books on training dogs and trained Coffee himself to be his hunting companion.

My mom, Inge Clody, became interested in showing, but Coffee did not have what it took for the conformation ring. Dad had no use for 'show dogs' but it would be okay if it could hunt too. The only way to do that and make them both happy was to have a Dual. After reading C. B. Maxwell's *The New German Shorthaired Pointer*, mom decided if she wanted a dual champion, the Greif line was the way to go since FC Greif v. Hundsheimerkogel (bred to Ch. Yunga War Bride) had produced four Duals and one champion. (Greif and Yunga War Bride are both All-Time Top Producers in the Hall of Fame, as previously mentioned.)

Ch. Minado's I-M Precious Crystal, dam of the top-winning GSP in the United States in the mid-1990s, Ch. Minado's Parade Drum Major. "Crystal" is handled here by Leanne Clody Farrell. *Joan Ludwig*

Ch. Minado's Parade Drum Major, top-winner of the mid-1990s with ten Bests in Show, was bred by Leanne Farrell (handling) and Inge Clody and owned by Barbara Caron. "Toby" was later handled to his outstanding show record by Valerie Nunes-Ewing. *Joan Ludwig*

In her search for a show pup, mom heard that there was a dog being campaigned in the shows that was a field champion, and his sire was Dual Ch. Oxton Bride's Brunz v. Greif, one of the Grief/Yunga duals. (Brunz is now also in the Hall of Fame, producing three dual champions, fourteen show champions and five field champions.)

Mom thought that this potential dual might be the sire of a recent litter so she and dad went to the next show and watched as he took the points. His name was FC Oxton's Minado v. Brunz. His owner/trainer/handler, Jake Huizenga of Oxton Kennels, had bred those four duals. After the show, they talked to Jake and asked him if Minado (Mac) had produced any litters lately. Jake asked what their interests were and they told him that they wanted to buy a dual potential pup. His response was that the only way to assure themselves of a dual was to buy one that was already half way there. He asked

Dual Ch. Oxton's Minado Von Brunz, shown in a win under Canadian judge Ted Gunderson at the KC of Pasadena with owner Inge Clody handling. *Joan Ludwig*

if they would like to buy Mac. After much discussion, my mom and dad decided to buy him. The following week they drove to Oxton Kennels to run Mac with Jake and learn the 'ropes'. We learned that Mac finished his field title at the age of two and a half with five puppy points (only two were allowable) and a four- and five-point major and was the youngest to qualify to run in the nationals.

This was our first 'show dog' and he could hunt! Within fourteen months Mac was a dual, finishing with back to back Specialty wins. Five of his sisters finished their championships as well.

Mac had been bred to Dean Tidrick's Dual Ch. Cede Mein Dolly Der Orrian while under the Huizengas' ownership. In that litter they produced Dual Ch. Dee Tee's Baron v. Greif (who had multiple Group Placements) and Ch. Dee Tee's Benedict v. Greif (1972 NGPDA Championship).

Along the way, he was bred to Dolly two more times to produce Dual Ch. Fagon Haag v. Greif, as well as Ch. Dee Tee's Fanny v. Greif, Ch. Dee Tee's Flash v. Greif, Ch. Dee Tee's Fason Jagerin v. Greif, Dee Tee's Fan Cede v. Greif and BIS winner Ch. Dee Tee's Flambeau v. Greif.

The second mating produced Ch. Dee Tee's Garbo v. Greif, Ch. Dee Tee's Gaea v. Greif who finished her championship at the 1975 GSPCA national Specialty, Ch. Dee Tee's Gypsy Rose v. Greif and BIS winner Ch. Dee Tee's Grandee v. Greif. (Minado is in the Hall of Fame as a Producer of three dual champions, thirty-one show champions, three field champions and one amateur field champion and Dolly is in the Hall of Fame as a Top Producer as well.)

Minado bred to Ch. Callmac's Victory v. Gardsburg produced our two foundation bitches: Ch. Callmac's Mariah v. Minado and Callmac's Mona Lisa. Mariah produced five champions, Mona six.

We bred a half-brother and half-sister (both out of Mona) and the Huizengas took a pup from that breeding. Jake had retired from professional training and trialing and just wanted a dog to train for his own personal use. The Huizengas named her Oxton Minado's Inga v. Greif. When Jake passed away, Mom called Sally to offer her condolences and found out that Sally was to have Inga spayed the next day and placed with a friend. She had had one litter and produced Ch. Oxton Inga's Brunz v. Minado owned by Jean Galli, Jake Huizenga's niece.

Dad did not have a hunting dog at the time and Inga was fully trained. Mom asked Sally if she would consider allowing us to have her for Dad to hunt with. Sally agreed.

We bred Inga to Ch. Marilee's Ziel v. Jango who traced back to Dual Ch. Cede Mein Dolly Der Orrian. From that breeding Inga produced Ch. Minado's Izabo v. Greif, SH, Ch. Minado's Diamond in the Ruff, Ch. Minado's Jake v. Greif II, and Minado's Sherman v. Greif.

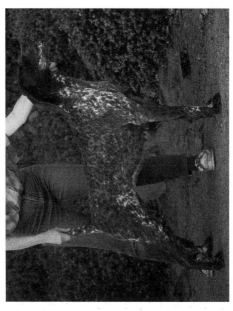

Oxton Minado's Inga v. Greif, tied for first as the breed's top producing dam of champions with twenty-five title holders to her credit. She was a foundation matron for Minado Kennels.

Pedigree of Oxton Minado's Inga v. Greif
#1 All Time Top Producer (Twenty-five Champions)

- DC Dee Tee's Baron v. Greif
  - DC Oxton's Minado v. Brunz
    - DC Oxton Bride's Brunz v. Greif
    - A/C Ch Sorgeville's Happy Holidays
  - DC Cede Mein Dolly Der Orrian
    - DC Zipper Der Orrian
    - DC Erdenreich's Jetta Beckum
- Ch Holiday's Sieglinde v. Greif
  - Edelmarke's Bismark v. Greif
    - FC Greif v. Hundsheimerkogel
    - Ch Yunga War Bride
  - DC Oxton Bride's Brunz v. Greif
    - Mutual Conservation
    - A/C Ch Sorgeville's Happy Holidays
      - Heidi Sorge v. Stettler

- Minado's Jack Daniels
  - DC Oxton's Minado v. Brunz
    - DC Oxton Bride's Brunz v. Greif
      - FC Greif v. Hundsheimerkogel
      - Ch Yunga War Bride
    - A/C Ch Sorgeville's Happy Holidays
      - Mutual Conservation
      - Heidi Sorge v. Stettler
  - Callmac's Mona Lisa
    - Ch Buck v. Gardsburg
      - Ch Red Velvet
      - Zukie v. Gardsburg
    - Ch Callmac's Victory v. Gardsburg
      - Ch Mark v. Waldhausen
      - Ch Heidi v. Waldhausen
        - Sadie v. Sirius

DC Duke Jager v. Sauffenberg
Ch Alta's Perfection
Moesgaard's Alta
Ch Ro-Shan's Jubilant Grenadier
Ch Storm King of Kaposia
Ch Kaposia's Ro-Shans Valdona
Ch Kaposia's Star Dancer
Ch Minado's Buc
DC Oxton Bride's Brunz v. Greif
DC Oxton's Minado v. Brunz
A/C Ch Sorgeville's Happy Holidays
Ch Callmac's Mariah v. Minado
Ch Buck v. Gardsburg
Ch Callmac's Victory v. Gardsburg
Ch Heidi v. Waldhausen CD

Minado Flying Chips
FC Greif v. Hundscheimerkogel
DC Oxton Bride's Brunz v. Greif
Ch Yunga War Bride
Ch Holiday's Sieglinde v. Greif
Mutual Conservation
A/C Ch Sorgeville's Happy Holidays
Heidi Sorge v. Stettler

Callmac's Mona Lisa
Ch Red Velvet
Ch Buck v Gardsburg
Zukie v. Gardsburg
Ch Callmac's Victory v. Gardsburg
Ch Mark v. Waldhausen
Ch Heidi v. Waldhausen
Sadie v. Sirius

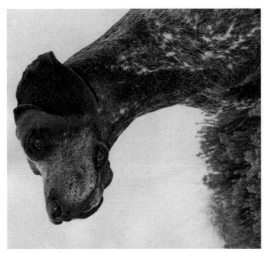

Dual Ch. Oxton's Minado Von Brunz, the signature dog of the venerable Minado Kennels of Leanne Farrell and her mother Inge Clody. Brunz was sired by Dual Ch. Oxton Bride's Brunz von Greif, one of the four dual champions from the FC Greif von Hundscheimerkogel ex Ch. Yunga Was Bride mating by Jake Huizenga. A Hall of Fame member, Minado sired three dual champions, thirty-one show champions and four field champions.

Pedigree of DC Oxton's Minado v. Brunz Minado's Foundation Sire

DC Oxton Bride's Brunz v. Greif

FC Greif v. Hundsheimerkogel
- Alf Gindl
  - Alex v. Holzgartl
    - Greif v. Herrnbaumgarten
    - Nora v. Laa
  - Flora (Singer)
    - Blitz v. Quadehugel
    - Flora (Budischovsky)
- Beria Spiesinger v. Pfaffenhofen
  - KS Markus Freising
    - KS Marko v. Schaumburg
    - Juno Freising
  - Gerda v.d. Forst Brickwedde
    - Artus v. Haseltal
    - Lotte Sudwest

Ch Yunga War Bride
- Major V S
  - Spokey v. Washington
    - Johann v. Schwarenberg
    - Misty Dawn
  - Cleve's Patches
    - Cleve v. Schwarenberg
    - Patsy v. Waldhausen
- Lassie v. Man O'War
  - Man O'War
    - Ch Paqina's Young Lover
    - Sue v. Dusseldorf
  - Ginger v. Denk

Brock's Rusty
Saddle v. Waldwinkel
Ch Pheasant Lane's Stormalong
Ch Pheasant Lane's Tomahawk
Ch Pheasant Lane's Deborah
Mela's Delight
DC Rusty v. Schwarenberg
Iowa Pride
Senta v. Hohenbruck
Mutual Conservation
Fritz v. Eberis
Tref Fra Engelbert
Kulla
Sieglinde of Lenair
DC Rusty v. Schwarenberg
Baroness v. Irma
Senta v. Hohenbruck
A/C Ch Sorgeville's Happy Holiday
Conrad v. Danenhorst
Danenhorst's Bright Tasso
Snow Park Farm heidi
Rip v. Danenhorst
Baron v. Vosburgh
Mutual Noweta v. Rustyburgh
Calla v. Brickwedde
Heidi Sorge v. Stettler
Buch v. Style
Bow View's Rex
Valle v. Style
Bow View's Roxy
A/C Ch Ludwig v. Saddler
Patsy v. Saddler
Jaeger's Pride of Marshland

Pedigree of Ch. Callmac's Mariah v. Minado & Callmac's Mona Lisa Minado's Foundation Bitches

DC Oxton Bride's Brunz v. Greif
- FC Greif v. Hundsheimerkogel
  - Alf Gindl
    - Alex v. Holzgartl
    - Flora (Singer)
  - Beria Spiesinger v. Pfaffenhofen
    - KS Markus Freising
    - Gerda v.d. Forst Brickwedde
- Ch Yunga War Bride
  - Major V S
    - Spokey v. Washington
    - Cleve's Patches
  - Lassie v. Man O'War
    - Man O'War
    - Brock's Rusty

DC Oxton's Minado v. Brunz
- Mutual Conservation
  - Mela's Delight
    - Ch Pheasant Lane's Tomahawk
    - Iowa Pride
  - Sieglinde of Lenair
    - Tref Fra Engelbert
    - Baroness v. Irma
- A/C Ch Sorgeville's Happy Holiday
  - Rip v. Danenhorst
    - Danenhorst's Bright Tasso
    - Mutual Noweta v. Rustyburgh
  - Bow View's Roxy
    - Heidi Sorge v. Stettler
    - Bow View's Rex
    - Patsy v. Saddler

Skriver's Seks

Skriver's Sofus

Skriver's Erte

Ch Red Velvet

Ch Rusty v. Schwarenberg

Freda v. Ludwick

Dorothy Buchwald Konigsweg

Ch Buck v. Gardsburg

Kobold v. Altenau

A/C Ch Coby v. Schnellburg

CH Bella v. Rheinburg

Zukie v. Gardsburg

Fieldborn Duke II

Susie VI

Fieldborn Duchess

Ch Callmac's Victory v. Gardsburg

Uncie v. Schoenweide

Ch Kurt II

Judy's Little Rye

Ch Mark v. Waldhausen

Ch Jim Dandy v. Roger

Topzi v. Waldhausen

Star-Lady v. Walshausen

Ch Heuidi v. Waldhausen, CD

McCarthy's Victory

Dan Siegfried

Tina Marlena

Sadie v. Sirius

Rocky of Malvern

Katrina R Flecken

Spritzeen v. Flecken

Inga's next breeding, an outcross, was to Ch. Maekenet's Flying Persuasion owned by Linda and Roger Armstrong. History was in the making and Inga became Top Producing Dam for 1990 with eight champions finishing that year. To date she is tied for the honor of being the breed's #1 All Time Top Producer of Show Champions producing twenty-five champions as follows:

(ex Inga by Mark's i-Wing Jarl)

Ch. Oxton Inga's Brunz v. Greif

(ex Inga by Ch. Marilee's Ziel v. Jango)

Ch. Minado's Diamond in the Ruff

Ch. Minado's Izabo v. Greif, SH

Ch. Minado's Shaman v. Greif

Ch. Minado's Jake v. Greif II

(ex Inga by Ch. Maekenet's Flying Persuasion)

Am/Mex Ch. Minado's Maekenet Mac

Ch. Minado's Maekenet My Memory, MH

Ch. Minado's Maekenet My Day

Ch. Minado's Maekenet Minerva

Ch. Minado's Maekenet Miss Molly

Ch. Minado's Maekenet Makai

Ch. Minado's Maekenet Minda, CD, SH

Ch. Minado's Maekenet Mallory

Ch. Minado's Maekenet Taylormade

Ch. Minado Maekenet My Marvel

Ch. Minado Maekenet's Mark

Ch. Minado Maekenet's Move

Ch. Minado's Fly'n Colors of Paladen, MH

Ch. Minado's Flying Ensign

Ch. Minado's Whitney v. Lieb'lhof

Ch. Minado's Wild Wings, BD

Ch. Minado's Brush Country Manana

Ch. Minado's Fliegen Hollander

Ch. Minado's Cascade v. Lieb'lof

(ex Inga by Ch. Minado's Dapper Can II)

Am., Mex. Ch. Minado's Boots De Codorniz

Another half-sister/half-brother breeding produced Ch. Minados I-M Precious Crystal (Am., Mex. Ch. Minado's Maekenet Mac ex Ch. Minado's Izabo v. Greif, SH) who when bred back to her grandsire, Ch. Maekenet's Flying Persuasion, produced six champions including Ch. Minado's Parade Drum Major, current top-winning GSP described earlier.

Crystal is the sister to Dual Ch. AFC Minado's Roman Adventure, MH, owned by Wayne and Sherrie Romanski. "Bones" was field trained and handled by his owner, proving the dual quality is still there for those who want to take these dogs to their full potential. Crystal has produced nine champions so far—all have finished young with Specialty wins in national competition.

RIVERSIDE KENNELS

In Putnam Valley, New York, a continent away from the Southern California home of the number-one All-Time Top Producing Dam Oxton Minado's Inga v. Greif, a beautiful bitch named Am., Can Ch. Cheza's Riverside Imp, Am., Can. CD was born in the same year, 1982. "Samantha" would be tied for All-Time Top Producing Dam of Show Champions with Inga. Actually, Samantha held the lead until shortly after 1994, when another champion finished for Inga to boost her into a tie. Get from both bitches are still being shown and the record could change. Inga died in 1992 and Samantha died in 1994.

Samantha was bred by Jane C. Rae of Cheza Kennels and at nine months of age, in the summer of 1983, was sold to Bob and Ann Keegan of Smithtown, New York. The Keegans operated Riverside Kennels, another highly successful establishment producing not only show champions but some of the top-winning Obedience Shorthairs of all time. Samantha was sired by Ch. Cheza's Billibong, UD ex Ch. Cheza's Windsong. The sire's side was

Am., Can. Ch. Cheza's Riverside Imp, owned by Mr. and Mrs. Robert Keegan, was tied for all-time top dam of champions with twenty-five progeny. She was also the dam of many outstanding Obedience winners. She is shown here finishing her championship under judge Robert H. McKowen. *Gilbert*

Ch. Riverside's Franz v. Minden, CD, owned and handled by Lt. Col. Obie D. Robinson, was #1 GSP in Obedience in 1994. This talented team was High in Trial at the national Specialty show. *Kohler*

as an amalgam of Gretchenhof/Columbia River/Kaposia, Int. Ch. Nessethal's Brown Mike and Ch. Shawn Haas v. Franzel. The dam's side was strongly Adam v. Fuehrerheim breeding through several different dams and sires.

Samantha produced her twenty-five champions out of forty-five puppies from her six breedings, a rate of more than 50 percent. Her six breedings were to six different sires. She was Top Dam of the Year twice, in 1985 with four champions and in 1989 with five. She is the dam of three five-champion litters and one six-champion litter.

Ann Keegan, who died in 1993, said she and her husband "wanted to bring in different lines to blend with their own, thus Samantha never had a repeat breeding." They felt that with different sires, she would prove that she was a major contributing factor to her offspring's quality.

The sires Samantha was bred to and outstanding get were:

Ch. Riverside's Sundance Kid (Am., Can. Fieldfine's Count Rambard ex Riverside's Calamity Jane): Out of this breeding were five champions, including the 1985 Winner's Bitch at the national Specialty, Ch. Riverside's Chocolate Chip. She, in turn, was bred to Ch. Kingswood's Maximilian and produced four champions, including the Keegans' first Group winner, Ch. Riverside's Country Legend, CD ("Willy"). When bred to the solid liver bitch Ch. Oaklore's Katja v. Shomberg, Willy sired the 1994 national Sweepstakes winner, Ch. Shomberg's Snowy River, who was Winners Bitch and Best of Winners at the same show!

Am., Can. Ch. Chances Are D.W. Crackerjack (Ch. Cedarpark Storm Warning ex Ch. Shaas v. Chances Are): This was Samantha's second five-champion litter, which included the multi Group, placing Ch. Riverside's Miss Trial with at least six champions to her credit. Ch. Riverside's C-Spot-Wyn, CDX, JH ("Spot"), owned and trained by George Anna Bobo of Houston, Texas, was the number-two Obedience GSP for 1990.

Am., Can. Ch. Lieblinghaus Flagstaff, CD (Ch. Indian Country Moon ex Ch. Lieblinghaus April Snow): From this breeding came Samantha's third five-champion litter, including the BIS bitch, Ch. Shannon's Riverside Ruffian, and Ch. Riverside's Song of the South, who was in the Top Ten GSPs for show points in 1990. Ruffian (known as "Amanda") has also made the All-Time Top Producer's list.

Ch. Crossing Creek's Homesteader, C.D. (Crossing Creek Hessian Baron ex Boulder Island Swanky Yankee): There were only six puppies in this litter, three of whom finished their championships. One of these, Ch. Riverside's Franz v. Minden, CDX, was one of the top Obedience GSPs of 1991 and the number-one Obedience GSP of 1994. He is owned and trained by Lt. Col. Obie Robinson of San Antonio, Texas.

Ch. Kingswood's Maximilian (Am., Can. Ch. Weinland's Matinee Idol ex Ch. Kingswood's Buffy of Geremy, CD): Out of nine puppies, six have finished and two more were close at this writing. Two were Top Ten GSPs for 1992: Ch. Riverside's Triple Threat, CD, JH, and a Group winner, owned, trained and handled by Rebecca Jacobs of North Port, Florida; and her sister, Ch. Riverside Moondust ("Velvet"), the number-three Show GSP for 1992, the number-one GSP in total points for 1993 and the number-one GSP bitch all-systems for that year. Velvet is also a BIS winner, a multiple Group winner and winner of some of the largest Specialty shows in the United States, and was Best of Opposite Sex at the 1993 national Specialty! She was kept as a replacement for her mother in the breeding program by the Keegans.

Am., Can. Ch. Nmk's Placer Country Snowbird (Ch. King v. Brandenberg ex Ch. Fieldfine's Lady of Adam): This was Samantha's last litter and consisted of only two puppies. Her last born, Ch. Riverside's Something Special, finished her championship in 1992.

Samantha's Champions and Their Other Titles

1. Ch. Riverside's Chocolate Chip (Winners Bitch 1985 national Specialty)
2. Ch. Riverside's Underdog, CD, JH
3. Ch. Riverside's Grouse Brook Big D
4. Ch. Riverside's Dark Star
5. Ch. Riverside's Willow v. Cheza
6. Ch. Riverside's Polly Purebred
7. Ch. Riverside's Miss Trial
8. Ch. Riverside's Jaylin Foy
9. Ch. Shannon's Riverside Ruffian (BIS winner)
10. Ch. Riverside's Jasper v. Cheza, CD
11. Ch. Riverside's Song of the South
12. Ch. Riverside's C-Spot-Wyn, CDX, JH
13. Ch. Riverside's Minado's Victoria
14. Ch. Riverside's Franz v. Minden, UD
15. Ch. Riverside's Briarwood's Madi, H
16. Ch. Lieblinghaus Riverside Riot, CD
17. Ch. Riverside's Promise to Cheza
18. Ch. Riverside's Moondust (BIS winner)
19. Ch. Riverside's Triple Threat, CD, JH
20. Ch. Riverside's Miss America
21. Ch. Riverside's Pale Rider, JH
22. Ch. Riverside's Bit O' The King and I
23. Ch. Riverside's Ragtime, CD
24. Ch. Riverside's Bit O' Hellsapoppin
25. Ch. Riverside's Something Special

Pedigree of Ch. Cheza's Riverside Imp

```
                              Gretchenhof Moonfrost
                    A/C Ch Gretchenhof Columbia River
                              Columbia River Della
          Ch Shaas River Racer
                              Adam v. Rollenberg
                    Ch Shawn Haas v. Franzel
                              Kindlein v. Franzel
    Ch Cheza's Billibong, CDX
                              Ch Ashbrook's Papageno
                    Nessenthal's Pinto
                              Nessenthal's Dawn
          Casandra
                              Nessenthal's R-Jon, UD
                    Nessenthal's R-Suzy
                              Nessenthal's Angel


                              Ch Rocky Run's Jason
                    Ch Windsong's Country Squire
                              Ch Windsong's Whispering Pines
          A/C Ch Kingswood's Windsong
                              Ch Adam v. Fuehrerheim
                    Windsong's Debbie
                              Windsong's Lady Heather
    Ch Cheza's Windsong
                              Ch Mr Jim of Rocky Run
                    Ch Rocky Run's Jason
                              Rocky Run's Gretchen
          Ch Windsong's Holy Terror
                              Ch Adam v. Fuehrerheim
                    Ch Windsong's Whispering Pines
                              Gretchenhof Tallyho
```

GENE SHULTZ'S GERMAN SHORTHAIRS

Not many people in German Shorthaired Pointers know of the extensive background in Obedience that Gene Shultz had among all breeds. Known primarily for show and field champions of national caliber, Gene was heavily involved in Obedience training for three decades from the 1950s through the 1970s and may have trained through his classes more titled dogs than anyone in history.

Gene served as president of the German Shorthaired Pointer Club of America for seven years, from 1985 to 1992, following my own term as president for the preceding five years, when we both strove to elevate Obedience in Shorthairs to a more respected level.

Gene's first Shorthair, Randy's Chocolate Chip, CD, was bred to his second, a bitch named Haney's Mona Lisa, to produce eight puppies, five of which became champions, among them Ch. Shultz's Coffee Royal, CD. Coffee Royal was bred to Ch. Callmac's Victory v. Gardsburg, which produced Callmac's Ivy v. Shultz. Ivy was bred NFC Thalberg's Seagraves Chayne, and this breeding produced FC Baron v. Shultz. Baron was bred to Shultz's Fire

Ch. Shultz's Coffee Royal, CD, a handsome foundation dog for Gene Schultz.

FC/AFC Shultz's Amber Lady, owned by Gene Schultz, was #1 gun dog in the United States two years in a row.

FC Schultz's Diamond Lil, runner up in the 1982 National Championship and top-winning field trial bitch owned by Gene Schultz.

Fly to produce FC Shultz's Amber Lady, and a repeat breeding produced FC Shultz's Diamond Lil.

Amber was the GSPCA number-one Gun Dog in 1980 and 1981 and was third in the National Gun Dog Championship in 1981. Diamond Lil was number two in the All-Age Dog of the Year rating in 1981 and second in the 1982 National All Age Championship, to Dual Ch. Ehrlicher Abe.

Coffee Royal was the great-great-grandsire of Ch. Donavin's Sir Ivanhoe, who was BB at the 1982 National Specialty. Sir Ivanhoe was bred by David and Susan Thompson and owned by David and Donna Gilliam and Valerie Nunes, who, at age eleven, handled him to win the coveted Junior Showmanship competition at Westminster. Ivanhoe, a BIS winner among his many wins, was by Ch. Geezee Super Chief ex Lady Plutonian Star Traveler.

Gene Shultz recalls:

My first experience in Obedience was with a Boxer bitch, which I trained in a novice training class conducted by William Koehler in 1950. She was High Scoring Dog at graduation and went on to earn the Utility Dog title.

My next dog in Obedience was my first Shorthair in 1952, "Randy's chocolate Chip." His biggest claim to fame was winning High Scoring Dog of the Day in the largest Obedience trial in history. That was the Hollywood Dog Obedience Club Trial, May 7, 1961, where we had 575 entries. To the best of our knowledge that is the largest Obedience Trial in history. His score was 199 ½ (I still have that score card).

I became involved with the administrative aspect of Obedience in my early days with Boxers. I was Obedience Chairman for the Boxer Club of Southern California for five years. During that time I also served as delegate to the Southern California Dog Obedience Council. That was an organization comprised of delegates from Obedience clubs throughout Southern California. I believe that there are over 40 clubs represented in that organization now. During 1956 and 1957 I served as President of the Council.

During this same period I was elected Vice President of the Hollywood Dog Obedience club and later served as President for two years. Those were the days when the Hollywood Club was the largest Obedience club in the nation and our trials usually had the biggest entry. We generally had 14 rings going. I also served as Chairman of this trial for several years.

In 1956 I was awarded the Will Judy Award for Outstanding Service to Dogdom. That was only the third time for that award to be presented on the West Coast. Previous winners were William Koehler and Carl Spitz. In 1959 I was awarded the first award from the Southwest Obedience Club for First In Dedication to Obedience (FIDO). In 1966 I was inducted into the Hollywood Dog Obedience Club Hall of Fame.

During 1951 or 1952 I began judging class graduations, practice matches and sanctioned matches. I kept track until I had judged over 3,000 dogs. I believe I judged about 5,000 dogs in the Obedience ring before I quit judging.

During the late 1970s I was the instructor for the Hollywood Club's Advanced Obedience classes (Open and Utility). I trained over 500 dogs and their handlers during a period lasting about five years. I also conducted a training class each year for 18 years, teaching people to train their Pointers in the field. Each dog was taught all of the novice exercises and many of the open exercises including forced retrieving.

Author's note: In the history of the Minado Kennels given earlier in this chapter, note the reference to the Clodys' taking their first German Shorthair to one of Gene's field training classes.

RUGERHEIM KENNELS

The history of Rugerheim Kennels is a love story blending triumph and tragedy, and as the owner of the dog chosen independently for breeding by both Janet and Terry, who were not aware of each other at the time, I was the man in between.

Janet Fiorina (now Janet Chandler) got her first German Shorthair, Ch. Flintlock's Anastasia, in 1970 in Hawaii for her birthday. Janet was very active in Junior Showmanship. She grew up showing German Shepherds, her family's principal breed. She trained and finished Anastasia as a show champion at the age of seventeen. When she turned eighteen, as a senior in high school, she was approved for her professional handler's license. As a high school graduation present, her parents, who had moved to Tucson, paid the stud fee for her to breed Anastasia to her grandsire, Ch. Adam v. Fuehrerheim.

Terry Chandler got his first German Shorthair in 1971 from his brother Ray. This dog, which had Greif ex Moesgaard breeding, began Terry's career in field trialing. In 1972, Terry bought his first brood bitch from Birdacre Kennels. In 1974, he and a friend drove this bitch from New Mexico to Pennsylvania to breed her to her grandsire, Ch. Adam v. Fuehrerheim. While Terry was in Pennsylvania, Adam died, the breeding hadn't taken and Terry began a search for an Adam granddaughter, bred to Adam, to fit his breeding program. He saw an ad for Janet's litter in a breed magazine and drove from New Mexico to Arizona to see the puppies. This led to the purchase of Rugerheim's Adament Eric and launched a four-year friendship between Janet and Terry culminating in their marriage.

Rugerheim's Adament Eric was Terry's first show champion, and in 1974 Terry also purchased an Adam daughter, Adam's Heller v Waldenburg, from Waldenburg Kennels as his second brood bitch. Her breeding on her dam's side was Greif ex Moesgaard.

From these four dogs—Ch. Flintlock's Anastasia, Ch. Rugerheim's Adament Eric, Birdacre's Summer Wind and Adam's Heller v. Waldenburg—Rugerheim Kennels began.

The Breeding Program

Because of Janet's extensive background in the show ring and Terry's background in the field, they decided that when they got married they wanted to produce "a bloodline that could excel in both show and field—that is dual champions." They both held a deep belief that dogs with correct conformation could compete in field trials, and that dogs that were competitive in field trials could *look like* a GSP and win in the ring. The dogs they began with were exceptional animals in a given arena, with bloodlines that amply supported their talents.

Terry said:

We chose Adam V. Fuehrerheim because of his prepotency and his exceptional qualities in the ring. He was a national Specialty show champion, and a better-than-average field dog, having won several points in the field. This was done with our original brood bitch, Ch. Flintlock's Anastasia, her son, Ch. Rugerheim's Adament Eric, and an Adam daughter, Adam's Heller V. Waldenburg. We chose the Kaposia bloodlines because of their soundness in the ring, their gorgeous head type, and their abilities in the field. Kaposia had produced several national Specialty winners, and several dual champions. We added the Kaposia bloodline through Birdacres Summer Wind and later on through Ch. Rugerheim's Autumn Wynd, who was out of Ch. Rugerheim's Adament Eric and Ch. Autumn Wynd's Magic Echo (a Ch. Kaposia Otsego daughter and Ch. Adam v Fuehrerheim granddaughter). On the field side, we chose the most competitive line in the U.S. at the time—Moesgaard. This was done by adding NFC Moesgaard's Cocoa. Moesgaard Kennels had produced several National Field Trial Champions, and a couple of duals. This bloodline was added with one of our original brood bitches, Heller. To top it off we added the Greif bloodline, via NFC Rip Traf V. Bess. We liked the Greif line because of its soundness in the field and its exceptional bird ability. This line was also added through Heller, and later from NFC/Dual Ch. Ehrlicher Abe.

What They Produced

Terry and Janet kept a puppy by Ch. Rugerheim's Adament Eric out of Ch. Autumnwynd's Magic Echo. She was Kaposia and Adam bred. This breeding produced Ch. Rugerheim's Autumnwynd, MH. Although "Ruger" never won his dual championship, Terry began entering him in hunting tests at the age of eleven years, and he obtained his Master Hunter title the following year. "Ruger" was bred to Adam's Heller v. Waldenburg, and this breeding produced Ch. Rugerheim's Amazing Nicola, Ch. Rugerheim's Bit of Whiskey, Mex. Ch. Rugerheim's Bit of Rum, CD, and Dual Champion Rugerheim's Bit of Bourbon.

Ch. Rugerheim's Adament Eric was also bred to one of the Chandlers' original brood bitches, Birdacre's Summer Wind. This breeding produced Ch. Chabar's Aurora. "Aurora" was bred to NFC/Dual Ch. Ehrlicher Abe and produced Dual Ch. Rugerheim's Fireboss, the number-one Gun dog in the United States in 1985.

Ch Rugerheim's Bit of Whiskey was bred to a linebred Kaposia bitch, Ch. Brandywine's Superspook. This breeding produced one of the Chandlers'

THE LEGACY OF
DUAL CH. RUGERHEIM'S BIT OF BOURBON

Dual Ch. Rugerheim's Little Lord, owned by Jack Marczeski.

Dual Ch. NMK's Star v. Rugerheim, owned by Hal and Lilianne Shepherd.

Dual Ch. Rugerheim's Ice Breaker, owned by Mike Franco.

Dual Ch. Rugerheim's Verys Pistol Pete, owned by Donald Marczeski.

Dual Ch. Rugerheim's Bit of Bourbon, owned by Terry and Janet Chandler, with six dual champion get, is the all-time leading sire of duals.

Pedigree of Dual Ch. Rugerheim's Bit Of Bourbon

     Int. Dual Ch Adam
    Ch Adam v. Fuehrerheim
     Tessa v. Fuehrerheim
   Ch Rugerheim's Adament Eric
     Warrenwood's Sir Flintlock Jager's Nama
    Ch Flintlock's Anastasia
     Ch Flintlock's Resando Bandita
  Ch Rugerheim's Autumn Wynd, MH
     Ch Kaposia's War Lance
    Ch Kaposia's Otsego
     Ch Kaposia's Star Dancer
   Ch Autumn's Majic Echo
     Ch Adam v. Fuehrerheim
    Ch Warrenwood Majic of Murphaus
     Ch Warrenwood's Kandy Kane

     Jack
    Int. Dual Ch Adam
     Heidi
   Ch Adam V Fuehrerheim
     Ch Baron v. Fuehrerheim
    Tessa V Fuehrerheim
     Ch Katrin v. Fuehrerheim
  Adam's Heller v. Fuehrerheim
     FC v. Thalberg's Fritz II
    NFC Rip Traf v. Bess
     FC Mitzi Grabenbruch Beckum
   Ch Fralene's Maybe
     NFC Moesgaards Coco
    Callmac's Katrina v. Moesgaard
     Ch Callmac's Victory v. Gardsburg

A truly thrilling portrait is Dual Ch. Rugerheim's Bit of Bourbon on point being backed by three of his dual champion sons. Bourbon is at the top right with Dual Ch. Rugerheim's Ice Breaker and Dual Ch. Rugerheim's Wisner behind him. Dual Ch. Rugerheim's Fireboss appears in the foreground.

most competitive field dogs, Dual Ch. Rugerheim's Wisner. "Wis" was winner or runner-up in five regional and national championships.

Dual Ch. Rugerheim's Bit of Bourbon was bred to many Rugerheim bitches and to Dual Ch. NMK's Brittania v Silbelstein (Terry trained Brittania and finished her dual championship). The breeding to Brittania has thus far produced three duals: Dual Ch. NMK's Irresistable v. Rugerheim, Dual Ch./AFC NMK's Whitney v. Rugerheim and Dual Ch. NMK's Shining Star v. Rugerheim. From these breedings, Britannia was awarded Dual Dam of the year twice. Bourbon was also bred to his niece, Ch. Rugerheim's Dash of Cinnamon (Ch. Rugerheim's Bit of Whiskey ex Ch. Chabar's Aurora), and produced Dual Ch./AFC Rugerheim's Little Lord, MH. He was bred to a Moesgaard-bred bitch named Checkmate's Daylight Katie, purchased by the Chandlers. This breeding produced Dual Ch. Rugerheim's Icebreaker. "Bourbon's" sixth dual champion was out of a Fireboss littermate, Rugerheim's Firesnapper. This breeding produced Dual Ch. Rugerheim's Verys Pistol Pete and made "Bourbon" the all-time top-producing Dual Sire in the breed, and the number-three all-time top producing show sire through 1994 with sixty show champions, behind only Adam and Adam's grandson Ch. Fieldfine's Count Rombard.

Accomplishments

Terry and Janet to date have finished over sixty-five show champions, more than thirty-five field champions and twelve dual champions. Their sires and dams have produced too many champions to count, but it is in the several hundreds.

"In the past twenty-four years, we have done what we set out to do," Terry said. "We have produced a bloodline that continually has dogs that excel in both arenas. Dogs out of this breeding are continually ranked in the top ten in both the show and field, and place among the top winners at both the Field Trial nationals and the national Specialty shows."

The Future

When I talked to Terry and Janet about the future, they both smiled and said that they had two dogs in their kennel that would most likely finish their dual championships in 1997, one of them a "Bourbon" daughter. One of the Chandlers' daughters, Kristina, is following in her parents' footsteps and is very active in both show and field competition.

Terry's goal is to win the GSP national field trials with one of his dual champions, and Janet said that she wanted to just keep showing and going to field trials with Terry. They said they were continually trying to upgrade their breeding program. They also said that the competition in both areas was getting tougher and more specialized, and that perhaps one day there would no longer be any dual champions. But then they both looked at each other, and Janet squeezed Terry's hand and said, "I bet that we will always have them."

DUAL CH. HILLHAVEN'S HUSTLER

With his impressive background of all-time greats, Dual Ch. Hillhaven's Hustler was destined to earn a place in breed history. He was bred in 1978 by Dave and Jan Hill of Wisconsin and sold to Helen B. Shelly and Randall Sime. Jan handled Hustler to his show championship in 1982, and Dave handled him to his field championship in 1983. After his dual championship was completed, Hustler's ownership was transferred to the Hills. Mrs. Shelly also owned Dual Ch. Waldwinkels' Painted Lady and, as mentioned earlier, Ch. Kaposia's Waupun II, the only dog to win three national Specialty Bests of Breed.

Hustler was by Hillhaven's Handsome ex Hillhaven's Mark V's Mandy. In the background is perhaps the greatest concentration of Germany's leading sire Axel v. Wasserschling through the Axel son, Peron, on both sire and dam's side of the sire and through Esser's Chick, another Axel son, on the dam's side. Hustler's great grandsire on the sire's side is Dual Ch. Erick v. Enzstrand twice in the fourth generation and FC Uodibar's Boss Man in the fifth generation. On Hustler's dam's side are NFC/FC Mark V's One Spot, NFC Blick v. Shinback and Dual Ch. Kay v.d. Wildburg. His pedigree includes six Hall of Fame members.

Hustler was a sire of the year for dual-type dogs, and many of his get went on to establish their own impressive records. His five dual champions were Hillhaven's Sunshine (owners Ed and Mary Ann Delker); Trekker v.

Dual Ch. Hillhaven's Hustler, owned by Jan and Dave Hill, is the breed's second leading all-time sire of dual champions with five. Hustler was equally at home in the show ring and the bird field and was shown to his championship by his owner Jan Hill.

Pedigree of Dual Ch. Hillhaven's Hustler

      Peron (German-Belgian Import)
    DC Erick v. Enzstrand
      Hope v. Luftnase
  A/C Ch Hillhaven's Chief Honcho
      Hillhaven's Rex v. Hohen-Strauss
    Hesgard's Mrs Mitz
      Queen Valley
Hillhaven's Handsome
      Peron (German-Belgian Import)
    DC Erick v. Enzstrand
      Hope v. Luftnase
  Hillhaven's Proud Mary
      FC Uodibar's Boss Man
    Hillhaven's T N T
      Saxony's Brandy

      Heller v. Hundscheimberkogel
    Roughshooter's John-L
      Chubby v. Greif
  FC/1975 NFC Mark V's One Spot
      DC Kay v.d. Wildburg (Germany)
    Ritzie's Freida v. Wildburg
      FC My Ritzie Fer Gitunburdz
Hillhaven's Mark V's Mandy
      Esser's Chick (Germany)
    FC/1969 NFC Blick v. Shinback
      Melissa v. Greif
  Blick's Mariah v. Jango
      Duke v. Schmoldt
    Val's Heidi v. Schmoldt
      La Richards Croquett

Dual Ch. Hillhaven's Hustler standing on point at right with two dual champion sons backing: (from right), Hustler, Dual Ch. Cebourn's Erick of Hustleberg and Dual Ch. Stradivarius Baroque.

Grumbaum, UD, MH; Cebourn's Erick of Hustleberg, JH (Charlie and Lynn Blackbairne); Dual Ch./Can. Ch./AFC Stradivarius Baroque CGC; and Kurzhaar's Ruger v. Haven, SH (Billard Dearse Collins). Of these duals, the two most famous were Stradivarius Baroque, owned by Jean-Pierre Turgeon of Hemmingford, Quebec, Canada; and Trekker, owned by David B. Deimoa of Chagrin Falls, Ohio. In addition, Hustler sired twenty-two show champions and nine field champions (five FC and four AFC).

Dual Ch./AFC Trekker v. Grumbaum, MH, UDOA, is one of the most titled dogs in GSP history. His lineage on the Hustler side was reported under Hustler's pedigree. His dam, Freigeist Begannte v. Laden, CD, JH, was by K.S. Voli Rothenuffeln ex Am/Can Ch. Laden Field's Cocoa Pebbles, CD. In the background of the dam are many famous stalwarts of the breed, including NSS BB Ch. Kooskia's Chief Joseph; Dual Ch. and NFC Erick v. Enzstrand; Am., Can. Dual Ch. Radbach's Dustcloud, TD; Ch. Ashbrook's Papageno and Ch. Kaposia's Star of the North.

Dual Ch./AFC Trekker v. Grunbaum, UD, MH, owned by David Deioma.

Trekker finished his dual championship at just two years, making him one of the youngest, if not the youngest, dogs to earn a dual. In his field trial career he earned ten first places, including five majors, and qualified as a Master Hunter in four consecutive weekends. His last leg was earned two hours before winning BB at the Western Reserve KC show. His was the first Utility Dog Obedience title earned by a dual champion. At the age of five years, he had already sired twelve champions. In 1997, Trekker added the new open Agility title to his long list of achievements.

ROBIN CREST KENNELS

Robin Crest Kennels produced an amateur-trained and handled dual champion in Robin Crest Chip, who was the foundation of some of the biggest-winning Shorthairs in the United States. Chip was owned by John and Rita Remondi of New York, now of Napa, California, and the kennel was named for their daughter Robin, also living in San Ramon, California, with her husband, Leo Siegel.

Chip was sired by the famous Alnor's Brown Mike out of their foundation bitch, Montreal Belle, a Canadian import. Chip earned his show title in 1958 and his field championship in 1967 to become a dual.

Chip was well on his way to establishing an extraordinary show record when at an age when most dogs have completed their field trial careers, someone told John his dog was not the equal of a field champion. That got John

Dual Ch. Robin Crest Chip, one of the most successful German Shorthaired Pointers in America in the field and on the show bench, was owned by John and Rita Remondi. *William Brown*

a little angry and he went to an experienced field man for instructions, finishing his field championship himself. He marched through the field in the same manner as he had done in shows. Chip was a fired-up, enthusiastic dog in the field, and it didn't take him long to finish.

Chip also won show championships in Canada, Bermuda and the Bahamas, where he also earned a CD, and he earned a CD, TD in the United States. He was king of the hill in the East in the late 1950s and '60s, battling with Carl Tuttle's Ch. Gunhill's Mesa Maverick (Winner of two NSS BBs) for top honors year after year. He won more than 200 BBs, including Westminster, had ninety-eight group placements, six Bests in Show and nine specialty show BBs. Chip produced one dual champion, DC Kajobar v. Stony Brook, who was owned and handled by H. Straus of Ridgewood, New York. His dam was Jodi v. Hohen-neuffen.

Among Chip's eleven show champions was Ch. Robin Crest Ringo Riant, who was the grandsire of Ch. Robin Crest Royles Royce, a BIS-winner, who sired Am., Can., Puerto Rican, S.A., Int. Ch. Robin Crest Lorein Corniche, the third all-time top-winning show GSP in history. "Cory"'s dam was Lorein's Alfa v.d. Norden Herbst. He was whelped in 1985 for breeders Elaine and Pam Hoffman and Pam Fullford and was co-owned by the Remondis and Anthony Attalla of Windham, New Hampshire, for most of his show career.

Cory died February 24, 1997, after establishing one of the best show careers on record. He ended his career with 23 Bests in Show, 88 Group firsts, 67 Group seconds, 60 thirds and 20 fourths. He won a total of 339 Bests of

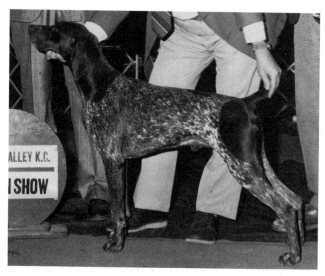

Ch. Robin Crest Lorien Corniche, one of the all-time top-wimming shorthairs in history, owned by John and Rita Remondi. He was among the "Top Ten" show dogs for all breeds during the late 1980s.

Breed, including Westminster 1988 and multiple Specialty Bests. Cory won BB at the 1989 national Specialty after going Best of Opposite at the 1988 national. He was the number-one GSP in 1988 and 1989 and number six for all breeds in 1988.

GERI AND DOYLE (BUCK) IRWIN

Two of the strongest supporters of the dual championship for more than thirty years were Geri and Doyle Irwin of Denver, Colorado. Geri served as secretary of the GSPCA for eleven years, from 1983 to 1994, when she resigned her position to move to Arizona after the death of her husband. Doyle, a championship shooter, was gun captain of many national field championships and served as coordinator of field trial dates for the parent club.

From the time they got started in GSPs in 1972, the Irwins finished four field champions, four amateur field champions, one dual champion and four show champions (shown by Geri). Their dual, amateur trained and handled by themselves, was Dual Ch. B-G's Jagerhund Gebhard, bred by Gary F. Short and Harriet M. Short of Iowa, who won all the national championships with their dogs. Geb sired three show and six field champions.

Geb was sired by FC Mark V's One Spot (Roughshooter's John L ex Ritzie's Freida v. Wildburg) ex Dual Ch./AFC Dee Tee's Baschen v. Greif (Dual Ch. Oxton's Minado V. Brunz ex Dual Ch. Cede Mein Dolly Der Orian). Two of the Irwins' field champions were sired by their Dual Ch. B-G's Trooper v. Gebhard and FC/AFC B-G's Ring, both out of AFC Moesgaard's Dandy's Cindy Lu.

In addition to serving as secretary of the parent club during a period of high accomplishment, Geri also was editor of the first parent club magazine, *Shorthair*, which continues today as the basic means of communication among the GSPCA's more than 2,000 members.

BIG ISLAND KENNELS

George De Gidio of Bloomington, Minnesota, advertises his Big Island Kennels as the "Home of the Duals," and with justification. It has produced four duals, a Hall of Fame dog, two field champions and five show champions. DeGidio, who has served as president of the Minnesota GSP Club five times, took over Big Island upon the death of George Ruidiger, one of the pillars of the Minnesota hotbed of Shorthair activity.

De Gidio got his first German Shorthair in 1949 while training young men for Golden Gloves boxing competition in the upper Midwest. He had been a boxing champion himself, with 129 amateur and 56 professional bouts, of which he won all but 4. He won the Minnesota and Northwest Featherweight Championship and was featherweight champion in the Maritime Service for three consecutive years. That sense of competition was carried over to dogs, in both the show ring and field trial activity.

George De Gidio's duals are Dual Ch. Ritzie (FC Chocolate Chip II ex Big Island Sheba); Dual Ch. Ritzie Oranien Rocco (Dual Ch. Richlu's Dan

Dual Ch./AFC B-G's Jagerhund Gebhard, owned by Doyle and Geri Irwin was owned, trained and handled by his owners. Geri served for many years as secretary of the GSPCA as well as the Colorado GSP Club.

This rare photo shows two-time national Specialty BB, Gene Ellis' Ch. Schatzie Ripper v. Greif (left) working on birds with three-time National Gun Dog Champion Gary Short's Dual Ch./NFC Bosslady Jodi v. Greif, in an Iowa grain field.

Dual Ch. Rocco's Diamond Kate v. Belle, one of five duals George De Gidio bred and handled at his kennel in Bloomington, Minnesota.

Dual Ch. Ritzie's Oranien Rocco, owned and trained by George De Gidio.

Oranien ex Dual Ch. Ritzie); Dual Ch. Roccoi's Diamond Kate v. Belle (Dual Ch./AFC Ritzie's Oranien Rocco ex Deering's Bell Waldwinkel, who was sired by De Gidio's Hall of Fame member Big Island Junker); and Dual Ch. The Flying Dutchman v. Rip Traf, who sired 1991 National All-Age Champion Desert Dutch out of White Smoke's Daisey Mae. Dutch is owned by Don Loyd of Olathe, Kan sas.

CROSSING CREEK KENNELS

One of the most important sires of the 1980s and 1990s was Ch. Crossing Creek Homesteader CD, CGC, TDI, MH, owned by Ken and Judy Marden of Crossing Creek Kennels, Titusville, New Jersey. Although not a dual himself (lacking one win in limited field trialing), Teddy was an important sire of dual-type dogs.

At Teddy's field trial peak, Ken Marden was elected president of the American Kennel Club and became ineligible to enter any of his dogs in competition. When he completed his term in 1990, it was too late to finish Homesteader. However, he earned his Master Hunter title to go with his Derby, Open and Amateur Field Trial wins and successes in the show ring.

Bred by the Mardens, Teddy was sired by Crossing Creek Hessian Baron ex Boulder Island Swanky Yankee. Behind these two dogs in three generations is a *Who's Who* of great duals, as shown by the pedigree on page 167.

As noted in the above pedigree, one of the foundation sires of Crossing Creek Kennels was the aforementioned Dual Ch. Biff Bangabird, who figures prominently in the mother line. Back in the fourth generation on the sire's side is the prepotent Dual Ch. Oxton's Bride's Brunz v. Greif, who launched nearly a half-century of outstanding dual-type dogs from California to Maine.

Ch. Crossing Creek Homesteader is tied for fourth among All-Time Top Sires of Dual Champions, with three. Through 1994, with some other get still being campaigned, he was tenth in all-time production of show champions, with thirty-two, and his offspring also included five field and amateur field champions.

In 1983, at a little over a year, he earned his show championship, was first in the Field Trial class at the GSPCA Specialty Show, earned a CD degree in Obedience, won field trial derby points and won the Eastern GSP Club's Derby Championship for combined show, field and water work.

Teddy's three duals were Dual Ch., AFC, Can. Ch. Shill Rest's Impressive and Dual Ch., AFC Briarwood's Shill Rest Roxie, CD, both out of Ch. Wildburg's Salt 'N Pepper, CD (Ch. Deitz vd Wildburg ex Ch. Kittlehersch Kelly's Revival), and Dual Ch. Kingswood Glen Kirk Zanzibar, out of Ch. Kingswood's Candy Kiss, CD (Am., Can. Ch. Weinland's Matinee Idol ex Ch. Kingswood's Buffy of Geremy, CD). He was 1987 and 1989 GSPCA Dual Sire of the Year, 1988 Hunting-Type Sire of the Year and 1991 and 1992 Obedience Sire of the Year. Teddy also worked as a therapy dog at hospitals and nursing homes.

Ch. Crossing Creek Home-steader, #4 all-time pro-ducer of dual champions with three, along with thirty-one show champions and five field champions. Teddy was owned by Judy and Ken Marden, former President and long-time Board member of the American Kennel Club.

Pedigree of Ch. Crossing Creek Homesteader, CD
1987 Sire of the Year (Dual Type)

Dual Ch. Oxton's Brides Brunz v. Greif

Dual Ch. Oxton's Minado v. Brunz

A/C Ch Sorgeville's Happy Holiday

Dual Ch. Dee Tee's Baron v. Greif

Dual Ch. Zipper Der Orrian

Dual Ch. Cede Mein Dolly Der Orrian

Dual Ch. Erdenreich's Jetta Beckum

Crossing Creek Hessian Baron

Ch Dax v. Heidebrink

Dual Ch. Richlu's Dan Oranien

Ch Richlu's Jill Oranien

Ch Crossing Creek's Kate

Dual Ch. Biff Bangabird

Ch Crossing Creek Molly Pitcher

Ch Jagers Dienstmadchen

Ch Kaposia's Oconto

Ch Ashbrook's Papageno

Ch Sieglinde of Ashbrook

Ch Crossing Creek Yankee Doodle

Dual Ch. Biff Bangabird

Ch Crossing Creek Molly Pitcher

Ch Jagers Dienstmadchen

Boulder Island Swanky Yankee

Axel v. Wasserschling

Esser's Chick

Jager's Nama

Taya v. Hohen Tann

NFC/FC Blick v. Shinback

Kline Madchen

Lady Vogel v. Hohen Tann

Ch. Crossing Creek Homesteader (left) and his many-titled son, Dual Ch./AFC Shill Rest's Impressive, with the day's catch. Homesteader was owned by Ken Marden and Impressive (Tory) was owned by Kathy Kurtz.

Marden has been a major influence in the advancement of the GSP in the United States since 1961. In addition to serving as AKC president for three years, he sat on the AKC Board of Directors for more than a decade and was AKC delegate from the GSPCA for over twenty-two years. He has served three consecutive terms on the Board of the GSPCA and as two-time president of the large Eastern GSP Club.

Ken and his wife, Judy, have been heavily involved in GSP Rescue for many years, helping to find homes for more than fifty lost or abandoned Shorthairs in conjunction with their good friend Rescue Chairwoman Nancy Campbell, owner of Homesteader Kennels in Redding, Connecticut, a leading producer of champions.

SHILL REST

Perhaps both the greatest challenge and the greatest satisfaction for an amateur is earning a dual championship with a dog trained and handled by him or herself. Kathy Kurtz of Mohrsville, Pennsylvania, whose family ran the well-known Shill-Rest restaurant near Reading, has done it twice and bred a third dual. Her two duals were homebred, sired by Ch. Crossing Creek Homesteader, and the third was by one of her own duals. Her first and most impressive dual was appropriately named Shill Rest's Impressive. He earned a dual championship, amateur championship, Canadian championship, CDX Obedience titles in America and Canada and a Master Hunter title.

What makes it that much sweeter is that Kathy did it all herself. She began with a show champion and decided to make a dual. She bought two horses

Dual Ch./AFC Briarwood's Shill Rest Roxie, owned by Jean and Thomas Cross, was a sister to Dual Ch./ AFC Shill Rest's Impressive, CDX, MH.

Dual Ch./AFC Can. Ch. Shill Rest's Cajun Queen, MH, bred by Kathy Kurtz. Sired by FC Dixieland's Rusty ex Shill Rest's Double Take.

Dual Ch./AFC Shill Rest's Lasting Impression (Dual Ch./AFC Shill Rest's Impressive, CDX, MH ex Jenny Kist Mi, JH, MH), bred by Frederick Paine.

Dual Ch./AFC Shill Rest's Impressive, CDX, MH, owned and handled by Kathy Kurtz, earned many wins and titles and sired a dual champion before his tragic accidental death at age six.

Pedigree of Dual Ch., AFC Shill Rest's Impressive CD, SH

                      DC Oxton's Minado v. Brunz
            DC Dee Tee's Baron v. Greif
                      DC Cede Mein Dolly Der Orrian
        Crossing Creek Hessian Baron
                      DC Richlu's Dan Oranien
            Ch Crossing Creek's Kate
                      Ch Crossing Creek Molly Pitcher
Ch Crossing Creek's Homesteader, CD
                      Ch Ashbrook's Papageno
            Ch Crossing Creek Yankee Doodle
                      Ch Crossing Creek Molly Pitcher
        Boulder Island Swanky Yankee
                      Esser's Chick
            Taya v. Hohen Tann
                      Kline Madchen

                      KS Pol v. Blitzdorf
            DC Kay v.d. Wildburg
                      Cora v. Wesertor
        Ch Deitz v.d. Wildburg
                      DC Gruenweg's Dandy Dandy
            Gruenweg's Bonnie
                      Ch Sobols Pointing Flecka
Ch Wildburg's Salt 'N Pepper
                      DC Kay v.d. Wildburg
            DC Frei of Klarbruck, CD
                      Ch Gretchenhof of Cinnabar, CDX
        Ch Kittlehersch Kelly Revival
                      Ch Lufkin's Big Mike
            Ch Kelly's Baby
                      Lufkin's Happy Contessa

and began serious training, making all the trials in her area. In between, she continued showing. Impressive was whelped in 1984, by Homesteader ex Ch. Wildburg's Salt 'N Pepper, whose lineage is strongly Dual Ch. Kay v.d. Wildburg. He earned all of his titles in the six short years he had before being killed in an accident in 1990.

Impressive was a natural in the field, and he passed his skill on to his children. I saw an entire litter of a half-dozen twelve-week-old puppies dropped on the course at the end of a field trial, and they pointed and backed scattered quail all over a wide area without even slowing down except to point or honor.

Impressive was the first dog of all hunting breeds to earn a Senior Hunter title, which he did at age two. He earned his dual championship at a little over two years; remember, this was by an amateur. Tory was GSPCA Sire of the Year for Hunting Type in 1990, 1991, 1993 and 1994, and Sire of the Year For Dual Type in 1993. He sired two dual champions, nineteen show champions, two field champions, eleven amateur field champions, eleven Master Hunters, twenty Senior Hunters, thirty-seven Junior Hunters, ten CDs, three CDXs and one UD, for a total of 106 titles in his short life.

Dual Ch./AFC Briarwood's Shill Rest Roxie

From the same litter of Impressive came Dual Ch./AFC Briarwood's Shill Rest Roxie, owned by Jean and Thomas Cross of Port Murray, New Jersey. Roxie finished her field title in 1989 under professional trainer Daniel Burjan and her show title under Peggy Rousch four months later. Kathy Kurtz handled Roxie to her amateur field championship one month later. It was the second dual for the Cross family, who also owned Dual Ch. Briarwood's Peppermint Patty, CD, who finished her dual championship in 1969, twenty years before.

Dual Ch. Briarwood's Peppermint Patty

"Babe," as Peppermint Patty was known, had an interesting history in the field. The second Shorthair owned by the Crosses, she was bought with the intention of making her a dual. A friend, Roy Schwartz of Hollabird Kennels in Dover, New Jersey, suggested that they look at a litter—the only one in the area at the time—bred by Vince De Marco, a Newark, New Jersey, police officer. They selected one of the two bitches left. Babe was sired by NFC Fritz v. Schmidt (brother of FC Tip Top Timmy) ex Sallie of Hollabird, who was by Dual Ch. Biff Bangabird.

Initially, Babe was strongly motivated to field work, and she was hunted and shown at the same time early in her active career, but she lost enthusiasm. When the Crosses sent her to a highly respected local trainer for field work, he told them after a while that he had four or five dogs in his kennel who were better than she and he felt she would be better off at home. So Tom and Jean took her back and worked with her in the field themselves. That

Dual Ch./AFC Briarwood Peppermint Patty, one of two dual champions owned by Tom and Jean Cross.

winter, a heavy snowfall tore down some netting at a nearby state pheasant farm and many mature birds escaped. The Crosses worked the escaped birds all winter and into the late summer. They met a man with a Pointer, and the two dogs had a great time pointing and backing without any pressure put on them. As a result of this lucky turn of events, Babe went off to their trainer's good friend and fellow professional Dick Johns for training and trialing. She clicked and finished her field and dual titles in October 1969. She also won the Eastern GSP Club championship that same month. I judged the field portion of the championship, which was based on ten categories with ten points each. I told my fellow judge, Herb Hollawell, I was going to award her 100 points with a perfect score, and he said, "You can't give 100 percent." I asked him to tell me what we should detract and after a few moments, he agreed. It turned out that she needed that perfect score, because another dog had been given too high a score in Conformation and would have won. Babe was a genuine Shorthair in both breed type, as well as in field performance. She was everywhere she was supposed to be without any letdown and had perfect manners on her many bird finds.

Dual Ch./AFC Shill Rest's Lasting Impression

When Dual Ch. Shill Rest's Impressive was bred to Fred Paine's Jenny Kist Mi, JH, Kathy got Dual Ch. and AFC Shill Rest's Lasting Impression, SH, a bitch who finished her dual in 1993, just a few months past her third birthday. Again, Kathy did all the training and handling. The dam goes back to Fieldfine lineage, including the GSPCA national Specialty BB Ch. Fieldfine's Lord Tanner.

It was a terrible shock for Kathy to lose Tory in his prime, and there is no telling what his production record would have been if he had lived to a normal age. However, he left a lasting impression that lived up to his name.

chapter 12

The Australian Connection

The first two American-bred German Shorthaired Pointers exported to Australia were an Adam grandson and an Adam son. Both caused a considerable stir in the land "Down Under."

"HANK THE YANK"

The first Shorthair to make the long trip was a seven-month-old puppy called Starlite's Greif v. Kazia, bred by Marcy Desmond of Starlite Kennels in Hayden Lake, Idaho. The dog who was to become known as "Hank the Yank" was sold to Lynn and Carolyn Butler of Kazia Kennels in Rouse Hill, New South Wales.

The first Shorthairs came to Australia from neighboring New Zealand, where the GSP was introduced in 1957, long after the breed was established in America. American lines were introduced in New Zealand through the Hank offspring Kazia Stars 'N Stripes and NZ. Ch. Kazia v. Jagenspiel, exported by breeders Lynn and Carolyn Butler. The first direct import from America was Pine Hill Trisha Blue, who arrived in 1985.

Hank the Yank was by Dual Ch. Schatzie's Eric v. Greif (Ch. Adam v. Fuehrerheim ex FC Schatzi Dem Balder v. Greif) out of the recent Hall of Fame inductee Ch. Schatzi v. Heiligsepp, CD (NFC V. Thalberg's Seagraves Chayne ex Rauke v. Heiligsepp, an Esser's Chick daughter). He was born September 3, 1977, and began his trip to Australia via England the following May at age seven months. Hank spent six months in strict quarantine and six more months out of quarantine in England, where he sired two litters; several from them went on to become champions. He was flown to Australia, where he spent three more months in quarantine before the Butlers were able to get him.

Starlite's Greif v. Kazia aka "Hank the Yank," owned by Lynn and Carolyn Butler of New South Wales and bred in the United States by Marcy Desmond, was the first American-bred GSP imported to Australia. He proved a great asset to the breed's gene pool in his new home as well as a peerless goodwill ambassador. *Lynn Butler*

Schatzi v. Heiligsepp, CD, dam of Starlite's Greif v. Kazia ("Hank the Yank"). Schatzi was owned by Marci Desmond. Hank was by Dual Ch. Schatzie's Eric v. Greif, an Adam son.

It took seventeen months to complete the trip from California because of the highly restrictive quarantine laws of the United Kingdom. Out of her only two litters, Ch. Schatzi v. Heiligsepp produced four champions and Hank from Eric and three champions from a breeding to Ch. Abiqua Diplomatic Super Kay, CD, another Adam son.

Once Hank arrived in Australia, he lived a happy and productive life, siring twenty show and field champions. He was the second-leading sire of champions in Australia in the 1980s and lived to be sixteen years old. The Butlers said of him in a letter to Marcy, "If all dogs had his temperament, the world would be a better place. He certainly made a lot of people very happy with his happy attitude to life and enormous amount of energy. He had quality of life right to the end."

Hank became world famous, but he almost missed coming into existence. Gene Ellis of Glastonbury, Connecticut, was a friend of Gene and Ercia Harden and got them to breed their FC Schatzi Dem Balder v. Greif to Adam in February 1970. The bitch was shipped to Gene at his home and he flew with her to Philadelphia, where I picked them up and drove to the nearby home of Gary and Betty Trumbow, who were to return on an early evening flight. The plane came in ahead of a predicted snowstorm, and timing was crucial. When Adam and Schatzi were introduced in the house, Adam showed no interest, and after about two hours, with the deadline for getting to the plane rapidly approaching, it appeared there would be no breeding.

Finally, I suggested we take them to the outdoor pen on the property and just let them alone. A short while later, we looked out and they were in a tie, which seemed to go on forever while the clock ticked on ominously. Finally, they broke. We gave them a few minutes' rest and then rushed madly to the airport. Gene's plane took off just as the forefront of the snowstorm was reaching the airport. From this mating, Schatzi produced three offspring— one dual champion and two show champions, the dual being Eric. That's how close Hank the Yank came to never existing. Who would have thought that that mating would result in a world traveler whose bloodlines influenced champions in many countries?

Thanks to modern science, the Butlers have found an easier way to bring over champion breeding from America: frozen semen. No more six-month quarantines for them. In 1995, they obtained frozen semen from Dual Ch./ AFC Trekker v. Grunbaum, UDX, MH, TD, one of the most titled dogs in German Shorthair history, to impregnate their Ch. Kazia Kavatina. That mating produced six offspring, from which came five champions—four Australian and one New Zealand. Trekker is a Dual Ch. Hillhaven Hustler son, owned by David B. Deioma of Chagrin Falls, Ohio.

INT. CH. ADAM'S HAGEN V. WALDENBURG

The Adam son who became the second American-bred export to Australia was another near miss. Am., Eng. Show Ch. and Aust. Ch. Adam's Hagen v.

Waldenburg was whelped May 7, 1974, and in his eleven short years established an amazing record on the international scene, but, like "Hank the Yank," the breeding that produced him was perilously close to not taking place. Hagen's dam, Ch. Fralene's Maybe, owned by Roy and Ursula Pletcher of El Cajon, California, was shipped across the country to Adam in Pennsylvania three times before a successful mating was consummated.

The first mating consisted of a very short tie with no results, and on the second try, we couldn't get a mating at all. I asked my veterinarian to examine the dam, and he determined she had a very high white blood cell count, which meant a possible infection. We thought an infection might have been triggered by Maybe's coming into season. But the third time was the charm.

The result, as it turned out, was worth a lot of aggravation. I still marvel at the Pletchers' patience. Five champions came out of that litter, including Adam's Hagen v. Waldenburg and another dog that would become famous in her own right, Ch. Adam's Heller v. Waldenburg, the mother of Terry and Janet Chandler's Dual Ch. Rugerheim's Bit of Bourbon, the greatest sire of dual champions in history. Also from that breeding came Pine Hill Apple Jack, a foundation bitch for Mary and Duane Sisson's Pine Hill Kennels, which produced a series of outstanding champions, including Am., Can., Mex. Ch. Pine Hill Apple Cider (ex Harriet v. Rossner) and Am., Can., Mex. Ch. Pine Hill Royal Star Brandy.

Ursula Pletcher owned, trained and handled Hagen to his American championship, achieved July 3, 1977. At the age of six, Hagen was sold to Dr. Michael and Georgina Byrne, who operated the highly respected Burnbrook kennel in western Australia. Georgina authored the beautiful, definitive book *The German Shorthaired Pointer* (1990), covering Shorthair breeding and activities all over the world.

The Byrnes owned Hagen when he finished his English and Australian championships. Hagen was shipped first to England for his six months' quarantine and was shown during his six-month residency period. Trained and handled in England by Mick and David Layton of Midlander Gundog Kennels, Hagen finished his English championship at age seven in 1981. He finished his Australian championship under the training and handling of Georgina in 1983. He won his English show title by winning all Challenges with Best of Breed, and he won multiple Group firsts while gaining his Australian championship at age nine.

Hagen was the only American-bred GSP to earn either an English or Australian championship. In 1983, he was the United Kingdom Sire of the Year. In 1984–85 he was West Australian Sire of the Year, and he is the All-time Top Four sire from only six litters in Australia, plus his overseas get for the whole of Australia. In addition to his two American champions, Hagen sired six show champions from four English-bred litters and ten from Australian litters, which included one champion in New Zealand. He died in 1985 at age twelve at home with the Byrnes. Hagen was inducted into the GSPCA

Am., Eng. and Australian Ch. Adam's Hagen v. Waldenburg (Ch. Adam v. Fuehrerheim ex Ch. Fralene's Maybe), England's 1983 Sire of the Year, was exported to Australia for Michael and Georgina Byrne. His breeders were Roy and Ursula Pletcher.

Hall of Fame in 1987, the only dog outside the United States to be so honored. However, he was a native son.

Hagen's grandsire, Int. Dual Ch. Adam, was considered the greatest dog in Sweden, and his importation to America was not without some sorrow. When he sired his first litter in England, a delegation from Sweden arrived to buy four puppies to take back home.

And finally, to close this chapter, a daughter of Hagen has come back to California. Ch. Burnbrook Alexandria (Hagen ex Australian Ch. Burnbrook Kalinda) is the dam of Ch. Enelrad Madmax Biyon Paladen, who was advertised in 1992 for breeding by Paladen German Shorthaired Pointers owned by Karen Detterich of Riverside. Madmax was by Ch. Paladen's Pine Hill Lone Star, going back to the original breeding that produced Hagen and helped establish the Pine Hill Kennels.

chapter 13

Obedience Winners

Three of the top-winning German Shorthaired Pointers of the late 1970s and early 1980s competing in Obedience came from Riverside breeding. They were from a breeding of Shaas Sundown, CD (Ch. Hollyhof Colonel Shaas ex Ch. Shawn Haas v. Franzell), who was purchased from Sandy Haas of Georgia, to Riverside's Painted Lady, whom the Keegans purchased in 1974 from George Pavlik of Scranton, Pennsylvania. These two dogs are still on the list of All-Time Top Obedience Producers in the history of the breed.

The first litter from Sundown ex Painted Lady was whelped in March 1978, and produced one of the first OTCHs (Obedience Trial Champions) for GSPs: OTCH Riverside's Pocono Breeze, UD, owned and trained by Karen Allen of Poolesville, Maryland. "Chance," as she was called, obtained this title in 1983.

Two sisters from the second breeding of Sundown and Lady, whelped in 1980, were the top Obedience performers Ch. Riverside's Rising Sun, UD, and Riverside's Sporting Chance, UD, owned and trained by Betty Lang of Sparta, New Jersey.

Ch. Riverside's Rising Sun, UD, when bred to Ch. Kingswood's Maximillian, produced an OTCH of her own: OTCH Sunreach's Ticked Tornado, UD (bred and owned by Karen Allen), plus another top Obedience winner, Sunreach's Hans v. Minden, UD, owned and trained by Lt. Col. Obie D. Robinson. Hans was the number-one Obedience GSP for 1991, edging out Ticked Tornado, who was second. Another Riverside dog, Ch. Riverside's Franz v. Minden, CD (also owned by Lt. Col. Robinson), was fourth. In 1994, Franz, who eventually earned a CDX, was the number-one Obedience GSP! Franz was sired by Ch. Crossing Creek's Homesteader, CD, and was out of the Top Producing Show Dam of All Time, Am., Can. Ch. Cheza's Riverside Imp, Am., Can. CD, TT.

Ch. Riverside's Rising Sun, UD, was also the dam of the littermates 1992 National Specialty Show Best of Breed, Ch. Sunreach's Flexible Flyer, CDX, and the Highest Scoring Dog in the Obedience Trial at the National, OTCH Sunreach's Ticked Tornado, UD! Both were owned by Karen Allen.

KAREN ALLEN

Probably the most prominent name in Obedience GSPs is Karen Allen of Poolsville, Maryland, who got her start with a dog from the Keegans' Riverside Kennels. Karen began with a GSP bought as a wedding present in 1970. In the latter years of the life of that dog, who lived to be 18 years old, Karen was dared to take the dog to an Obedience match. "I went and got High in Trial and I was hooked," she said.

Her second Shorthair, OTCH Riverside's Pocono Breeze, UD, CGC, Can. CD ("Chance"), was one of the early GSPs to win an Obedience championship. She won HIT at the 1979 GSPCA National Specialty Show from the Novice class. Chance won a total of thirteen HITs and two *Dog World* Awards, and in 1997 was the only GSP to ever place in an Obedience Classic.

A first was achieved for Karen Allen at the 1992 GSPCA National Specialty. Her Ch. Sunreach's Flexible Flyer CDX (right) won Best of Breed and her OTCH. Sunreach's Ticked Tornado, UD (left), was High in Trial for a Specialty their owner will never forget.

Karen also owned a Chance full sister, Ch. Riverside's Rising Sun, UD, who was also a multiple HIT winner, including HIT at the 1981 National Specialty. "Spring" was the dam of a history-making duo, by Ch. Kingwood's Maximilian, OTCH Sunreach's Ticked Tornado, UD, Can. CDX, CGC, and Ch. Sunreach's Flexible Flyer, CDX, TT, CGC.

In 1992, Flexible Flyer won BB at the GSPCA National Specialty show and Ticked Tornado went HIT in the Obedience Trial at the same show, the first and only time a brother and sister owned by the same person ever accomplished the feat. It was the largest specialty in history.

Spring is the number-three All-Time Top Obedience Dam. She also went HIT in the 1987 national Specialty, among her twenty HITs. She was Obedience Dog of the Year in 1987, 1988, 1989 and 1991. The dam of a 1990 litter, she was the youngest as well as the first homebred Obedience Champion GSP at 4 years of age.

Sunreach's Ticked Tornado is the dam of Sunreach's Dawg Gone Good, CDX ex Ch. Cheza's Billibong, UD, who won six HITs through 1997, including the the 1993 HIT in Novice and 1995 HIT in Open at the GSPCA National Specialties.

In the course of her career, Karen has trained two OTCHs, three UDs, six CDXs and ten CDs. She has won forty-five HITs, seven GSPCA Specialty HITs, four Obedience Dog of the Year titles, one Gaines Classic placement (being the only GSP to place) and multiple Gaines Regional placements.

OTCH EBEL FELDZUG SCHULTZ

The first Shorthair to earn an Obedience Trial championship was Ebel Feldzug Schultz, owned by Carl W. Johnson. Ebel went HIT at the 1983 National Specialty. He was bred by Louis Kassab and was by Squantum Streaker Bud ex Dawn v. Ranger. The most recognizable ancestors are in the third and fourth generation on the dam's side: FC Hewlett's Stoney v. Bess, Dual Ch. Hewlett Girl Pebbles and FC Moesgaard's Doktor. Whelped in 1976, Schultz died in 1989. Johnson said he was bought for hunting and taken to Obedience classes as a preliminary for field training. The instructor, Susan Strickland, noticed his potential, and he went on to his place in history.

OTCH BRIARCLIFF SASSAFRAS

Born in 1976, the same year as Ebel, OTCH Briarcliff Sassafras, TD, was the first GSP bitch to earn an Obedience Trial championship. She was bred by Patricia Miller and owned by Emory Shipley of Frederick, Maryland. "Twiggy," as she was known, was in a tight race to become the first GSP to earn the difficult Obedience Trial championship. She just missed but did become the first bitch to do so.

Twiggy was by Lee McKowen's Ch. Adam's Vindicator ex Ch. Jiff's Tanglewood, with strong lines to Ch. Adam v. Fuehrerheim on both sides

OTCH Ebel Feldzug Schultz, owned by Carl Johnson, was the first German Shorthair to earn an Obedience Trial championship.

OTCH Briarcliff Sassafras, UD, owned by Mr. and Mrs. Emory B. Shipley, Jr., was the first German Shorthair bitch to win an Obedience Trial championship.

along with Ch. Gunhill's Mesa Maverick and Dual Ch. Dino v. Albrecht on the dam's side. Vindicator was sired by Derek v. Dorjan, Adam's litter brother out of an Adam daughter, Ch. Adam's Sweet N' Sassy. At his first show, the national Specialty in Waterloo, Iowa, "Vince" went BOW and easily made his championship. His daughter Twiggy made us all proud.

Owned, trained and handled by Shipley, Twiggy earned her American CD in 1977, her American CDX in 1978 and her American UD in 1985. She earned her Bermudian CD in 1982, her CDX in 1983 and her Bermudian UD in 1985. Her OTCH was completed in 1982 and her Tracking Degree in 1985. She was the 1980 and 1981 GSPCA Obedience Dog of the Year, earning a total of eleven titles over the course of her career.

OBIE ROBINSON

The chairman of the GSPCA Obedience Committee, Lt. Col. Obie Robinson of San Antonio, Texas, has placed consistently among the leading Obedience performers. His Sunreach's Hans v. Minden, UDX, was the first GSP in history to win the UDX title. Hans won High Combined in the 1992 National Obedience Trial, with littermates going HIT and Best of Breed. Obie's Ch. Riverside's Franz v. Minden, CDX, went HIT in the 1997 National Specialty Obedience Trial to add to his glowing list of winning performances.

To place the OTCH title in perspective in terms of difficulty, through 1993 only seven sires and dams had produced an Obedience champion. The sires are Ch. Kingwood's Maximilian; Shaas Sundown, CD; Ch. Adam's Vindicator; Shikar's Sargent Pepper Duff; Lord Shannon III; Ch. Lowenbrau's Ben v. Greif, a BIS winner; and Squantum Streaker Bud. The dams are Ch. Riverside's Rising Sun, UD; Riverside's Painted Lady; Jif's Tanglewood; Champagne Lady; Dawn v. Ranger, Lady Velvet VI; and Dual Ch. NMK's Brittania v. Silbelstein.

CH./OTCH NMK'S SHARWILL V. LOWENBRAU

Against the strong competition of established Obedience performers going into the mid-1990s came a truly outstanding bitch named Ch./OTCH NMK's Sharwill v. Lowenbrau, UD, JH, CGC, the 1990, 1992 and 1993 Obedience Dog of the Year. "Zoe," as she was nicknamed, is the first GSP in the history of the breed to earn both a Conformation championship and an Obedience championship. She was royally bred, sired by the handsome BIS winner Ch. Lowenbrau's Ben v. Greif (Ch. Lucas v. Lowenbrau, CDX ex Ch. Lowenbrau's Yahtzee v. Greif, CDX) out of the All-Time Top-Winning GSP Dual Ch. NMK's Brittania v. Silbelstein. Breeders were Carol Chadwick and Dr. Gary Stone, and the owners are Bill and Sharon Asbell of San Anselmo, California.

Zoe finished her show championship in 1989 and her OTCH with six Highs in Trial and twelve High Combineds in 1993. She was HIT at the 1991

OTCH/Ch. NMK's Sharwill v. Lowenbrau, UD, JH, CGC, is the first GSP in history to earn both a Show championship and an Obedience championship. "Zoe," owned by Bill and Sharon Asbell, earned her OTCH with six High in Trial scores in 1993.

National Specialty Trial and was a Gaines Classic placer the same year. She earned a Junior Hunter title in four tests, proving her field ability as well as her aptitude for conformation and Obedience.

The All-Time Top Sire of Obedience title holders is Ch. Strauss's Happy Go Lucky, one of the biggest-winning show dogs in the history of the breed. "Lucky" has sired dogs with a total of twenty-eight Obedience titles, one more than close runner-up Ch. Sure Shot's Bounty Hunter, UD. Both dogs are in the Hall of Fame.

Lucky was bred by Del Glodowski of Wisconsin, one of America's early GSP breeders, and was acquired at 8 weeks of age by Ann Serak. She founded the Serakraut Kennels of Sturdevant, Wisconsin, with Happy as the foundation stud. His sire was Strauss's Viktor ex Strauss's Teora. Viktor was by Dual Ch. Hans v. Eldridge, CD (whose grandsire was Dual Ch. Baron v. Strauss ex FC Gretel v. Ahornstrasse). The dam, Strauss's Teora, was by Dual Ch. Esso v. Enzstrand ex Strauss's Jennalee, which goes back to Dual Ch. Baron v. Strauss.

Lucky was the fourth All-Time Top Sire of Champions through 1994 with forty-eight (since surpassed by Ch. Huntabird's Main Reason), including some of the top winners of the time. He was the number-one Show GSP in 1968,

Sandy, UD, one of the first two dogs elected into the Obedience Hall of Fame in 1996. Sandy was owned by June Herziger.

Bjarke's Sargent Pepper, UD (Sarg), was elected into the first Obedience Hall of Fame in 1996. He is owned by Michelle Burns.

1969 and 1970. He won four all-breed BISs, twenty-eight Group firsts out of eighty-two Group placings, thirteen Specialty Bests of Breed, 185 BBs (including Westminster 1969) and two BBs at the large Eastern GSPC Specialty, and was 1973 Show Sire of the Year and 1975, 1976 and 1977 Obedience Sire of the Year.

Serakraut Kennels is operated by Ann Serak and her daughter Margie, who do most of their own showing all over the United States.

AM., CAN. CH. SURE SHOT'S BOUNTY HUNTER

Interestingly, the second-place All-Time Top Sire of Obedience titles, Am., Can. Ch. Sure Shot's Bounty Hunter, UDT, MH, goes back to Lucky in the fourth generation on the sire's side. Owned by Patricia Witkiewicz of Wadsworth, Illinois, Bounty Hunter went into the Hall of Fame in 1993 after establishing an impressive winning record in versatile competition. He was the first Ch./UDT/MH of any breed in AKC competition and the youngest Ch./UDT in history. He was number-one Obedience dog in 1986 and Sire of the Year for Obedience titles in 1986, 1987 and 1990, and is the All-Time Top Producer of Hunting Test titles with fifty.

Bounty Hunter was sired by Sure Shot's Country Squire, UD ex Larson's Brandy. Squire lists among his ancestors FC, AFC, NAFC Moesgaard's Coco, FC Checkmate's Dandy Dude, FC Moesgaard's Ruffy, Dual Ch. Tip Top Timber, FC Moesgaard's Angel's Deejay and Ch. Happy Go Lucky.

OBEDIENCE HALL OF FAME

In 1996, the GSPCA Board of Directors established the GSPCA Obedience Hall of Fame. The first two inductees were OTCH Bjarke's Sargent Pepper, UD, and Sandy, UD.

Sarge was owned by Michelle Bjarke Burns of Los Alamos, New Mexico, and was bred by Charles Cockerell. He was sired by Shikar's Sargent Pepper's Duff ex Lady Velvet VI.

Sandy, who lived to be almost 17 years old, was whelped in 1963 and died in 1979. She was owned by June Herziger of Santa Barbara, California, and trained and handled by her 15-year-old son, John. Sandy, who competed under an Indefinite Listing Privilege (ILP) with pedigree unknown, was the GSPCA's Obedience Dog of the Year for four consecutive years, 1973–1976, and was in the Top Ten Obedience Sporting Dogs in 1974 and 1976. The Herzigers' daughter, Laurie, taught her to sing, play the piano, jump rope and ride a skateboard. She marched in parades wearing a hat, sunglasses and red boots. She had a wonderful life and because of her, so did her devoted owners.

The 1968 National Championship winners included three dual champions in second, third and fourth places. First was NFC v. Thalberg's Seagraves Chayne, second Dual Ch. Richlu's Dan Oranien, third Dual Ch. Bo Diddley v. Hohen Tann and fourth Dual Ch. Tip Top Timber.

Three dual-champion litter sisters owned by Gene and Ercia Harden, (from left): Dual Ch. Oxton's Leiselotte v. Greif, Dual Ch. Madchen Braut v. Greif and Dual Ch. Schoene Braut v. Greif.

The Dual Champions

During the early part of my career with Shorthairs, I entered the Saw Mill River KC show in White Plains, New York, in March 1963. When it came time to show the Shorthairs, there was great excitement about a dog called Biff Bangabird, who was going for a dual championship. Biff was owned by Chick Gandal, the young veterinarian at the Bronx Zoo, and was the subject of a *New York Times* feature before the show. If Biff went Winners Dog, he would finish his show championship to become a dual champion. There was great tension until the judge pointed to Biff and the arena erupted into a roar of applause while Chick jumped up and down with happiness. Biff went on to become an outstanding sire and was elected to the GSPCA Hall of Fame in 1982.

My dogs were braced with Biff in several field trials, and I remember him as a methodical hunter with great retrieving ability. In those days, the handlers did their own gunning in retrieving stakes and Chick was not very accurate, so his birds frequently went sailing over the horizon after the shots. Chick would look at the judges and tell them, "I think I got him. I'm going to send my dog." Biff would disappear in the distance and, after what seemed a very long time, would reappear with the live pheasant in his mouth. He was what many of us thought a Shorthair should be.

The wonderful thing about Biff's earning a dual championship was that his owner trained and handled the dog for both show and field competition, as had Jack Shattuck with the first dual, Rusty v. Schwarenberg in 1947. Biff was number fifty in a line of great dogs before him. Number 100 to finish a dual was, fittingly, Dual Ch./AFC Albrecht's Tena Hi in 1972, one of six duals to come from the famous Albrecht Kennels in Kansas.

Biff was whelped in 1958. His sire was Chadwick of Hollabird and his dam was Grousewald's Berta. Chadwick was sired by Ch. Alnor's Brown Mike, and his background included Dual Ch. Rusty v. Schwarenberg, Dual

Dual Ch. Biff Bangabird, owned by Dr. Charles Gandal. Biff was owner-trained and -handled in dog shows and field trials.

The 100th Dual Champion, Dual Ch./AFC Albrecht's Tena Hy. Tena, the dam of three duals, was bred by Myron Albrecht and owned by Myron and Lorraine Albrecht.

Ch. Blick v. Grabenbruch, Sepp v. Grabenbruch and Nanny v. Luckseck on the dam's side.

Although a number of people have finished duals that they trained and handled themselves, most have been trained and handled by professionals in either or both show and field. Since Jack Shattuck showed the way with Rusty, only 188 dogs have earned dual championships through 1996 out of the 500,000 GSPs registered in the last fifty years.

Among the champions sired by Biff Bangabird was Dual Ch. Hewlett Girl Pebbles, for breeder-owner Herman Levee of Long Island, New York. Levee started out in field trials and became interested in shows. His first dual was Dual Ch. Hewlett Girl Greta (Long Island Dutch ex Queen XVIII). Greta was bred to Biff to produce Pebbles. Pebbles was bred to FC Mitzi Bo Jack v. Bess to produce FC/AFC Golden West Greta Hewlett, who became the 1971 Amateur Field Trial Dog of the Year. She was bred by Levee and owned by Steve and Patricia Sue Pasas of San Diego.

For many, the most difficult part of the dual title is the field championship. You may recall how in the Minado story, veteran Jake Huizenga advised the Clodys to get a dog that was halfway there if they wanted a dual. The dog he sold them was already a field champion. The late professional show handler Eric Thomee once told me, "If it's got four legs and a tail, I can finish it." To be realistic, a few of the duals are just average in both conformation and field ability, or strong in one and average in the other, while some are strong in both departments. Some dogs with the greatest genuine dual potential never do make the grade for some reason. But the jealous criticism of duals, claiming that they are mediocre, is not correct. All have met at least the minimum standards for field and show championships. Many duals have been great performers and contributors to the big winners we have today.

For everyone interested in the future of the German Shorthaired Pointer, great encouragement should be given for earning a dual championship. The GSP should be a capable hunting companion and should look like a Shorthair. It is easier to train a dog for shows, since equipment and space are not a critical part of the equation. Unless it's a good specimen, a dog is subject to criticism through close inspection by not only the judge but everyone at ringside. Field trials, by contrast, require space, birds and the ability to get up on a horse as well as experience and the knowledge of training. And, of course, it takes a great deal of time and money to finish a dual. The all-walking trials offer encouragement in the field. Professionals perform a service by lending their expertise in both show and field training and the handling of dogs that might never have had an opportunity to compete because of their owners' limitations. However, there is great personal satisfaction in doing it all yourself.

Of the 188 duals currently listed, some have remarkable records and have produced other duals, field and show champions of note. Some national field

Dual Ch. Oxton Bride's Brunz v. Greif, owned by Jake Huizenga, was a prepotent sire of dual champions.

Dual Ch. Erick v. Enzstrand, a GSPCA Hall of Fame dog owned by Dave and Janice Hill.

Dual Ch. Esso v. Enzstrand, owned by Del J. Glodowski.

Dual Ch./NFC Checkmate's Challenger, winner of the 1983 National All Age Championship. Challenger was owned by John and Irene Voglein.

Dual Ch. Gert's Duro v. Greif, owned by Mr. and Mrs. Ralph Park, Sr. The Parkses owned five American and Canadian dual champions.

champions with little show stock in their backgrounds have produced a number of good dual champions. I have already covered many of the great ones. I cannot profile them all, unfortunately, although I will highlight a few for which information is available. All of the duals to date are listed in the back of this book, and their backgrounds can be researched in the GSPCA Yearbooks. Also listed are the leading sires and dams of duals.

In the 1990s, there was a duel of duals for the honor of being the number-one All-Time Top Sire of dual champions between Dave and Jan Hill's Dual Ch. Hillhaven's Hustler and Terry and Janet Chandler's Dual Ch. Rugerheim's Bit of Bourbon. They were both tied with four duals along with old FC Greif v. Hundscheimerkogel (who held the title for three decades), Dual Ch. Kay v.d. Wildburg and FC Lutz v. dem Radbach. Both Hustler and Bourbon were outstanding winners in field and show, and both were sires of many champions. Finally, Hustler broke the grip with his fifth dual to go to the top, only to have Bourbon tie him with his fifth and finally move ahead with six in the mid-1990s.

Both the Hills and the Chandlers are husband-wife teams. Dave Hill does the field trialing and Jan the showing; the same arrangement is in place with Terry and Janet Chandler. Terry was a professional field trainer based in Las Cruces, New Mexico. A college graduate with a major in computer science, Terry gave up a solid career in computers to become a professional field trial trainer, his first love. While still in college, he drove to my home to breed a bitch to my Adam. The Chandlers' interesting story of developing an outstanding line to produce duals is best covered in the Rugerheim section in Chapter 11.

OTHER OUTSTANDING DUALS

The Duals of Hidden Hollow

Living close to the Mardens was another first-time amateur owner to finish a dual champion. Ellen Cavalla of Flemington, New Jersey, got her own Shorthair from Herb and Elaine Hollowell's Hidden Hollow Kennels in 1973, after she and her mother had bought a puppy from the Hollowells as an early Christmas gift for her father.

The new dog became Dual Ch./AFC Hidden Hollow's Pleasure, nicknamed "Shamrock" for the shamrock-shaped patch on her side that initially attracted Ellen. She was on the Top Ten Gun Dog list for three years, earning more than 110 broke dog placements, and was New Jersey's number-one Walking Shooting Dog for 1981.

Shammy was sired by Ch. Warrenwood's Alfie (Ch. Adam v. Fuehrerheim ex Ch. Warrenwood's Kandy Kane) ex Ceres of Hidden Hollow (Knight ex Middleton's Girl). Shammy's dam, Ceres, has no recognizable ancestors in four generations, but she became the foundation of the Hidden Hollow Kennels, which would become a leader in field trial champions in the East. Ceres produced one dual, two show champions and fourteen field and amateur field champions to become the third leading dam of field trial champions and a member of the Hall of Fame. She was the granddam of another dual, Dual Ch. Hidden Hollow's Ronlord Ruler, bred by Ron Dombrowski and owned by Elaine Hollowell. Ruler was by FC Checkmate's Dandy Dude ex FC Pilar of Hidden Hollow, Ceres' daughter. Ruler, who is also in the Hall

Dual Ch./AFC Hidden Hollow's Pleasure, owned and handled by Ellen Cavalla.

of Fame, sired FC and AFC Hidden Hollow's Hot Shot, who won the 1983 National Gun Dog Championship for his owner/handler, Craig Little, DVM, of Whitehouse Station, New Jersey. Hot Shot's dam was P.J's Hot Pants of Hidden Hollow, who was by another of Ceres' famous sons, FC/AFC Pretty Boy of Hidden Hollow. Dr. Little also owned Dual Ch./AFC Hidden Hollow's Classy Sassy, a Ruler granddaughter. Ruler also sired Dual Ch. Princess Pepper V, bred by John C. Werren and owned by Robert A. Leonard, DVM, of Frederick, Maryland, and Dual Ch./AFC Hidden Hollow's Rowdy Bess out of Ray Mac's Ginger Bred, owned by Elaine Hollowell and Anne-Louise King.

Dual Ch. Richlu's Dan Oranien

Shirley and Cle Carlson of St. Paris, Ohio, owners and publishers of *The GSP News*, were strong proponents of the dual champion as evidenced by their two duals, Dual Ch. Richlu's Dan Oranien and Dual Ch. Richlu's Terror. Dan, a Hall of Fame member, was a natural and broke field dog and outstanding performer in trials. He was twice runner-up in the GSPCA national championship in 1968 and 1969 and was number one in the Top Ten Puppy-Derby rankings at the time.

Bred by Dick and Lonnie Sylvester, Dan was sired by Ch. Dax Heidebrink (Dual Ch. Blick v. Grabenbruch ex Betsy v. Heidebrink) ex Ch. Richlu's Jill Oranien (Ch. Richlu's Jeffson ex Ch. Richlu's Jan Oranien-Nassau). Jeffson was sired by Lonnie and Dick Sylvester's famous Dual Ch. Sager v. Gardsburg. Dan sired one dual and seven field champions.

Dual Ch. Richlu's Dan Oranien, owned by Shirley and Cle Carlson. Shirley, who published the *German Shorthaired Pointer News,* handled Dan in shows and Cle did the same in trials. Dan was runner-up at the National Championship two years in a row.

Dual Ch. Richlu's Terror, owned by Shirley and Cle Carlson, was the second dual owned and trained by the Carlsons.

The Carlsons' second dual was Dual Ch. Richlu's Terror, who was sired by Dual Ch. Sager v. Gardsburg (Ch. Buck v. Gardsburg ex Ch. Richlu's Jan Oranien-Nassau). Jan was sired by Dual Ch. Al-Ru's Erich ex Ch. Xenia Oranien-Nassau.

Of Dan, Cle said, "He was probably the smartest dual ever. He broke himself after one lesson; he just knew you didn't move." I saw him perform in the 1968 national, and he had numerous finds in the third series and never moved an inch while Cle hunted them out no matter how long it took.

One of the strongest supporters of the breed through their magazine and personal handling and judging in field and shows, Shirley died in 1995. Those of us who knew her will always remember her.

Dual Ch. Golden West Chucko

Dual Ch. Golden West Chucko was a true All-Age dog who goes back to FC Greif v. Hundscheimerkogel; the first dual, Dual Ch. Rusty v. Schwarenburg; and Dual Ch. Blick v. Grabenbruch. He was the 1980 All-Age Dog of the Year. He was bred by M. and P. Kuykendall and owned by Kay and the late Marlin Thrasher of Killeen, Texas. Chuck was handled in the field by John Merrell. He finished his amateur field championship in 1982 at age eleven because of the difficulty in finding All-Age Amateur Stakes at that time. Chuck

Dual Ch./AFC Golden West Chucko, owned by Kay Thrasher.

Dual Ch./NFC Erlicher Abe, owned by Patrick and Linda Cross.

was sired by Golden West Blick's Fritz (NFC Blick v. Shinback ex Sierra Apollo Rae, an NFC v. Thalberg's Seagraves Chayne daughter) ex Waldenburg Chayne's Beasley (NFC v. Thalberg's Seagraves Chayne ex FC/AFC Golden West Skoan Y Bob's Rebel).

Dual Ch./AFC/NFC Erlicher Abe

Dual Ch./AFC/NFC Erlicher Abe was bred by Mr. and Mrs. Paul J. Ashley and was owned by Patrick and Linda Cross of Boise, Idaho. He finished his field championship, handled by Dave McGinnis, in 1980 and his show championship in 1981. He won the GSPCA National Championship in 1982.

Abe was sired by FC Ammertal's Lancer D (NFC v. Thalberg's Seagraves Chayne ex FC/AFC Kitt v. Shinback, who was sired by Esser's Chick) ex Ch. Misty Fer Gitunburdz (Dual Ch. Tip Top Timber ex FC Kay Fer Gitunburdz, who was sired by Dual Ch./NFC Kay v.d. Wildburg).

Abe sired two dual champions, six show champions and ten field and amateur field champions, and he was named to the Hall of Fame in 1995. He is the grandsire of FC/AFC Beier's Evolution, who is fast moving up in the standings as a leading sire of field champions at this writing.

NAFC, NFC Beier's Evolution

NAFC, NFC Beier's Evolution was owned by Dr. Jim McCue, Jr., of Idaho Falls, Idaho, and was bred by Rafael Beier. He was sired by Beier's Ace ex

FC/AFC Beier's Evolution, owned by Dr. J. G. McCue, Jr. A top-producing sire and member of the Hall of Fame, Evolution won the 1986 National Gun Dog Championship and the 1985 National Amateur Championship.

Neika Meister Jagerin. Ace goes back to NFC Frulord's Tim and FC Shilo v. Hessenwald. Neika was sired by Abe ex Neika Jager v. Shilo.

Evolution won the 1985 National Amateur Championship and the 1986 National Open Gun Dog Championship. He was the top all-age dog in the nation in 1987 and 1988, and he won the NGSPA National Chukar Championship in 1988. He was named to the Hall of Fame in 1997.

He is the sixth-place All-Time Top Sire of Field Champions with thirty-four, along with two dual champions and two show champions. His duals are Dual Ch. Beier's Misty Blu, JH, and Dual Ch. Ziel v. Feinschmecker.

Misty Blu was bred by Catherine Black and is owned by Charlene E. Smithgall of Lakewood, Colorado. Her dam is AFC Mywar's Prairie Reaper, by FC/AFC Rieko v. Shinback ex Cinders Shadow Beapa's Baby. Ziel's dam is FC Brookvue's Gerda Garbo, SH, bred and owned by Eva Gorbants and S.L. Babinski, DMD.

Evolution also sired NFC/AFC Timberdoodle's Holiday Edition, who won the first AKC National Gun Dog Championship in 1994 and finished second in the fourth AKC National Gun Dog Championship in 1997. Holiday Edition was out of Timberdoodle's Crackerjack, bred by Dot and Dick Kern of New Jersey and owned and handled by Dino Russo.

The Kerns owned FC/AFC Timberdoodle's Bee-Line out of the same breeding. They also owned Dual Ch. Timberdoodle's Lancer's Answer, who died in 1994 shortly before his sixteenth birthday. He was bred by Frank Critelli and handled in the field by Dick Kern and in the show ring by Dot.

Lancer was sired by NFC Ammertal's Lancer D (NFC v. Thalberg's Seagraves Chayne ex FC Ammertal's Kitt v. Shinback) ex Da-Lors Brandie v. der Wildburg (Dual Ch. and NFC Kay v.d. Wildburg ex Dual Ch. Fee v. der Wildburg).

V. Hainholz Kennels

The V. Hainholz Kennels of Daisy Schapeer, Lancaster, California, is the home of three duals. Her foundation sire was Dual Ch. and German K.S. Ybold Rothemufflen, a dog imported from Germany after winning the German K.S. title in 1982. He won his American show championship, handled by Clay Coady, in September 1982 and his FC, handled by Heinz Schapheer, in 1985. The only dog to hold a K.S. and dual title, he was named to the GSPCA Hall of Fame in 1995.

Dual Ch. Captain v. Winterhauch, owned by Millard W. Axelrod, shown here with his legendary handler Hollis Wilson, who later became an all-breed judge. *Frasie*

Ybold sired one dual champion, twenty-three show champions and seven field and amateur field champions. His dual was Dual Ch. Ybold's Graf v. Hainholz, who was bred by John Vukson out of Katie Blue v. Hainholz (FC/AFC Dutch v. Hainholz ex Bonnie Blue v. Hainholz, MH).

Ms. Schapheer also co-owned, with Brent Henry, Dual Ch. Bodo v. Waldbrand, MH, who was bred by Herbert Nowak. Bodo was sired by Arco v. Den Sieben Brunnen ex Nixe v. Huenenbrink.

THE LEADING DAMS OF DUALS

Ch. Yunga War Bride (discussed in an earlier chapter) has held the record for Top Dam of Dual Champions for more than forty years, with four duals from five champions and four field champions. She was owned by Jake Huizenga.

Right behind her, tied with three duals each, are FC Albrecht's Contess Tena, who was elected to the first Hall of Fame; Dual Ch. Cede Mein Dolly Der Orrian, also in the first Hall of Fame; Dual Ch. Gretchen v. Greif, also in the first Hall of Fame; and Ch. Suzanna Mein Liebchen. All but Dolly and Suzanna have been discussed in earlier chapters.

Dual Ch. Cede Mein Dolly Der Orrian, owned by Dean Tidrick. Dolly is tied for second All-Time Lading Producer of Duals with three. She also produced twenty-one show champions and four field champions.

Dual Ch. Cede Mein Dolly Der Orrian

Dolly, bred by C. D. Lawrence and owned by Dean Tidrick of Iowa, was sired by Dual Ch. Zipper Der Orrian ex Dual Ch. Erdenreich's Jetta Beckum. In addition to being number two in the production of dual champions, she is also the number-three All-Time Producer of Show Champions, with twenty-one, and produced four field and amateur field champions. Dolly was Dam of the Year for Dual Types in 1972, 1973, 1976 and 1978, and she was 1974 Dam of the Year for Show Champions.

Ch. Suzanna Mein Liebchen

Ch. Suzanna Mein Liebchen was owned by Ted and Maxine Collins of Newaygo, Michigan. Maxine was editor and chairman of the *GSPCA Yearbook* for twenty-one years. Suzanna's sire was Pat of Sonja Lee Lodge ex Pal of Sonja Lee Lodge, with no titled forebearers in three generations.

Her three duals were Dual Ch. Marmaduke Mein Liebchen, Fritz of Hickory Lane Farm and Gustav Mein Liebchen. Marmaduke was sired by Ch. Fieldborn Tempo II, whose pedigree contains Ch. Waldo v.d. Goldenmark, Timm v. Altenau and Waldwinkel and Schwarenburg bloodlines. Fritz and Gustav were sired by Dual Ch./NFC Dandy Jim v. Feldstrom.

Leading Field Trial Shorthairs

Field trials and hunting tests are the proving ground for the German Short-haired Pointer's ability to perform its traditional function and, with sixty-eight member clubs operating under the umbrella of the American parent club, there are hundreds of trials and tests for the 15,000 GSPs registered each year with the AKC.

From these events emerge dogs that demonstrate outstanding abilities in the field. In this chapter you will learn who some of the leading dogs were and what made them such standouts.

FC DIXIELAND'S RUSTY

As noted earlier, FC Uodibar's Boss Man was the all-time leading sire of field champions until the 1990s, with forty-three field-titled offspring, two duals and four show champions. However, in the last decade of the twentieth century, he was passed for the number-one spot by a new leader who literally burst into the forefront. FC Dixieland's Rusty, carrying many of the great foundation dogs in history in his background, produced an astounding sixty-nine field champions, two duals and two show champions, and the roster is growing as this is being written. Rusty's get have virtually dominated the national championships for nearly a decade.

Rusty was bred and owned by Ron Herman of El Dorado, Arkansas, and he was trained and handled by Ed Husser of Covington, Louisiana. He was whelped May 2, 1978, finished his field championship in 1982 and died on November 11, 1991, at age eleven and a half years.

Rusty was sired by JG's Ludwig v. Duesenburg (FC Brown-L ex Dual Ch./AFC Kerlacres Tell's Moonbeam) ex Leighton's Ace Mona (FC Moesgaard's Ace ex Jimmy's Fieldacres Joy). In his fourth generation are FC

FC Dixieland's Rusty, sire of the unbelievable total of sixty-nine field trial champions. The all-time leading sire of field trial champions, Rusty is owned and bred by Ronald Herman.

Fieldacres Ib, FC Fieldacres Ammy, Dual Ch./NFC Moesgaard's Dandy, FC Tell, FC Moesgaard's Ruffy, Int. FC Moesgaard's IB and Big Island Junker. His breeding traces back almost exclusively to Danish bloodlines.

For his outstanding performance in the field and as a sire, Rusty was inducted into the GSPCA Hall of Fame in 1997.

In addition to sheer numbers, Rusty's get and grand-get excelled in quality with numerous national titles and records of achievement. Rusty's own achievement awards and national championships and the awards of his get and grand-get are given by year in the listing which follows.

Year	Get and Grand-Get
1987	Sire of National Amateur Champion Big Oak's Irish Mist (ex Big Oak's Bitsha), owner/handler Vern Grimslid, West Allis, Wisconsin.
1989	Sire of National Amateur Champion Lars Agnes v. Rusdelite (ex FC Dixieland's Mocha Delight, a Rusty daughter), owner/handler Dr. M. Parl Larson, Pinetop, Arizona.
	GSPCA Sire of the Year for Field Type, with fourteen field champions and one show champion.

Year	Get and Grand-Get
1990	Sire of the Year for Field Type with nine field titles.
	Sire of National Amateur Champion and National Gun Dog Champion Lars v. Rusdelite (given).
1991	Sire of FC Uodibar's Koonas, Sire of the Year for Field Type and National Gun Dog Champion Uodibar's Stub A Dub (ex FC Brownhaven Mellifluous), owner, Kent Kislingbury, D.V.M., Fairmont, Minnesota.
	Sire of the Year for Field Type.
1992	Grandsire of Gun Dog of the Year and Amateur Gun Dog of the Year FC and AFC Erdenreich's Navigator (FC Uodibar's Koonas ex FC/AFC Erdenreich's Neika Ptarmigan), owner Lou Tonelli, San Francisco.
	Sire of the Year for Field Type with two duals, and five other field titles. Two dual champions: Dual Ch./AFC Shill Rest's Cajun Queen, MH (given in duals), owner/handler Kathy Kurtz, Pennsylvania; and Dual Ch./AFC Rusty Spur (ex Sier Apollo Fancy Fancy Free), breeder John Merrell. Owned by Darwin Oordt, Blue Earth, Minnesota.
	Grandsire of Dual Ch. Voglein's Billy of Sundance (FC Uodibar's Koonas ex FC Sundance Gypsy Lee), breeder/owner John Voglein, Zion, Illinois.
1993	Grandsire of Gun Dog of Year FC/AFC Lars Kandu Quails (Quail Ridge Sundance Rusty, sired by Rusty, ex Quailrun's Roxy Roller sired by FC Jigg's White Smoke), owned by Dr. M. Parl Larson, Pinetop, Arizona.
1994	National Gun Dog Champion FC Windjammer's Tina (ex FC Wildfire's Windjammer), breeder/owner Terry Zylgalinski.
1997	Induction into the GSPCA Hall of Fame.

Rusty's record is especially spectacular considering that he was bred and kept for hunting, without much thought given to field trialing. Owner Ron Herman sent him to Ed Husser to train him as a hunting dog. Herman said that after Ed had him for a short time, he asked Ron, "Do you know what you have here?" Herman said all he had planned for Rusty was quail hunting in Louisiana. Even though he had served as president of the New Orleans GSP Club, he did not consider trying for a field championship. "I just kind of fell into it," Herman said.

Ed Husser said, "We got him at five months, and we sort of raised him here. We felt he was too nice a potential and needed to be used for more than hunting. He would just go, go, go." It was that go that attracted him to so many breeders.

Rusty's biggest win as a competitor was the NGSPA National Championship.

Husser said his wife Linda "adopted him and put him in the house. He protected her and became our house dog.

"When he retired, he was to come back home for the last two years of his life, but he died six months after he came back. He was kind of special to us."

FC BIG OAK BUMPER

Given the fact that a female is limited in the number of offspring she can produce with prudent breeding in a lifetime, it is remarkable to see the production records of all the All-Time Top Dams. In the number-one spot through 1994 records is FC Big Oak Bumper, with eighteen field and amateur field champions, just two ahead of second-place Quailrun's Roxy Roller, with sixteen.

FC Big Oak Bumper was bred and owned by Michael Walsh of Arlington Heights, Illinois. She was whelped in 1976, two years before the birth of all-time top sire Rusty. She finished her field championship in 1983. Bumper

FC Big Oak Bumper, All-Time Top-Producing Dam of Field Champions with eighteen, owned by Mike Walsh.

was Dam of the Year for Field Type in 1984, 1985 and 1989. She was elected to the Hall of Fame in 1995.

Bumper was sired by FCD Moesgaard's Madchen Ruffy (FC Moesgaard's Ruffy ex FC Madchen Wenwald Leica) ex Little Bobbie's Jodi Girl (FC Windy Hills Toby, who was sired by Windy Hill Prince James) ex Big Oak Little Bobbie, going back to FC Moesgaard's Ruffy.

QUAILRUN'S ROXY ROLLER

Quailrun's Roxy Roller was bred by Robert and Sandy Deitering of Huachua City, Arizona. She was sired by Hall of Fame members FC Jigg's White Smoke (FC Moesgaard's Jigg's ex Schatten's JJ) ex Freedom's Candy (Hickory Ridge Hank ex Timmy's Little Bit of Freedom, who was sired by Dual Ch. Timber Top Tell, CD). She was 1991 Dam of the Year for Field Type.

MAJOR WINNERS

Rawhide Kennels

Don Paltani, who operates Rawhide Kennels in LaPlatte, Nebraska, with his wife, Pam, has had great success with several top-winning dogs of national caliber. Four of the most recent top winners in his kennel are NFC Rawhide's Clown, NFC Stuka of the Knight, Dual Ch./FC Desert Dutch and NFC Rawhide's Mo-Reen.

NFC Rawhide's Clown set a new record in 1994 by winning his third GSCA National All Age Championship, becoming the only dog in history to win the National All Age three years in a row. He also won in 1992 and 1993.

Clown was bred by Paltani and Marty Wyant and trained and handled by Don Paltani for owner Dierk Davis of Terre Haute, Indiana. He was sired by the Paltani-bred Hall of Fame member FC Jigg's White Smoke (FC/AFC Moesgaard's Jigg's ex Schatten's JJ) ex FC Josie Wells (FC Smokey Ike's Blaze ex FC Moeswinkle's Dutchies v. Jake). Jake and Blaze go back to Ruth John's Betti, who was sired by Int. Ch. Adam.

To go along with his history-making win in 1994, Clown had three of his get finish their championships that same year: FC Fennenberg's Georgia Girl, FC North Texas Crude and FC Ruby's Little Clown.

"Not only is Clown a legend in field trials, but also a great hunting partner," Don said. "Clown is truly a master on wild birds, pheasants, grouse and especially quail." This refutes the frequent claim by outdoor writers that field trial dogs do not make suitable hunting companions.

FC Stuka of the Knight won the 1989 GSPCA All Age National Championship. Stuka was bred by J. L. Craig and owned by Stanley Rys of Omaha, Nebraska. He finished his field championship eleven days before winning the national championship under Paltani's handling.

NFC Rawhide's Clown, owned by Dierk Davis, was handled to three straight National All Age Field Trial Championships (1992, 1993, 1994) by Don Paltani.

Dual Ch./ NFC Desert Dutch, owned by Don Lloyd and bred by George De Gidio, won the 1991 National All Age Championship handled by Don Paltani.

Stuka of the Knight, owned by Stanley Rys and handled by Don Paltani, was the 1989 AKC National All Age Champion.

Stuka was sired by FC Craig's Moontige (FC Brown L ex Dual Ch./SFC Kerlacres Tell's Moonbeam) ex Rawhide's Pamela Jean (FC Jigg's White Smoke ex Craigs Tige F.R. Mae).

Dual Ch./NFC Desert Dutch was bred by George De Gidio, owned by Don Lloyd of Olathe, Kansas, and handled by Paltani. He was sired by Dual Ch. The Flying Dutchman v. Rip Traf v. Bess (FC v. Thalberg's Fritz II ex FC De Gidio's Will-O-The-Wisp Wendy) ex White Smoke's Daisy Mae (FC Jigg's White Smoke ex Craig's Tige ex F.R. Mae). The lineage goes back to the breed pillars Greif v. Hundscheimerkogel, Grabenbruch, Moesgaards, Radbach and Dual Ch./AFC Kerlacres Tell's Moonbeam. Dutch was the fifth National All Age champion handled by Paltani in six years.

Don Lloyd also owns 1996 National Gun Dog Champion NFC Rawhide's Mo-Reen, who also won the 1996 NGSPA National Quail Shooting Dog Championship. She was sired by FC Rosehill's Cosmo (FC/AFC Craig's Moontige ex FC Brown L's Ruby) ex Rosehill's Dizzie Lizzie, who was sired by FC Dixieland's Rusty).

Lloyd owned another dual champion, Dual Ch. Apocalypse v. Greif, who finished both titles in 1984. Apocalypse was bred by Ken Sanderson of Olathe, Kansas, and handled in the field by Paltani and in shows by Larry Hitchcock. He was sired by Dual Ch. and NFC Erlicher Abe ex Giner v. Hessewald, who counts NFC Blick v. Shinback and NFC Rip Traf v. Bess in her background.

NFC Buckville's Maggie Mae

The 1993 National Gun Dog Championship was the largest in history with 100 entries. It was won by NFC Buckville's Maggie Mae, owned by Joe Minard of Clear Lake, Iowa, and trained and handled by Bob Merkel of Jessup, Iowa. NFC Buckville's Maggie Mae, who finished her field championship in 1992, was sired by FC Dixieland's Luke (FC Dixieland's Rusty ex FC Leipchen Buddendorf) ex Vivid Dixie.

FC/AFC Bluemax Spitfire v. Greif

FC/AFC Bluemax Spitfire v. Greif, bred and owned by John and Linda Nickerson of Overland Park, Kansas, and trained and handled by Keith Gulledge of Blue Dawn Kennels, Eureka, Kansas, has won many titles and placements in the nine years since his birth in 1988.

Spitfire was sired by FC Sieg Heil (Julson Jesse ex Ginger v. Hessenwald ex FC Heide Ho-Pinehurst) (Julson Jesse ex FC/AFC Erbe's White Streaker, by Jigg's White Smoke). He was named the GSPCA All Age Dog of the Year in 1992. He finished his AKC field championship in 1990 and added the AFC in 1996. Much of Spitfire's activity has been in American Field Trials conducted by the National German Pointing Dog Association (NGPDA) and the National German Shorthaired Pointer Association, where he has been very successful.

FC Bluemax Spitfire v. Greif won many field trial championships in AKC and American Field Trial formats. Spitfire was owned by John and Linda Nickerson and handled by Keith Gulledge.

FC Heide Ho-Pinehurst, owned by John and Linda Nickerson and bred by Ken Sanderson.

Spitfire won the NGPD National Championship in 1992 and the National Shooting Dog Championships in 1994 and 1995, and was runner-up for the National Championship and National Shooting Dog Championship in 1993.

In NGSPA competition, Spitfire was named All Age Dog of the Year in 1992, Shooting Dog of the Year in 1993 and Amateur Shooting Dog of the Year in 1996. He won the National Shooting Dog Championship in 1997 and was runner-up in 1993. He won the National Amateur Shooting Dog Championship in 1996 and was runner-up in 1991. He also won the National Chukar Shooting Dog Championship in 1993 and 1994 and the Quail All Age Championship in 1995.

FC Heide Ho-Pinehurst

Spitfire's dam, FC Heide Ho-Pinehurst, also owned by the Nickersons, is fifth in the All-Time Dam's list for field trial champions with twelve. She was bred by Ken Sanderson of Olathe, Kansas, and trained by Keith Gulledge. She was by Julson Jesse (FC/AFC Moesgaard's Jigs ex FC/AFC Mac The Knife) ex Erbe's White Streaker (FC Jigg's White Smoke ex Rawhide's Blazing Annie v. Jake).

Heide won an AKC National Futurity Championship and an NGSPA National Shooting Dog Championship, and was twice NGSPA National Futurity Top Producing Dam. Her list of titled get is exceptional in the national quality of their wins. Heide's mating to NFC Sanjo Sin City Slicker produced in 1991 two national winners among the other national-placing field champions in the litter. They were NFC Heide's Mighty City Slicker and NGSPA National All Age Champion FC BMK's Strike the Gold.

The sire of this exceptional litter, NFC Sanjo Sin City Slicker, won the 1990 GSPCA All Age Championship, handled by John Steger for owner Stephen C. Harold of Terre Haute, Indiana. Michael Brittain was the breeder. Slicker was sired by Blue Bayou (Colonel of Belle-Arch ex Alexandria v. Snifter) ex Kiss Me Kate (FC Wolfjaeger's Nikki v. Spee ex FC Uodibar's Rachel).

NFC Heide's Mighty City Slicker was owned by Robert Thompson of Stafford, Missouri, and trained and handled by Keith Gulledge. He won the GSPCA All Age Championship, the NGSPA National Shooting Dog Championship and the NGSPA National All Age Championship in 1995, the NGSPA National Amateur Championship in 1966 and the NGSPA National All Age Championship again in 1997. Slick is one of only three dogs to win all three national championships.

Slick's litter brother, FC Strike the Gold, was owned by Brian Nail of Leawood, Kansas, a long-time treasurer of the GSPA, and was trained and handled by Keith Gulledge. Strike the Gold won the 1966 NGSPA National All Age Championship and the 1993 NGSPA National Pheasant Shooting Dog Championship. He was runner-up to his brother for the AKC 1995 National All Age Championship and the 1997 National Shooting Dog Championship.

NFC Heide's Mighty City Slicker, owned by Robert Thompson and bred by Linda Nickerson, was one of only three dogs to win all four national championships: NGSPA National Shooting Dog Champion, AKC National All-Age Champion, NGPD National All-Age Champion, and NGPC National Amateur Champion.

FC BMK's Strike The Gold, owned by Brian Nail.

NFC/AFC Lars Agnes v. Rusdelite, owned by Parl Larson, won the 1989 National Amateur Championship and the 1990 National Amateur and National Open Gun Dog Championships.

Lars Kennels

Dr. Parl Larson of Bluegrass Ranch in Pinetop, Arizona, has one of the two best records for an amateur trainer and handler in national events. His most outstanding dog was NFC Lars Agnes v. Rusdelite, who won back-to-back National Amateur Championships in 1989 and 1990 and the National Open Gun Dog Championship in 1990.

Agnes was bred by Michael LaRose in 1986 and owned and handled by Dr. Larson. She was sired by the All-Time Top Sire of Field Champions FC Dixieland's Rusty ex FC Dixieland's Mocha Delight, a Rusty daughter.

Bred to Larson's FC/AFC Lars Kandu Quails Quail Ridge Sundance Rusty ex Quailrun's Roxy Rover, she produced 1995 National Gun Dog Champion FC K-Hawk's Kandu Kandy, owned by Kem Kisingbury, D.V.M. Quails was the GSPCA Gun Dog of the Year in 1993.

"Agnes was a once-in-a-lifetime dog that would rise to the big occasion and provide so many thrills and so much pride for an amateur trainer/owner/handler and family," Dr. Larson said.

Dr. Larson served as chairman of the GSPCA Hall of Fame and Honorary Lifetime Committee for nearly fifteen years, and he was vice president and a board member of the GSPCA for many years. Now retired on his ranch high up in the White Mountains in eastern Arizona, Dr. Larson remains an active field trialer through the publishing of this book.

Frank Alexander

Frank Alexander, of Albuquerque, New Mexico, has been a prominent fixture on the national field trial scene for many years, quietly smoking his pipe in front of his big Bluebird motor home while the hubbub of field trial activity swirls around him. His dog NFC Windswept's Little Big Man won the National All Age Championship at Fort Huachuca, Sierra Vista, Arizona, in 1985 shortly before the nationals picked a permanent site at Eureka, Kansas. Little Big Man was bred by Robert Perlin in New Jersey in 1979, and he was handled by Dave Peck, who moved out West from the East Coast. The judges were Joe Vicari of Illinois and Bill Mengert of New Jersey, both of whom have won national championships and have dogs in the Hall of Fame. Vicari's NAFC P.J. Wildfire was elected in 1991 and Mengert's FC/AFC Stoney's Jake v. Hewletts, the grandsire of Little Big Man, in 1988.

Eleven years later, in 1996, Alexander again won the National All Age Championship with NFC Alamo Magic (NFC Uodibar's Koonas ex FC/AFC Brownhaven Mellifluous), handled by Ron Schaitel.

Dual Ch./NFC Bosslady Jodi v. Greif, owned by Gary and Harriet Short, won the 1979 and 1981 National Amateur Championships and the 1980 National Open Gun Dog Championship.

Lika Buckskin, 1979 National All Age Champion, owned and handled by Gary Short.

chapter 16

The National Field Trial Championships

The German Shorthaired Pointer Club of America offers three annual National Championship trials and one National Futurity. The first National Championship was held in 1953, with Dr. Clark Lemley's NFC Dandy Jim v. Feldstrom winning the title to take his place in history. There was only one National Championship until the National Amateur Field Championship was inaugurated in 1966, when the judges withheld the title because of what they considered lack of merit. The first winner came the following year, when Lloyd Sanders' NAFC Moesgaard's Coco earned the title.

A National Gun Dog Stake was added in 1977, with the first win going to FC Patar's Chocolate Chip, owned by Ernie Kolb. The American Kennel Club refused to grant a Gun Dog Championship, so first place was simply listed as Winner of the Stake. It was recorded as a Limited Gun Dog Stake. The AKC's position was that there were too many national championships and another one would dilute the honor of winning a national title.

The problem was that the National Championship was usually judged on an all-age basis, and dogs of gun dog range and application found it difficult to win the championship. They could win a National Amateur Championship, which might be based more closely on a gun dog performance, but it was not an open stake. When I was president of the GSPCA, I went to New York on two occasions to get the AKC to reverse its position, to no avail. When I became vice president of Performance Events at AKC, I convinced the Board to grant a National Gun Dog Championship title effective in 1990, so the winner of this trial is now listed as National Gun Dog Champion.

In 1961, the GSPCA established a National Futurity Championship for dogs up to 2 years old from Futurity-nominated litters. For many years, the Futurity was held successfully in the spring in Wisconsin under the guidance of Jack Pomrening. The first winner was Schultzie v. Hohen Tann, owned by Ray Bauspies. The Futurity was run as a single stake until 1978, when it was won by Erlicher Abe, who later won the National All Age Championship and became a dual champion. Abe was owned by Patrick and Linda Cross.

There was a great deal of controversy about the manner in which the Futurity was judged. Almost without exception, the dog closest to approaching all-age potential became the winner. It was then decided to hold two Futurity stakes, one for all-age potential and one for gun dog potential. The Futurity was judged in this manner until it was cancelled in 1983 because the entries had fallen far below the number considered to be of national championship caliber. I believe the entries had dropped to about eleven or twelve in each stake.

The membership of the GSPCA was polled to find out if it wanted the Field Futurity to continue, and the majority voted in favor. Don Higgins and I put together the present format, stipulating that the dog displaying the best potential, including gun dog potential, should be declared the winner. That criterion is still in place, although most judges today still put up the biggest-running dog that shows acceptable bird work or in some cases, even poor bird work.

In lieu of the Futurity in 1983 and 1984, there was a National Derby Classic and a National Puppy Classic. These also drew low entries, hence the poll to determine whether a one-stake Futurity should be renewed.

All-age dogs are expected to run to the limits of the course in a determined search for birds, but they should be under control and appear in front unless they are on point or take a cast beyond their handlers' hearing. At that point a scout is dispatched to locate the dog and report back that it is either on point or moving in a certain direction. The scout should return to his or her position behind the handler and not attempt to handle the dog. This requirement is frequently violated, with the scout helping to bring the dog around.

A gun dog should hunt more to the handler and appear frequently in front so that it can keep moving in the direction of the handler on course. Scouts operate in the same manner. The gun dog usually handles more kindly, although both types are expected to demonstrate impeccable manners on birds and respond to the handler's commands.

The American Field licenses several national championships under two organizations: the National German Shorthaired Pointer Association and the National German Pointing Dog Association. It lists them as National Champion (for all-age dog) and National Shooting Dog Champion. The shooting dog is defined as being similar to the AKC gun dog in performance, except that it usually ranges farther. Since the same dogs compete in both AKC and American Field championships, it's all in the eyes of the judges. The American Field also licenses a number of regional and national championships (both all-age and shooting dog for different species of birds, such as the National Chukar Championship, National Pheasant Championship and National Quail Championship).

chapter 17

The Show Ring and the Shorthair

While field trials and hunting tests evaluate the German Shorthaired Pointer's hunting ability, dog show competition measures the quality of its conformation. Do the dogs look like Shorthairs, and how do they compare to other GSPs in competition? To provide that competition, thousands of AKC all-breed shows and hundreds of Specialties are held annually for all AKC-recognized breeds. The most basic aim of most competitors is to have their dogs earn a show championship. Some exhibitors "campaign," or continue showing champions for Bests of Breed, Group placings and Bests in Show, to have their dogs ranked nationally. For the Shorthair fancy as a whole, the show year culminates in the national Specialty, held on Memorial Day weekend and rotating around the country from year to year. The outcome has great bearing on future breeding and rankings of dogs. The national Specialty is also a "gathering of the clan," to renew old friendships, forge new ones and see the new dogs and old favorites.

Although many people have contributed to the success of the national Specialty, the man credited with starting it is Gene Ellis, an honorary life member of the GSPCA and owner of two-time national Specialty winner Ch. Shatzi's Ripper v. Greif.

Gene got his first Shorthair in 1954 from his father, but found it difficult to finish her championship because of lack of entries in all-breed shows in the Northeast. As a member of the Farmington Valley Kennel Club (Connecticut), he generated trophy donations for the GSP entry, and so built up entries in area shows. The dog finished to become Ch. Merrymaker's Nutmeg, and is far back in Ripper's family. Gene thought the GSPCA should hold a national Specialty show, and he mailed cards to all members of the reorganized GSPCA in 1963 to attend and support a national Specialty show in 1964. The Specialty was held in Farmington, Connecticut, where Gene lived at the time.

In addition to gathering trophies, Gene also arranged for a pre-show get-together on the eve of the event and set up a post-show banquet at which C. Bede Maxwell, the Australian author of *The Complete German Shorthaired Pointer,* agreed to speak. Gene had hoped for an entry of 100, and that magic number was achieved. Many of the people and dogs from other areas that we had only read about were there. In addition to the outstanding competition, it was a successful social affair. Gene attended every Specialty for a period of about fifteen years before missing one, as they rotated around the United States.

From the impressive entry of 100 in 1964, the GSPCA Specialty has grown to as many as 900 entries and is held over two days. Winning is difficult in such strong competition, and going for the gold is the ambition of everyone who shows dogs.

Although Gene had won placements at the National (in fact, most of his dogs' points were earned at Specialties), it took him twenty years to win BB, and then he did it two years in a row. I gave his Ripper BB in 1984 on his excellent type and flawless movement in spite of Gene's rather limited handling abilities. *The dog showed Gene very well!* Helen Case, who had a three-time national Specialty winner, gave Ripper BB at the 1985 National in Phoenix.

The first national Specialty was won by Ch. Jones Hill Jay, bred by Amelia F. Jones and owned by William McLoughlan of Troy, New York. Jay also won the Sporting Group that day, and I believe he was never shown again. The judge was the former professional handler Hollis Wilson, in his second assignment with Shorthairs. Jay's sire was Dual Ch. Junker v. Grabenbruch, a son of Dual Ch. Blick v. Grabenbruch and grandson of Dick Johns' K.S. Sepp v. Grabenbruch ex Nanny v. Luckseck. The dam, Ch. Jones Hill Coco, CD, was sired by FC Zitt v.d. Sellweide, Col. Larry Keith's German import.

Long-time GSPCA secretary Irene Pauly presented the award, a beautiful sterling hand-hammered family heirloom bowl donated by Camilla Lyman, owner of Ch. Ricefield's John. The bowl, which had to be won three times by the same owner, was retired by Helen Case, one of the original attendees. Also attending were Don and Betty Sandberg from Minnesota; P. Carl Tuttle from New Jersey, who later won two national Specialty BBs; Bob Arnold and Al Maurer, both from Pennsylvania, who later became distinguished multiple-breed judges; Ruth Eitel and Ken and Judy Marden from New Jersey; Ercia Harden from California; and, of course, Gene and Shirley Ellis.

Ch. Jones Hill Jay also had the distinction of being listed in the first *GSPCA Yearbook,* published in 1964, and in each succeeding year until 1993, one year after long-time editor Maxine Collins resigned after twenty-three years of service. No yearbooks were published for three years, which proved a tremendous handicap in updating the information in this book. No one can

Dual Ch. Kaposia's Firebird (Ch. Count Snooper v. Dusseldorf ex Dual Ch. Lucky Lady v. Winterhauch, CD), GSPCA Hall of Fame member and foundation dam for Don and Betty Sandberg's Kaposia Kennels. She is shown here in a circa 1955 photo after winning a field trial with her owner-handler Don Sandberg.

Ch. Kaposia's Waupun II, owned by Helen Case and bred by Kaposia Kennels, was the only dog to win three GSPCA national Specialty BBs.

Ch. Kaposia's Dacotah Star, one of over a hundred champions bred by Kaposia Kennels in forty years of activity. Kaposia Shorthairs trace back to the breed's early foundation stock from the Upper Midwest. Dacotah Star is presented as an example of the family's type and closeness to the GSP Standard. *Booth*

appreciate the work of the Yearbook Committee, especially the editor, until the need to look up something arises. Those who compile GSPCA statistics, such as Julia Carroll and Terri Everwine, compiler of the GSPCA Reference Index, can never be adequately compensated for their dedication to this arduous task.

The chairman of the first yearbook was Robert F. Snyder of Cleveland, Ohio, owner of Hall of Fame member Am., Can. Ch. Fliegen Meister's Gunner, number nine in all-time production of champions with thirty-seven show champions, two field champions and one dual. The committee included Lorraine Albrecht, Jerry Bingham, Mildred Cellura, Gerald Green, Elizabeth Richmond and Phil White.

In 1964, the president of the newly organized GSPCA was Ralph Park, Sr., of Seattle, Washington, owner of the many Am., Can. dual champions mentioned earlier. Vice president, soon to become president, was Dr. Lewis Kline. Secretary was Irene Pauly and Treasurer was William Woods, the successor to Parks as president. Directors were Richard Sylvester, Gerald Godwin, Bernie Elder and Chuck Peterson.

FC Shockley's Pride, bred and owned by Luther Shockley of Crete, Illinois, and handled by Pete Kainz, won the National Field Championship that year. Show Dog of the Year was Ch. v. der Tol Kierkhof, owned by Kenneth Winterle of Farmington, Michigan. In a five-way tie for sire of the year were Ch. Hans v. Nitschke, owned by Bill Jensen of Nine Mile Falls, Washington; FC Skriver's Streak (sire of Dual Ch. Streak's Herbst Versprechen), owned by Carl Schnell of Fraser, Michigan; Ch. Big Island Spotter, a grandson of Dual Ch. Big Island Spook, who was tied for fourth in all-time production of dual champions with three duals, seven show champions and five field champions, owned by Houston Carter of Raytown, Missouri; Int. Dual Ch. Adam, a Swedish import, owned by John H. Wilkins, Jr., Remington, Virginia; and Dual Ch. Biff Bangabird, owned by Dr. C. P. Gandal, of Pleasantville, New York. Dam of the Year was Ch. Tessa v. Abendstern, owned by Ralph Z. Neff, of Canton, Ohio.

Dual Champions finishing in 1964 and listed in the first yearbook were NFC Moesgaard's Dandy, owned by Dr. Lewis Kline of Orlando, Florida; Dual Ch. Erdenreich's Eartha, a daughter of the famous Am., Can. Ch. Erdenreich's Die Zweite, CD, owned by Irene Pauly of Sonoma, California; Dual Ch. Dino v. Albrecht, son of Ch. Big Island Spotter, owned by Kenneth Hopper of Denver, Colorado, at the time; Dual Ch. Kay v.d. Wildburg, owned by Dick Johns of Benton, Pennsylvania, and Joe Eusepi of Oswego, New York; Dual Ch. Bee's Gabby v. Beckum, sired by NFC Bobo Grabenbruch Beckum, owned by Don Briggs of Arcadia, California; and Streak's Herbst Versprechen, owned by Jack Meredith of Dayton, Ohio.

Since the beginning, there have been thirty-four national Specialty shows, reaching a high of 901 entries in 1986 when Ch. Echo Run's Corteze's Choice, owned by Neil Ritter of Pittsburgh, was BB.

Ch. Columbia River Lightning, a multiple BIS winner and a foundation sire for Columbia River Kennels owned by Van McGilbry, shown handling. *Norman*

Ch. Gretchenhof Moonshine, owned by Walt and Joyce Shellenbarger, was a truly memorable Shorthair. A Hall of Fame member and an all-time top-winning show dog among all breeds, she was from Columbia River breeding.

Ch. Gunhill's Mesa Maverick, owned by P. Carl Tuttle, winner of two GSPCA national Specialty BBs and an all-time top-winning Shorthair.

THE SPECIALTIES—SOME MAJOR PLAYERS

Up N' Adam

Sometimes an individual with one or two dogs gets an outstanding specimen that wins the National. Sometimes the winner is the result of careful breeding over the years with that goal in mind, as it was with Up N' Adam Kennels, founded by Katrin Higgins Tazza of Connecticut.

Up N' Adam Kennels was based largely on Ch. Adam v. Fuehrerheim and Gretchenhof bloodlines through their get, such as Kingswoods Windsong, Windsong's Holy Terror and Gretchenhof Westminster. This line of breeding produced Ch. Up N' Adam Barbara, CD (inducted into the Hall of Fame in 1997), who, when bred to Ch./K.S. Zobel v. Pregelufer, a German import, produced fourteen champions in successive breedings. Out of this breeding came Dual Ch. Up N' Adam, UD, JH, who won BB at the 1990 National Specialty in Houston.

Barbara's fourteen champions from those matings placed her in a tie with Gretchenhof Tallyho for seventh place among the All-Time Top Dams list of champions. This breeding also helped launch Zobel's career at stud. Zobel was seventh on the All-Time Top Sires of Champions list through 1994, with thirty-nine show champions, one field and one dual champion.

The Tazzas' breeding program has been highly successful, with one Hall of Fame bitch, Barbara, and a national Specialty winner, Up N' Adam, who earned a UD in Obedience and completed his dual championship in 1995, close to becoming the breed's first triple champion.

Ch. Conrad's Brio

While the Tazzas built their breeding program over a period of years, Nancy and Galen Conrad of Hummelstown, Pennsylvania, gained a national Specialty winner in two breedings. They won the 1977 national Specialty in Bridgewater, New Jersey, with their homebred, owner-handled Ch. Conrad's Brio. Coincidently, at that same National, Katrin Higgins, now Tazza, went High in Trial in Obedience with her first champion, Ch. Higgins Up N' Adam, the namesake of her 1990 Specialty winner.

The Conrads bred their Conrad's Dutchess to Nevins Maximilian, a son of Am., Can. Ch. Fliegen Meister's Gunner, to get Ch. Missy v. Nevins, their first champion. Missy was bred to Ch. Mika v. der Gartenstole (Ch. Hungerlighter's Jug O' Punch, an Adam son, ex Ch. Becky v. Dutchwood) to produce Brio. Brio became the eleventh all-time top sire of champions with twenty-eight, won a BIS and was elected into the Hall of Fame.

Dutchwoods

The Dutchwoods Kennel was owned by the late Jim Dietrich and his wife, Judy, of Sinking Springs, Pennsylvania. And after many years of breeding

Ch. Kooskia's Chief Joseph, owned by Margaret and Nolan Noren. Winner of the 1978 national Specialty show under author-judge C. Bede Maxwell, Chief Joseph came from Radbach/Kaposia bloodlines.

Ch. Strauss's Happy Go Lucky, a Hall of Fame Top producer and an all-time top winner, bred by Del Glodowski and owned by Ann Serak.

Dual Ch. Up N' Adam, UD, JH (Ch./K.S. Zobel Vom Pregelufer ex Ch. Up N' Adam Barbara, CD), Katrin Higgins Tazza's first dual, was BB at the 1990 national Specialty and was elected to the GSPCA Hall of Fame in 1997. *Nugent*

champions, they produced a dog carrying the Dutchwood's bloodline that won the 1993 National Specialty, Ch. Intrepids Headline Hunter. Hunter was owned by Kim Edwards of Lawrenceville, Georgia. He was sired by Ch. Snowcreek's Tracker (Ch. Kooskia's Chief Timothy ex Abiqua Breezy Rebecca, CD) ex Dutchwood's Instant Replay, CDX. The breeders, Johal R. and Martha H. Boteler, were friends of the Dietrichs, whom they had met in the military in North Carolina.

Ch. Nock's Chocolate Chip

Ch. Nock's Chocolate Chip, owned by Jack and Sherri Nock of Jupiter, Florida, was one of the biggest-winning dogs through the 1970s and 1980s. Although he was not fortunate enough to win the National Specialty, he was elected to the GSPCA Hall of Fame in 1987 for his outstanding record. Whelped in 1974, Chip won 5 all-breed BIS, 29 Group firsts, 142 BB and 2 Specialty Bests. He sired seventeen champions, including Ch. Nock's Chocolate Morsel, who was the Show Dog of the Year.

Chip was bred by K. Lytle. He was by Ch. Baron Marquis of Ashbrook (Ch. Kaposia's War Lance ex Ch. Sieglinde of Ashbrook) ex Wild Winds Mitzi (Ch. Gunner v. Hackenschmidt ex Megarys Dasher).

Multiple Winners

Only two people have won three National Specialty BBs with dogs they owned, and only three have won twice. Ruth Ann Freer won number three in 1997 with Ch. Lieblinghaus Chief Executive, CD, JH, and Helen Case Shelly won three with her Dual Ch. Kaposia's Waupun II, as previously reported. The two-time winners are Carl Tuttle with Ch. Gunhill's Mesa Maverick, Susan Harrison with Ch. Windsong's Misty Memories and Ch. Wyndbourne's Keepsake in 1994 and Gene Ellis with Ch. Schatzi's Ripper v. Greif.

All-Time Sires and Dams

As the twentieth century moved to a close, Ch. Adam v. Fuehrerheim remained strongly in place as the top sire of champions with 115, followed by his grandson Ch. Fieldfine's Count Rambard with eighty-nine and in third place by another grandson, Dual Ch. Rugerheim's Bit of Bourbon, the all-time top sire of dual champions with four duals, sixty champions and seven field champions.

But moving rapidly up the ladder in the late 1990s was Ch. Huntabird's Main Reason, bred in 1987 by Herman Tekelve and owned by Patti Keller of Paris Crossing, Indiana. Ch. Huntabird's Main Reason was sired by Ch. Huntabird's For All Reasons (Ch. Huntabird's Sporting Chance ex Ch. Huntabird's Born A Star) ex Ch. Huntabird's The Farmer's Daughter (Ch. Huntabird's Billy Jack ex Huntabird's Heidi Ho). This line of breeding also goes back to Adam v. Fuehrerheim and Columbia River lines begun by Eve Spanic in the late 1970s.

Ch. Huntabird's Main Reason, owned by Patti Lohr Keller, is the youngest German Shorthaired Pointer in history to win a Best in Show, doing so at just fifteen months old. When this book went to press he was the third leading sire of champions with sixty-three through 1997.

Am., Can. Ch. Tabor's Zephyr of Orion, multiple BIS winner for breeders-owners Joan and Joel Tabor.

Ch. v. Eugen's Easy Goer, owned by David Gontz, finished his championship with three five-point majors, all in Specialty shows. He is shown going BOS at the Long Island GSP Specialty in 1990 under veteran breeder-judge Bob Arnold. *John Ashbey*

In 1994, Ch. Huntabird's Main Reason was in ninth place with thirty-three champions, but fourteen of his get finished championships in 1995 and sixteen earned titles in 1996, giving him a total of sixty-three to move into third place ahead of Bourbon. Main Reason was Sire of the Year for both 1995 and 1996.

For All-Time Top Dams, Ch. Cheza's Riverside Imp and Oxton Minado's Inga v. Greif remained tied with twenty-five champions each. The closest with still active get was Dual Ch. NMK's Brittania v. Silbelstein, with nineteen through the 1994 tabulations.

Present and Future Development of the German Shorthaired Pointer in America

There is a verse that nicely describes the development of the German Shorthaired Pointer in America:

> The race is not always to the swift,
>   nor yet riches to the wise.
> Time and chance happens to us all
> They also serve who only stand and wait.

Standing in someone's backyard somewhere in the United States today is a dog that is superior to anything carrying multiple titles and impeccable credentials. This is a dog with conformation described as the ideal, that much-sought-after natural hunting ability that requires little training and the desire to please. It will be a good citizen in its habits, a protector of family and property, yet not be aggressive or vicious. Along with all of these attributes, it will possess elegance. This dog will never be known outside of its family, except perhaps through a local breeding to someone who wants a hunting dog or to earn some money selling puppies. Maybe one of its puppies will rise from the mist of obscurity to distinguish itself and contribute to the advancement of the Shorthair; most likely it will not.

A dog cannot contribute to the gene pool unless someone knows it's there and can recognize its qualities. Likewise, a dog cannot win unless it is placed in competition, and it probably will never win big unless its owner and/or handler knows how to properly train, condition and present the dog. Finally, the dog will advance only as far as its owner's will and financial resources allow. Being able to promote a dog—making it known and broadcasting its accomplishments—requires expenditures beyond the means of most owners, as well as ability and expertise most owners cannot command. It is obvious from this that without someone with the desire and money who pushes it to the fore, even a talented Shorthair will not progress very far.

Duke II Polovanie v. Wagger, owned by Fred Singer, the respected Shorthair historian who helped with the history of Charles Thornton that appears in this book. This liver male is line bred back to the Thornton imports of the 1920s.

Ego drives us all to a greater or lesser extent, and we want a winning dog because it pleases us and gives us status, albeit in a rather limited segment of society. The dog world as a whole, and the GSP fancy specifically, mirrors the larger society. So, in the narrowly defined world of the dog sport—but a universe to its enthusiasts—people from every walk of life meet on an open playing field. In our mundane lives, we have the opportunity to gain Andy Warhol's "fifteen minutes of fame" through our dogs.

Out of all of this—from rich or poor, small breeder or famous kennel—will come the progenitors and the breeders or owners who will continue to advance the GSP towards the elusive ideal, the perfect Shorthair, a 150-year quest going into the twenty-first century.

Yes, there are many people motivated to develop the best Shorthair possible, and their objective from the start is to contribute to the advancement of the breed. Others contribute through their desire to gain their fifteen minutes of fame. But all this effort, no matter the motive, results in better Shorthairs, because their supporters get them out of the backyard and into the public arena where they can be seen and used. Some eager participants come and leave after a few years—in fact, most last about three to five years—but others persevere, and these are the people and dogs you met throughout this book. Through their sustained efforts, it is possible for the average Joe or Jane to own a good hunting Shorthair that is also an ideal family companion, dual roles most fill so well.

The late Ercia Harden, a gracious lady, said it rather well some years ago: "A lot of good dogs will never get a chance because their owners don't have the money to campaign them." It was a simple but pithy statement coming from a lady who should know. Ercia was the wife of Gene Harden, a highly successful California cauliflower grower. The Hardens owned five dual champions and campaigned their dogs extensively. Their best-known was NFC Rip Traf v. Bess. But Ercia recognized that the race does not always belong to the swift. They have to be given a chance to run.

Time and chance abound in the Shorthair world. In the 1950s, Tom Getler, an early trainer, was out running a dog in the fields near his New Jersey home when a Shorthair came out of nowhere from behind him. The dog passed his dog and continued forward until it suddenly snapped into a point, standing there until its owner came up to flush the bird. Tom learned that the dog had no known immediate antecedents, but he decided then and there he wanted to breed to it. The result was FC Tip Top Timmy, one of the most influential sires in breed history.

Another successful Shorthair of note mentioned throughout this book is FC Greif v. Hundscheimerkogel. Imported from Austria, he was sold and resold as a backup hunting dog and not started in field competition until age six. However, with limited breeding, he became a household word, albeit hard to pronounce, and one of the great pillars of the breed in America.

Ch. Sheridan Brandy v. Fieldfine, owned by Michael Coniglia, is an early champion daughter of Am., Can. Ch. Fieldfine's Count Rambard, the number two All-Time Top Sire of Champions. This multiple BB winner was BOS at the 1985 national Specialty, under judge Helen Case, owner of three-time national Specialty BB Ch. Kaposia's Waupun II. *Kohler*

Ch. Adam v. Fuehrerheim was another "Cinderella story": Out of a large litter bred by a sporting goods store owner in Virginia, he was one of four his breeder was unable to sell. I bought him for $100 to replace a pheasant dog that had died, and Adam became the All-Time Top Sire of Show Champions in the world.

The list goes on and on, but one of the most remarkable examples of time and chance is FC Dixieland's Rusty, the All-Time Leading Sire of Field Champions. Rusty was bred and kept as a hunting dog. When he was sent to a trainer to acquire some polish, the trainer recognized his field trial potential and suggested trialing him. He was seen, was bred to and clicked. For more than a decade, his get have dominated major pointing dog trials in the United States.

So, we see that the Shorthair comes from carefully choreographed matings and from unions of happenstance. But none of these dogs can get very far without being out where they can be seen, and those that can be campaigned with strong financial backing have a much better chance to succeed than others. This is especially true in the rarefied atmosphere of conformation shows.

FC/AFC Hidden Hollow's Ronlord Ruler, a top-winner and strong producer owned by Elaine Hollowell.

Dual Ch./Can. Ch. NMK's Rustic Country Charm, MH, owned by Carol Chadwick, was yet another notable son of Am., Can. Ch. NMK's Placer Country Snowbird.

Every February annual award dinners, with corporate sponsorship, are important fixtures of the Westminster weekend to honor the top-rated show dogs in America. These gala black-tie affairs come complete with live music, masters of ceremonies, spotlights and considerable fanfare. Unlike the Academy Awards, at which the winners don't know who wins until the names are announced at the ceremony, the dogs' owners and handlers already know; oh, how they know! They will fly all over the United States in December seeking last-minute points to boost their position for that year; cost is no object.

In this hallowed company are the aristocracy of the dog show world, the successful people with the means to promote their standard bearers either from a desire to improve dogs and make a contribution to help recognize great ones or for their fifteen minutes of fame. As the owners, handlers and associates are announced and come to the stage to the accompaniment of a drum roll and the glare of lights, some break down and cry. I would cry, too, if I had just spent $250,000 campaigning a dog for this brief moment of recognition. Some of these dogs are, of course, worthy specimens of their breeds, while others might not be able to achieve these heights without power behind them. All this happens because of ego, the thirst for that brief moment of fame and a place in the spotlight during the great social whirl that is Westminster weekend.

It is not wrong to put money behind a good dog to see that it is promoted to get its recognition. If the dog is a good one, it will contribute greatly to the breed because it gets the exposure to impact the gene pool. But the point to be made is that all potentially great dogs do not come to the fore, because many had no backing or their owners did not know what they had. Sometimes these highly promoted dogs really are the best or among the best. A dog's real contribution, after gaining recognition, is in producing. And that's where the truly good ones leave the others behind. Some of the biggest-winning dogs in America are on the top sires and dams lists, but others surpass them in terms of quality that is passed on through their get.

As to the Shorthair, it is still a functional dog able to perform the task for which it was developed. It's true we see many show champions that will never be trialed or maybe even hunted, but almost every Shorthair still has hunting instincts. Its performance may not be field-trial quality, but it will hunt. All show champions are not special material, but they do meet championship standards. The same is true with big field trial winners. Some defy description, but many do look like Shorthairs and a number are capable of winning show championships to become dual champions.

One of the greatest programs ever developed by the American Kennel Club is the Hunting Test for pointing breeds, launched in 1986. The Hunting Test's growth since its inception has been phenomenal. Many dogs that ordinarily would never have participated in organized field events are now out earning Hunting Test titles, proving their ability to perform the work for

Can. Ch. Buck Hollow's Force of Destiny, bred by Julia Carroll of Buck Hollow Kennels, Mohnton, Pennsylvania, who keeps records for the GSPCA and helped with late statistics for this book. "Bart" sired more than twenty American champions and numerous Canadian champions including Am., Can. Ch. Malhaven's Pied Piper, the top-winning Shorthair in the Canadian show ring during the late 1980s.

Am., Can. Ch. Malhaven's Pied Piper, owned by Mitch and Mabel Ferguson, was a top-winning GSP in Canada. His frozen semen was used to impregnate Ch. Breckenridge Mara, the top GSP in New Zealand for 1991 and 1992. From this breeding came Ch. Breckenridge Strauss, the number-one show GSP in New Zealand in 1996. *Mikron*

which they were bred. I joined the AKC staff in February 1988 to set up and manage the Performance Events Division, which administers the Hunting Test program; needless to say, I am personally gratified by my part in the program and by the dogs that have successfully participated in it.

Hunting Tests are not competitive. Dogs need not defeat other dogs to earn qualifications toward titles. In field trials and shows, dogs must defeat other dogs to earn championship titles. In Hunting Tests, dogs must meet minimum standards to earn the three titles of Junior Hunter (JH), Senior Hunter (SH) and Master Hunter (MH). They compete against a standard that becomes progressively more difficult as the dogs advance through the titles. A dog capable of earning a Master Hunter title is quite capable of being field trialed in competition to earn a field championship. Championship titles go before a dog's name and Hunting Test titles follow the name. A number of Shorthair owners have been motivated by the Hunting Tests to enter field trials and have been successful.

At the time the Hunting Test program became effective, field trials had been losing entries, primarily because people had become discouraged with the direction in which they were going. In order to train and handle a dog in trials, an individual almost needed to own a horse. This meant that owners had to stable, feed, groom and tend to the horse's other management and health needs, as well as to own a trailer in which to transport the horse. Alternatively, you could train your dog on foot at home and rent or borrow a horse at trials to handle it off horseback or on foot. The rules state that the horse is to be kept at a flat walk and used only as a means of conveyance, not as an aid to handling. They also state that the foot handler sets the pace. However, in reality, it's difficult to run a dog in field trials without owning a horse, so the owner could either get a horse or get a professional trainer and handler. Finally, an owner who does buy a horse is going to find that the flat walk of a Tennessee Walker is quite a bit faster than that of a regular saddlebred or quarter horse and there is a gait known as an extended walk that covers ground much faster without appearing to be moving beyond a walk. So even those who want to trial a dog themselves can be easily discouraged by the fast pace that judges, in many instances, fail to keep under control. Instead of letting a dog hunt out likely places, it is continuously pushed at a pace beyond its scenting ability. In addition to the dogs that are pushed by fast-moving horses, there are also runoff dogs—dogs that bolt out of sight and have to be double handled by scouts to be herded around the course. They've been trained to stay on point once they point a bird, but the only birds they can find are those that happen to come into their line of fire. Their handlers keep up a steady singsong, ostensibly to "keep in contact" but in reality to make the dog think the handler is watching its every move so that it doesn't go into the next county. At the most recent GSPCA National All Age championship, many dogs disappeared and did not come back on course.

Many GSP handlers believe their dogs need to emulate Pointers and Setters in run. However, in the big American field trials for these breeds, the dogs must be under control whether they run big or not. American Field–licensed GSP trials are a different matter altogether as far as controls by the licensing body are concerned. The AKC has a field staff that attends trials on a spot basis to assess judging in such matters as control over pace and other elements of the trial, as well as to provide assistance.

At first glance for the newcomer this is intimidating and discouraging, but most who stick with competition find they can fit in and achieve success. Except for the amateur stakes, they must compete against professional trainers who have the training and handling expertise that gives them an edge. However, amateurs can become quite good at training and handling dogs, and most professionals will help them. Lest the reader go away with the thought that all field trials are like a giant race with dogs running off into the horizon and horses galloping across the landscape after them, most trials are under control. But they do run big in All-Age and sometimes too big for the Gun Dog Stakes, which are supposed to be modeled on actual hunting conditions.

Most reasonable people know that dogs need to move out to find birds, whether field trialing or hunting. The GSP was not developed to be underfoot, but there is common sense about what constitutes too much run and failure to hunt and find birds.

Most good dogs can achieve their field championships as they do their conformation titles. However, some very fine Shorthairs fail to become field champions through no fault of their own. Not having become a field champion does not mean that the dog lacks field ability or is incapable of transmitting that quality in breeding.

During my nine-year term as vice president of Performance Events at AKC starting in 1988, we also helped the GSP and other pointing breeds by adding extra walking stakes for trials and, finally, adding a third all-walking field trial. Previously, clubs were limited to two trials a year, which could be all-walking, horseback or combinations of walking and horseback handling stakes. However, if a club wishes to hold a third field trial, it must be all-walking.

While the majority of people interested in field performance were happy with the new events, some of the old hands were highly critical. They said dogs would get titles in hunting tests that would be interpreted as being equal to a field championship and that the walking trials and stakes were not the equal of horseback trials. They overlooked the fact that only the dogs are being judged, not the horses. The foot-handled trials were usually filled within a few days of receiving the entry forms, and they became very popular because it grew possible for the average owner to participate in trials without needing a horse. This expanded the club memberships and provided enough workers to put on both field trials and hunting tests.

Until the mid-1960s, there were horses for the judges but eveyone else walked. At that time, parking lots at field trials were filled with station wagons, small trucks and some vans and automobiles. By the 1970s, those same lots were filled with horse trailers and rigs that included living quarters, kennels and horse stalls, along with vast fleets of motor homes, vans and trucks. An empty field one day would be a city the next.

Conformation shows underwent a similar metamorphosis, but the trend in vehicles here was to motor homes, trailers and vans. Show grounds, like trial grounds, were converted to cities overnight. Benched shows, where dogs are required to be on public display in numbered stalls until a specified release hour, were almost nonexistent by the 1980s. Only Westminster and a few other large shows remain benched. This format allows spectators to see the dogs up close in addition to seeing the actual judging. They can talk to exhibitors about breeds they are interested in, arrange breedings or negotiate to purchase dogs. Exhibitors can explain the merits of the various breeds. Now, most exhibitors arrive, are judged and, unless they win the breed and stay for Group judging later in the day, leave. Often by the time the Groups and Best in Show roll around, few people remain to see the finalists being judged and receive proper appreciation for their wins.

More single-breed and all-breed publications are now much in evidence where once there were only a few, such as the *AKC Gazette, Dog World* and *Popular Dogs*. Now we have many publications, including some that, through their editorial content, pursue an aggressive agenda of indignation. Today, judges receive numerous complimentary dog magazines filled with eye-catching displays advertising featuring dogs being actively campaigned in Group and Best in Show competition around the United States and Canada. All too often, advertisers hope judges will recognize their dogs in the ring from their ads and allow themselves to be swayed by previous well-heralded achievements. This practice becomes especially feverish before the year's end to advance in the annual standings and before the most important shows.

Although the best dogs do not always win, they are on display in shows and field trials, and people can make up their own minds about the dogs they want to own and use in their breeding programs. In seventy-five years of the GSP in America, it is still amazing to see the great ones of today trace their ancestry to some of the very first imports of Charles Thornton's breeding in remote Montana and to other greats that came before and after World War II. Based on these great dogs, people established their own breeding programs, and some of the early kennels are still in existence today while other successful programs continue to arise.

A number of dedicated men and women have worked diligently to preserve and improve the qualities of the Shorthair, and many programs exist today to help them in that purpose. As long as there are people who realize that the GSP was developed for hunting and for an attractive appearance as

Int. Ch. Count v. Herrenhausen, a grandson of German import K.S. Yoli Rothenuffeln, owned by Denny and Barbara Young-Smith. Count won a Prize 1 Natural Ability Test administered by the North American Versatile Hunting Dog Association.

Ch. Anja Rothenuffeln, a daughter of German import K.S. Yoli Rothenuffeln, owned by Denny and Barbara Young-Smith. *Mikron*

well as a pleasing temperament, the breed will continue to advance. But we face problems if we allow fads to dictate appearance and dogs continue to run bigger and bigger as available trial grounds continue to shrink. These problems could result in a split in breed type, as has happened in too many other Sporting breeds. It is the obligation of the entire membership of the German Shorthaired Pointer Club of America to see that such a split does not happen here.

Among the severest critics of field trials and conformation shows that provide competition to encourage breed improvement are dog writers for outdoor magazines. A recent example appeared in the August 1997 issue of *The American Hunter,* a publication of the National Rifle Association. In response to a reader asking what breed would be best for quail hunting in the South, the answer concluded with this advice: "Whatever breed you choose, be sure that the dog comes from proven hunting lineage, not from harder-to-control field trial or bench show stock."

Where do these writers think the hunting dogs come from, and how do they think the dogs prove themselves? Not many field trial dogs would win if they couldn't be controlled. While some may run big, they usually work to the gun when hunted. The dogs that don't are in the minority. Several of the biggest-running field trial dogs in the country are used for personal hunting. In fact, the late, highly regarded trainer Dave McGinnis trained most of his trial dogs by hunting wild chukars in the Idaho hills. Don Paltani hunted over three-time National All-Age Champion Rawhide's Clown.

After delivering all the pronouncements you read in this chapter, I'll close with an amusing story. One of the biggest-running field trial Shorthairs I ever saw was Tough Mike, owned by a man named Fred Hunt (not to be confused with the late show judge of the same name). Hunt ran Mike in a trial I judged in Baldwinsville, New York, years ago. Mike wore a large blaze-orange ribbon tied in a big bow around his neck so that his owner could see him. Fred had extremely poor eyesight and wore glasses that resembled inverted Coke bottles. During those days, handlers did their own shooting in retrieving stakes. I noticed on this occasion Fred had a pump shotgun, a dangerous weapon.

As we rode out, he kept asking if I could see the dog. I would see the big orange ribbon making big casts into the cover way up front, going off to the left and right, but always appearing up front to check on his half-blind owner. Mike went on point and I told Fred where he was on the other side of a hedgerow in front of us. I shepherded Fred in the direction of the dog and Fred said, "I've got him." But he was headed in a different direction. Finally, I got him up to the hedgerow, held his horse as he dismounted and took his gun out of the scabbard and pumped a shell in the chamber. I kept telling him, "I'm right behind you." He got the bird in the air and fired a shot, only he was shooting in a different direction from the bird's flight. I knew we had a problem. But Mike stood firm through all of this. He moved on when sent and continued to search the country in front. Finally he went across a cut cornfield and slammed into a point facing a large beech tree. I got Fred into position, off his horse, and gave him instructions. I asked him if he saw the beech tree and told him the bird was moving toward the tree. "Aim your gun at the other side of the tree near the ground. I'll tell you when to shoot." As the bird emerged on the other side, I yelled for him to shoot. Fred turned to me and asked, "Did I get him?" I told him to send his dog, and Mike picked the bird up and presented it to Fred. He was placed and made it to the national championships in this, his last try. I could have enjoyed hunting over that big-going dog.

Hoss v. Emil, owned by Neil Nacchio of Virginia and handled by Bob West of Iowa, earned a perfect score and title of Versatile Hunter in the difficult 1996 North American Versatile Hunting Dog Association International Invitational. *Dave Meisner, Pointing Dog Journal*

chapter 19

Conclusion

This book has endeavored to describe the intrinsic qualities of the German Shorthaired Pointer and trace its history in America. While most of the influential dogs and Shorthair people are included, obviously not all the good ones have been mentioned. That many thousands of champions could not be listed represents purely a spatial constraint. I would like those who read this book to come away with a sense of what German Shorthaired Pointer fanciers are, where we've been and where we're going. No one created a Shorthair out of thin air. We are all indebted to the dogs and people who have gone before just as those who come after us will, we hope, be indebted to us for our contributions.

A number of people were helpful in compiling information, especially Julia Carrol and Debbie Burgess with last-minute additional records of dogs not covered beyond the 1993 yearbooks. I thank all those who sent me kennel information and photographs. Several people involved with prominent dogs promised to send information and photos but never did. I wish they would have, but that's why their dogs are missing from the foregoing.

I also thank Howell Book House executive editor Seymour Weiss for his patience and forebearance in granting me many extentions to get the book written.

One thing I cannot overemphasize is that the GSP was brought to America and developed here for the specific purpose of hunting. It is, first and foremost, a field dog and should be bred for that purpose. It should also look and perform like a Shorthair. German Shorthaired Pointers are not natural show dogs; they will show with dignity and style, but they are mostly bored by the procedure and only do it out of a sense of loyalty to their handlers. Few will "cakewalk" like some other breeds that do not seem to have any duty other than to please their owners. To be sure, that can be enough if it's

Al Sause (right), an early breeder of foundation German Shorthairs in America and importer of top German dogs, with friend Ozzie Raith in 1992 at an Eastern field trial, shortly before he died.

all one wants, but don't waste a Shorthair as a lap dog. Let it do what it was bred to do: hunt or compete in trials or tests. At the very least, make sure your Shorthair gets a suffient amount of running and other kinds of regular, vigorous exercise.

It is encouraging to see that some of the most ardent show people with many years in the ring have now joined the ranks of those with dual champions or are competing in trials of hunting tests. Ruth Ann Freer, Katy Tazza, Jim and June Burns and Mary Beth Kirkland, who have outstanding, successful show dogs, now have dual champions and hunting test titles.

Information in this book is based strictly on the records and some personal observations, and I have not attempted to interject any negative personal opinions. I liked some of the dogs better than others, but these are personal opinions and have no place in a book of records. The records prove that these dogs accomplished something positive to have reached their place in breed history, even though some may have had more opportunities than others to demonstrate their talents.

For veterans, this book will be a reminder of what went before and what is going on today; and for newcomers thinking about buying a Shorthair for

Richard S. Johns, importer of the first German K.S. in America, is shown at his home in Benton, Pennsylvania. An outstanding trainer of field champions and dual champions, he is also a keen student of military history.

Author Bob McKowen (right) shown with famous breeder and trainer Richard S. Johns during a 1997 visit to Johns' home in connection with research for this book.

the first time, it will provide a basis on which to select the puppy. People should understand, however, that even with a lot of knowledge, they are pretty much in the hands of a breeder when they go to buy a puppy or an older dog. Therefore, they should be careful about where they buy from. Buy from a breeder who can show you at least the dam and explain who the sire was if he is not in residence. Under no circumstances should you ever buy a dog from a retail establishment. You will have no idea where the dog came from, and you are likely to be charged many times over the asking price of a good dog from a legitimate breeder. The initial cost of a dog is the smallest expense over the its lifetime. Start with a good dog and make sure it is well cared for. Do not chain the dog to a doghouse out back. If that's all you can provide, don't get the dog.

The American Kennel Club is responsible for the registration of dogs in the United States. It has spent millions of dollars attempting to ensure the integrity of the registry. However, the AKC is not responsible for the physical condition of the animals it registers and the conditions under which they are raised. The AKC's only enforcement power is to cancel faulty registrations and ban registrations from kennels where conditions are unsatisfactory. It maintains a staff of inspectors for that purpose, but they cannot cover every breeding situation, and not all mass breeders are in violation. That is really the job of the United States Department of Agriculture, which says it doesn't have enough inspectors either. So the buyer has to be informed, and the best rule of thumb is to buy from a creditable breeder.

Most German Shorthaired Pointers I have observed in recent years, competing in both dog shows and field trials, have been of good quality. Some are overly large, display faulty fronts or have tails curving over their backs. Some are too long, while some are too leggy. Some have poor heads, and some move like they have one too many. But, for the most part, I believe they are good specimens in general and have good temperaments and intelligence. I believe the average Shorthair will hunt for its owner given any kind of opportunity with minimum training. Obviously, the better bred and the better trained, the better the dog will perform.

This book is not meant to give the step-by-step details of how to train your Shorthair. You will have to get out and learn. The best way is to put your dogs on birds no matter how you get that done. If the puppy or young dog—or even an older dog—is taken out where there are birds or they are placed before it, it will usually demonstrate some interest by chasing or pointing. Either way, it's a start. But never put down birds that the dog can catch, or it may give up pointing or never start pointing at all. The dog may figure, "Why bother pointing birds if I can catch them?" You have to get into the field for real experience. Go to a friend who knows (join a club and meet such people), or to a professional who has credentials.

In the matter of discipline, no one should ever beat a dog for any reason. There is nothing wrong with correcting a dog with a slap on the rump if it

Author Bob McKowen with Tom Getler at the 1997 AKC Gun Dog Championships in New Jersey, thirty-five years after first meeting this handler of Hall of Famer, FC Tip Top Timmy.

Author Bob McKowen at the 1997 AKC Gun Dog Championships on the English Setter Club grounds in Medford, New Jersey, site of the first AKC field trial in America in 1924.

has really committed a crime, but there are many gentler ways to train a dog, and most pros know how. But be sure you know your pro or know someone who knows the pro. The best way to correct mistakes in training is not to make them. It is harder to correct unwanted behavior than it is to prevent it. Read all the training books you can get your hands on and take all the advice knowledgeable people give you. If you are still stumped, stop and find out what you are doing wrong and how to do it right.

If you want to trial your dog or run it in hunting tests yourself, have at it. After all, the Shorthair was meant to be easy to train. But get all the help and experience you can. Don't be critical of judging until you understand the game. The Shorthair was meant to cover a lot of ground and go to the likely places where game might be, but it was not meant to run into the next county or need the services of a second handler (sometimes referred to as a scout) to get it herded around the course.

Clubs need to select judges who will judge according to the rules and not allow handlers to race all over the course away from the line of march and yell continuously at their dogs. Scouts have only one function. They ride behind the handler and are sent only with permission from the judge to locate the dog that has gone out of sight for a time. The scout reports back that the dog has been found and is moving or is on point. The scout should not attempt to handle the dog in any manner. Does this go on? The official report of the 1994 GSPCA National All Age Championship indicates that over 80 percent of the dogs in competition ran off and were lost and most of those that did make it around the course had a scout act as a second handler to get it turned.

Some Shorthairs are not very good bird finders (possibly a result of being pushed too fast to hunt out the areas) and some lack style on pointing and handling birds. These are problems that will have an effect on all GSPs at some time. Presently, however, the Shorthair is still in great shape in field trials and in everyday hunting. It is discouraging, however, to see some of the wild riding that goes on at some trials. The clubs and judges can stop it by simply learning and obeying the rules. It is in everyone's interest to maintain the field quality of the Shorthair, and quality is not limited to range or endurance alone.

Dog shows present their own set of problems. No matter how much money the AKC spends on education or how restrictive it is with approvals, a number of judges simply will never be qualified to judge Shorthairs. They do not know what they were bred for and how to judge that quality in the ring.

They confuse animation with correct movement, and many depend on pictures in dog magazines and the reputation of the handler to help them make their choices. However, amateur handlers should not be discouraged at losing to some dogs of lesser quality, because there are enough good judges around to give every deserving dog its day. Finally, don't be kennel blind and blame judges for poor quality or poor showmanship. Learn to stack and move your dog properly. Go to classes. Practice in front of a mirror. If you can't show a dog properly, hire a professional to handle for you. It may be less expensive for you in the long run.

The German Shorthaired Pointer Club of America is the governing body for Shorthair matters in the United States and is responsible for the Standard and the well-being of the breed. It is an elective body, so if you don't belong to the parent club or do not exercise your vote, you have no grounds to complain about what happens in the breed.

Finally, do not take out your frustrations on your dog. It wants only to love you and to be loved in return. The German Shorthaired Pointer is a gift to us, and we should be grateful for the privilege of being owned by one.

Not every dog is destined to be a champion or a big winner, but all dogs can bring great happiness to their owners. Of all the trophies and titles won, perhaps none is more precious than the saving of a master's life, as in the case of a Shorthair named Red whose mission in life was hunting and taking care of his master.

On November 28, 1973, a rainy, miserable day, Phil Schreyer and Red went hunting on a vast public hunting ground in New Jersey. As a result of the bad weather, they were alone in the forested area surrounded by fog. Although a veteran hunter, Phil slipped and his shotgun accidentally discharged, almost severing his leg. He wrapped a shoelace above his knee to stop the bleeding and started to crawl back to his car. However, he became disoriented and did not know which way to go. He told the dog to go home while he crawled behind him, but Red took a shortcut directly to a highway and stood in the middle of the road barking until a car stopped and the driver heard Phil yelling. Another car stopped and they got him to a hospital. The leg had to be amputated, but Phil made a rapid recovery. When interviewed by a local newspaper, Phil asked, "Do they give medals to dogs? I think Red deserves one." The Eastern German Shorthaired Pointer Club secretary contacted the Pedigree Dog Food Company, suggesting that Red be considered for the Lassie Gold Award for heroism. In early May of the following year, Red was awarded a medal that said on the front, "For Meritorious Action— Lassie Gold Award." Inscribed on the back were the words "Awarded to Red, owned by Philip Schreyer, for giving meaning to the tradition that Man's Best Friend Is His Dog."

As recipient of the Lassie Gold Award, Red was automatically eligible for the Recipe National Gold Award, which is presented annually to the dog judged "Best of the Best." He was chosen from among six heroic dogs nominated to receive this honor in 1974. On July 22, 1974, Rudd Weatherwax, trainer and owner of Lassie, presented Red the Recipe National Gold Award in San Francisco. The award included transportation and accommodations for the Schreyer family and Red in San Francisco, $1,000, a year's supply of dog food and a gold statue inscribed "To Schreyer's Red Baron for unfaltering loyalty, deep love, and keen intelligence."

So the race is not always to the swift, nor yet riches to the wise; they also serve who only stand and wait. Philip Schreyer's nine-year-old hunting companion earned the greatest award of all, his master's life.

The GSP has come a long way in seventy-five years in America, and one hopes it will continue to improve and find a happy niche in the purebred family. The German Shorthaired Pointer is the finest breed in the world, and its basic desire is to love and be loved.

Appendix A

ALL-TIME TOP DAMS OF DUAL CHAMPIONS

Compiled by Julia M. Carroll

Name of Dam	Dual Ch. Get	Show Ch. Get	Field Ch. Get
1. Ch. Yunga War Bride	4	5	4(FC-4)
2. FC Albrecht's Countess Tena	3	5	6(FC-5/AFC-1)
DC Cede Mein Dolly der Orrian	3	21	4 (FC-3/AFC-1)
Dual Ch. Gretchen v. Greif	3	6	6 (FC-6)
Ch. Suzanna Mein Liebchen	3	4	3 (FC-3)
3. Da-Lors Brandie v.d. Wildburg	2	2	2 (FC-2)
Dual Ch./AFC Dee Tee's Baschen v. Greif	2	2	4 (FC-2/AFC-2)
Duchess v. Hotwagner	2	5	2 (FC-2)
Ch. Erdenreich Die Zweite, CD	2	7	3 (FC-3)
Freigeist Bekannte v. Laden, CD	2	2	3 (FC-2/AFC-1)
Gretchen v.d. Zigeuner	2	3	5 (FC-4/AFC-1)
Ch. Katinka of Sycamore Brook, CD	2	3	3 (FC-3)
Dual Ch. NMK's Brittania v. Sibelstein	2	19	2 (FC-2)
FC Tina of Sleepy Hollow	2	2	6 (FC-6)
Weidenbach Suzette	2	3	2 (FC-2)
Wendy v. Enzstrand	2	2	2 (FC-2)
Werren's Little Bit More	2	2	3 (FC-3)
Ch. Wildburg Salt 'N Pepper, CD	2	5	4 (FC-2/AFC-2)

Appendix B

DUAL CHAMPIONS 1947 THROUGH 1996

Name	Date Finished	
	Show	Field
Rusty v. Schwarenberg	7/10/42	10/6/47
Schatz v. Schwarenberg	8/22/48	10/2/49
Valbo v. Schlesburg	8/5/50	4/24/49
Buck v. Grabenbruch	9/9/50	3/11/51
Searching Wind Topper	3/12/50	9/16/51
Valkyrie v. Grabenbruch	9/16/51	3/9/52
Baron v. Strauss	8/25/47	9/20/53
Big Island Spook	5/17/53	10/11/53
'53 NFC Dandy Jim v. Feldstrom	12/13/53	9/13/53
Doktorgaarden's Caro (Denmark)	6/13/54	10/2/54
Riqa v. Hanen Tann	1/30/55	11/12/54
'54 NFC Wendenheim's Fritz	6/18/55	9/12/54
Trailborn Mike, CDX	8/20/55	9/11/55
Junker v. Grabenbruch	5/29/55	10/30/55
Fritz of Sleepy Hollow	9/25/55	12/4/55
Kaposia's Firebird	4/13/57	4/7/57
Jones Hill Friedrich	10/19/57	3/27/55
Peter Bruner	5/23/57	10/20/57
Captain v. Winterhauch	5/3/53	10/22/57

| Name | Date Finished | |
	Show	Field
Gretchen v. Suthers	2/24/57	11/3/57
Gretchen v. Greif	2/9/58	3/27/55
Strauss's Working Boy	3/10/57	9/21/58
Oxton's Lieselotte v. Greif	7/17/57	10/12/58
Al-Ru's Erich	6/18/56	10/12/58
Heidie v. Marvon	11/6/55	10/19/58
Oxton Bride's Brunz v. Greif	5/3/59	3/22/59
Lucky Lady v. Winterhauch, CD	5/9/59	9/28/58
Sager v. Gardsburg	2/24/57	4/10/60
Flick v. Heidebrink	1/30/60	4/24/60
Timberlane's Ace	7/14/57	5/6/60
Baron v. Turn and Taxis	9/18/60	11/2/58
Able v. Eltz	6/12/60	9/18/60
Madchen Braut v. Greif	9/5/60	12/4/60
Hans v. Eldridge, CD	6/1/58	4/16/61
Big Island Recs	11/9/58	4/23/61
Alfi v.d. Krunnenmuhle	11/4/56	4/23/61
Rommell v. Rumpelstilzchen	6/11/60	5/26/61
Grousewald's Blitz	7/2/61	10/9/60
Dallo v. Hesselbach, CD	2/23/61	9/8/61
Woody v. Ronberg	6/4/61	9/24/61
Miss B'Haven v. Winterhauch	2/24/57	9/30/61
Schone Braut v. Greif	6/28/59	10/15/61
Ski-Do's Bonnie Karin	3/18/62	10/8/61

| Name | Date Finished | |
	Show	Field
Fritz of Hickory Lane Farm	4/10/60	4/29/62
Wag-Ae's Snowflake, CD	10/14/56	5/13/62
Gustav Mein Liebchen	8/9/59	10/4/62
Esso v. Enzstrand (Germany)	9/1/58	11/4/62
Marmaduke Mein Liebchen	3/30/58	12/2/62
Brunnenhugel Balder	9/31/62	2/3/63
Biff Bangabird	3/10/63	10/29/61
Brunnenhugel Jan	7/27/63	4/1/62
Albrecht's Baroness Cora	11/3/63	9/29/63
Albrecht's Baron Cid	11/24/63	4/16/61
'62 MFC Moesgaard's Dandy	1/13/64	2/18/61
Erdenreich's Eartha	4/7/63	3/22/64
Dino v. Albrecht	5/26/63	4/19/64
Kay v.d. Wildburg (Canada)	5/23/64	5/17/59
Bee's Gabby v. Beckum	6/14/64	3/31/63
Streak's Herbst Versprechen	11/19/61	10/11/64
Robin Crest Chip, CD, TD	11/2/58	3/28/65
Baron Fritz v. Hohen Tann	11/25/62	4/25/65
Fieldacres Katia	9/4/60	5/1/65
Hewlett Girl Pebbles	8/15/65	9/12/65
Zipper der Orrian	2/29/64	9/19/65
Kamiak Desert Sand	10/4/64	9/26/65
Satan v. Schnellberg	12/4/65	11/24/63
Lucy Ball	1/20/66	12/5/65

Name	Date Finished	
	Show	Field
Radbach's Arko	3/27/66	3/29/64
Janie Greif v. Heisterholz	12/5/65	4/17/66
Ritzie	9/6/64	5/1/66
Erdenreich's Jetta Beckum	6/11/66	3/6/66
Gruenweg's Dandy Dandy	5/2/64	9/25/66
Richlu's Terror	8/22/64	10/23/66
Arrak v. Heisterholz (Germany)	11/20/66	9/15/63
Richlu's Dan Oranien	3/22/67	9/5/65
Rambling Rock	9/3/67	10/11/64
Blitz v. Jaegershebe	6/30/63	9/17/67
Hochlandjager's Titelhalter	9/4/67	9/17/67
Cede Mein Dolly Der Orrian	9/18/65	10/1/67
Big Island Silver Deuce	3/17/68	4/23/67
Hurckes Steel Victor	4/4/65	4/14/68
Bo Diddly v. Hohen Tann	6/29/68	3/12/67
Gert's Dena v. Greif	3/19/67	9/29/68
Kajobar v. Stony Brook	7/18/67	3/20/69
Oxton's Minado v. Brunz	4/21/69	11/26/67
Radbach's Dustcloud	7/27/69	5/5/68
Fee v.d. Wildburg	7/27/69	8/30/69
Gert's Duro v. Greif	9/11/69	9/11/66
AFC Briarwood's Peppermint Patty, CD	9/3/66	10/26/69
Ridgeland's Frauline	5/17/70	11/9/69
Tip Top Timber	7/12/70	4/6/69

| Name | Date Finished | |
	Show	Field
Timberlane's Fritz	7/24/70	9/7/69
Telstar Direct	10/16/65	9/6/70
Frei of Klarbruk, UDT	1/14/66	10/10/70
Dee Tee's Baron v. Greif	9/19/71	9/5/71
Dino's Baroness Marta	5/29/66	10/10/71
Roger's Hans	11/28/71	4/26/70
Eastwind's TK Dandy	2/15/72	4/27/69
Big Island Sass-A-Frass	3/23/72	4/25/71
AFC Albrecht's Tena Hy	3/5/66	4/2/72
AFC Dee Tee's Baschen v. Greif	3/28/71	4/16/72
AFC Ricki Radbach v. Greif	4/23/72	3/3/69
Waldwinkel's Painted Lady	7/24/66	5/21/72
AFC Fritz v.d. Zigeuner	9/24/67	9/17/72
Fritz v. Trekka Radbach	5/6/73	9/14/69
AFC Ritzi's Oranien Rocco	6/18/72	9/23/73
Eastwind's TK Rebel	7/13/73	10/7/73
Gruenweg's Dandy's Brodie, CDX	5/31/70	4/14/74
Erick v. Enzstrand	5/25/74	9/23/73
'79 NFC Lika Buckskin	7/7/73	9/15/74
Peter v.d. Zigeuner	2/23/75	9/27/74
Patche Prince James	4/26/75	4/22/74
AFC Albrecht Marta's Dino	9/18/71	11/2/75
AFC Herr Hans of the Barretts	10/11/70	11/16/75
Kerlacres Tell's Moonbeam	4/3/76	3/15/75
Jager Albrecht's Baron	9/15/73	4/25/76

Name	Date Finished Show	Field
Esser's Duke v.d. Wildburg	4/25/76	5/23/76
Timbertop Tell	7/28/74	5/30/76
Schatzi's Eric v. Greif	8/6/72	9/19/76
Bar Nuth'n Sandy	6/1/75	4/9/78
Fagon Haag v. Greif	9/2/73	4/16/78
Erdenreich's Marz Marsh	5/12/78	12/12/76
Uodibar's PDO v. Waldtaler	8/31/74	9/17/78
Ammertal's Candy Cane	5/27/77	10/7/78
JD Babe's Drifting Toby v. Greif	8/24/75	3/18/79
Treff Marimax v.d. Wildburg	9/16/78	4/22/79
Golden West Chucko	5/22/79	2/16/75
'79 ANFC and '81 ANFC Bosslady Jodi v. Greif	8/11/79	10/1/78
Rocco's Diamond Kate v. Belle	6/10/79	8/25/79
AFC Hidden Hollow's Pleasure	4/15/76	10/20/79
Eva v. Kieckheter	6/11/77	4/12/80
Eden's Lightning Snapper	6/29/80	11/4/79
Milane Candyman's Beau Geste	11/15/80	9/7/80
J B II	12/13/80	8/19/79
'82 NFC Ehrlicher Abe	5/19/81	8/23/80
Checkmate's August Dog	6/21/81	10/11/80
Wolfgang Radloff	8/29/81	3/12/78
Soc's One Shot	7/11/82	11/29/81
'83 NFC Checkmate's Challenger	12/6/81	5/15/82
Hillhaven's Hustler	6/20/81	3/19/83

| Name | Date Finished | |
	Show	Field
AFC B-G's Jagerhund Gebhard	2/19/78	4/17/83
AFC Lyon's Holy Smoke	11/20/82	10/16/83
Goldies Sam v. Pecos	2/4/84	3/7/82
Apocalypse v. Greif	6/30/84	5/6/84
Wilkinson's Yue-He	7/30/84	8/14/82
Timberdoodle Lancer's Answer	8/4/84	6/4/83
Werren's v. Nordhof	11/17/84	3/4/83
Ybold Rothenuffeln (Germany)	9/25/82	1/5/85
Moesgaard's Deejay's Derek	2/3/85	10/30/83
AFC Becky's Baroness Hightail	7/8/84	3/10/85
AFC Buck v. Greif	4/7/85	10/12/85
The Flying Dutchman v. Rip Traf	10/19/80	4/19/86
Princess Pepper V	8/16/86	5/25/85
Rugerheim's Bit of Bourbon	4/3/83	11/10/86
Wil-Lyn's Sparkling Nugget	8/14/83	2/21/87
AFC Shill Rest's Impressive, CDX, MH	5/3/86	10/3/87
Ybolds Graf v. Hainholz	8/10/86	2/20/88
AFC Hidden Hollow's Rowdy Bess	8/12/85	4/23/88
AFC Hidden Hollow's Classy Sassy	4/23/88	10/2/83
'87 NFC Liebchen Buddendorff	9/22/88	3/3/84
AFC Briarwood's Shillrest Roxie	9/29/89	5/20/89
Rugerheim's Wisner	4/12/90	
Hillhaven's Sunshine	10/84	10/15/90
Rugerheim's Ice Breaker	12/2/90	4/15/89

Name	Date Finished	
	Show	Field
Rugerheim's Fire Boss	1985	12/22/90
Cebourns Erick of Hustleberg	1987	5/4/91
High Rollin, SLD	5/5/91	1988
Stradivarius Baroque	1990	10/5/91
Rugerheim's Little Lord	4/13/91	10/19/91
Bandit's Traveling Gypsy	6/22/88	11/16/91
Kingswood Glinkirk Zanzibar	8/6/87	4/3/93
NFC Desert Dutch	10/3/93	
NMK-RD's Rustic Country Charm, JH	9/29/91	11/13/93
Rugerheim's Verys Pistol Pete	1991	11/20/93
AFC Shill Rest's Lasting Impression, SH	12/19/93	4/3/93
Lieblinghaus Hunter's Moon, SH	1994	
Kurzhaar's Ruger v. Haven, SH	1994	
Longacres Moment in Time	1994	
NMK Irresistible v. Rugerheim	1994	
Odyssey's Saint Blitz	1994	
NMK's Shining Star v. Rugerheim	1995	
Up N' Adam, UD, JH	1995	
NMK's Whitney v. Rugerheim	1995	
Bodo v. Waldrand, MH	1996	
AFC Stones River Destroyer, MH	1996	
Ziel v. Feinschmecker	1996	

Appendix C

NATIONAL SPECIALTY SHOW WINNERS

Year (Entries)	Best of Breed / Best of Opposite	BB Owner / BB Breeder
1964 (111)	Ch. Jones Hill Jay / Ch. Richlu's Becky Oranien	William P. McLoughlan / Amelia F. Jones
1965 (118)	Ch. Gunhill's Mesa Maverick / Ch. Erdenreich's Keesje v.d. Greif	P. Carl Tuttle / P. Carl Tuttle
1966 (209)	Ch. Gunhill's Mesa Maverick / Ch. Gretchenhof New Moon	P. Carl Tuttle / P. Carl Tuttle
1967 (183)	Ch. Whispering Pines Tally-Hi / Gunhill's Flying Dutchman	Mrs. S. Conroy / Rudolph Jordan
1968 (212)	Ch. Adam v. Fuehrerheim / Ch. Birdacre's Gay Princess	Robert H. McKowen / Charles H. Jordan
1969 (163)	Ch. Kaposia's Waupun II / Ch. Gina Braun v. Greif	Helen B. Case / D. and B. Sandberg
1970 (132)	Ch. Kaposia's Waupun II / Ch. Weidenbach Bridget	Helen B. Case / D. and B. Sandberg
1971 (179)	Ch. Whispering Pines Ranger / Ch. Whispering Pines Tally-Hi	Bernard Ginsberg / Rudolph Jordan
1972 (123)	Ch. Kaposia's Waupun II / Ch. Hi My Sudwind v. Kaposia	Helen B. Case / D. and B. Sandberg
1973 (283)	Ch. Kaposia's Tucumcari / Ch. Gretchenhof Moondance	D. and B. Sandberg / D. and B. Sandberg
1974 (123)	Ch. Cede Mein Chat Nuga Chu Chu / Ch. Leiblinghaus Snowstorm	C. D. Lawrence / C. D. Lawrence

Year (Entries)	Best of Breed / Best of Opposite	BB Owner / BB Breeder
1975 (166)	Ch. Jillard of Whispering Pines Ch. Serakraut's Hot Shot	S. and P. Nannola J. F. Potash
1976 (125)	Ch. Gretchenhof Columbia River Ch. Hi My Sudwind v. Kaposia	Gretchenhof Kennels L. W. Gilbry
1977 (268)	A/C Ch. Conrad's Brio Ch. Fieldfine's Foxy Lady	Galen and Nancy Conrad Galen and Nancy Conrad
1978 (109)	Ch. Kooskia's Chief Jospeh Ch. Bud Creek's Bertha	Margaret and Nolen Noren Margaret Noren
1979 (185)	Ch. Windsong's Misty Memories Ch. Fieldfine's Lord Tanner	Susan Harrison John and Helen Herring
1980 (228)	A/C Ch. Fieldfine's Lord Tanner Ch. Fieldfine's Foxy Lady	Leonard S. and Mark R. Shulman Leonard W. Seither
1981 (240)	Ch. P.W.'s Challenger v. Fieldfine Ch. Fieldfine's Ribbons	Larry Berg Bevan Ehrich
1982 (181)	Ch. Donavin's Sir Ivanhoe Ch. Fieldfine's Ribbons	D. and D. Gilliam and V. Nunes D. and S. Thompson
1983 (603)	Ch. Kingswood's Miss Chiff Ch. Broker's Best Offer	R. and C. Green June and Jim Burns
1984 (429)	Ch. Schatzie's Ripper v. Greif Ch. Kingswood's Miss Chiff	Eugene W. Ellis Debra Goodie
1985 (424)	Ch. Schatzie's Ripper v. Greif Ch. Sheridan Brandy v. Fieldfine	Eugene W. Ellis Debra Goodie
1986 (901)	Ch. Echo Run's Corteze's Choice Ch. Shannon's Scarlett O'Hara	Neil Ritter and D. McMullen Kathleen Carling
1987 (901)	Ch. NMK's Brittania v. Sibelstein Ch. Robin Crest Lorien Corniche	Dr. G. B. Stone and Carol Chadwick Kathy Sibley
1988 (404)	Ch. Lieblinghaus Here's To Freedom Ch. Robin Crest Lorien Corniche	Ruth Ann Freer S. and D. Urbanczyk and Ruth Ann Freer

Year (Entries)	Best of Breed / Best of Opposite	BB Owner / BB Breeder
1989 (778)	Ch. Robin Crest Lorien Corniche Ch. Lieblinghaus Here's To Freedom	A. Attila and J. and R. Remondi E. and D. Hoffman and P. Fullford
1990 (595)	Ch. Up N'Adam, CD, JH Khrispat's Mohave Valley	Katrin Higgins Tazza Katrin Higgins Tazza
1991 (568)	Ch. Maekenet's Flying Persuasion Ch. Tuckoma Shade Mtn Dawn	Linda M. Armstrong L. M. and R. K. Armstrong
1992 (869)	Ch. Sunreach's Flexible Flyer Ch. Wyndbourne's Keepsake	Karen L. Allen Karen L. Allen
1993 (711)	Ch. Intrepid's Headline Hunter Ch. Riverside's Moondust	Kim Edwards J. R. and M. H. Boteler
1994	Ch. Wyndbourne's Keepsake Ch. Pawmarc's Sierra Mtn Song	Susan Harrison Susan Harrison
1995	Ch. Roscommon At Birchwood, JH Ch. Homesteader's Merry Magdaline, JH	John and Wilma Sarna Jinny and Jack Nealon
1996	Ch. Pawmarc's Sierra Mtn Song Ch. Wyndbourne's Keepsake	Benny L Conboy and Margaret Sylvester Paula Williams and Pat Wilaby
1997	Ch. Lieblinghaus Chief Executive, CD, JH Ch. Kan-Point Enchanted Reason	Ruth Ann Freer and Jolene Whitfield Ruth Ann Freer

Appendix D

NATIONAL AMATEUR FIELD CHAMPIONS

Year	Name	Owner
1966	Championship Withheld	
1967	Moesgaard's Coco	Lloyd Sanders
1968	Pentre Bach Coco	W. R. Pritchard and Charlene Potts
1969	Speck v. Goldenmark II	James Lockett
1970	Schling v. Shinback	Don Nicely
1971	Andora v. Holkenborn	Al Holk
1972	Moesgaard's Wrenegade	Robert A. Merkel
1973	Jetta Liz Fesmire	Robert and Bernice Fitzgerald
1974	R. D.'s Rex v.d. Hirschau	Helmut Brosi
1975	Herr Hans of the Barretts	Betty and Don Barrett
1976	v. Thalberg's Gip's Jaxel	Warren Palmer
1977	Retzbach's Baron v. Fritz	George Wilson
1978	Retzbach's Baron v. Fritz	George Wilson
1979	Bosslady Jodi v. Greif	Gary F. and Harriet M. Short
1980	P. J. Wildfire	Patricia Vicari
1981	Bosslady Jodi v. Greif	Gary F. and Harriet M. Short
1982	FC/AFC Fleeta v. Bossman	Marie V. Mayo
1983	October's Punkin	Dr. John Baillie
1984	Breakaway's Princess Jessica	John Tomanski

Year	Name	Owner
1985	Beier's Evolution	Jim McCue and Ron Laird
1986	FC/AFC Edlou's Supersonic	Ed and Lou Lilly
1987	FC/AFC Big Oak's Irish Mist	Vern Grimslid
1988	FC/AFC Ranger's Essergreif Gabbe	Kevin P. Waide
1989	Lars Agnes v. Rusdelite	Dr. M. Parl Larson
1990	NAFC Lars Agnes v. Rusdelite	Dr. M. Parl Larson
1991	FC/AFC Wildfire's Angel	Joseph and Patricia Vicari
1992	Markar's Radioactive	Mark Oakley
1993	FC Tea Creeks' Big Bad Jayne	Lanny Silks
1994	FC Antrim's Wayside Willie	Rob Creany
1995	FC Markar's Maximum Heartbreaker	Mark Oakley
1996	FC and AFC Pipeline Jake On The Make	Marc McKinley and Kiyoski Mazaki

Appendix E

NATIONAL OPEN GUN DOG CHAMPIONS

Year	Name	Owner
1977	Patar's Chocolate Chip	Ernie Kolb
1978	October's Victory v. Greif	Dr. Stan Haag
1979	Uodibar's Mouse	Dr. John and Sandy Burk
1980	Bosslady Jodi v. Greif	Gary and Harriet Short
1981	Whitmer's Savage Sam	Carl Morreale
1982	FC Lancer's Royal Scout	Sandy Kimball
1983	FC & AFC Hidden Hollow's Hot Shot	Craig Little, D.V.M.
1984	FC Esser Wendy v. Wildburg	Robert Ryan
1985	FC Moesgaard's Deejay's Sin	John and Susan Rabidou
1986	FC & AFC and 1985 NAFC Beier's Evolution	Ron Laird and Dr. James McCue
1987	Pipeline's Bobtail Bandit	Steve Woudenberg
1988	Radbach Kizzy's Kunta	William H. Miller
1989	Wingfield's Lucky Putney	Hank and Heather Noble
1990	FC and AFC and 1989 NAFC Lars Agnes v. Rusdelite	Dr. M. Parl Larson
1991	Uodibar's Stub A Dub	Kent Kislingbury
1992	Blitz's Molly Be Good	Joseph Vicari
1993	FC Buckville's Maggie Mae	Joe Minard
1994	FC Windjammer's Tina	Terry Zygalinski
1995	FC K-Hawk's Kandu Kandy	Kent Kislingbury, D.V.M.
1996	FC Rawhide's Mo-Reen	Don Lloyd

Appendix F

NATIONAL FIELD CHAMPIONS AND NATIONAL ALL AGE CHAMPIONS

Year	Name	Owner
1953	Dandy Jim v. Feldstrom	Clark Lemley, M.D.
1954	Wendenheim's Fritz	Frank Nuzzo
1955	Gunmaster's Jenta	James A. Karns
1956	Traude v.d. Wengenstadt	Oliver M. Rousseau
1957	Bobo Grabenbruch	Dr. William Schimmel
1958	Dixon's Sheila	Russell Oixon
1959	Oloff v.d. Schleppenburg	Roy J. Thompson
1960	v. Saalfield's Kash	Walter Seagraves
1962	Moesgaard's Dandy	Dr. and Mrs. Lewis L. Kline
1963	Moesgaard's Angel	Donald Praeger
1964	Shockley's Pride	Luther Shockley
1965	Onna v. Bess	R. G. Froehlich
1966	Fieldacres Bonanza	Harold and Jean Dowler
1967	Rip Traf v. Bess	Gene and Ercia Harden
1968	v. Thalberg's Seagraves Chayne	Don Miner
1969	Blick v. Shinback	Brad Calkins
1970	Championship Withheld	
1972	Wyatt's Gipp v. Shinback	Mickey and Warren Palmer
1973	Patricia v. Frulord	Mrs. Gladys Laird
1971	Patricia v. Frulord	Mrs. Gladys Laird

Year	Name	Owner
1974	Cede Mein Georgie Girl	R. A. Flynn and W. P. Troutman
1975	Mark V's One Spot	Ronald Rainey
1976	Frulord's Tim	Fred and Gladys Laird
1977	Jocko v. Stolzhafen	Dr. J. S. Brown
1978	Championship Withheld	
1979	Lika Buckskin	Gary F. and Harriet M. Short
1980	Ammertal's Boss Ranger	Gary Nehring
1981	Checkmate's White Smoke	Steve Lyons
1982	Dual Ch. Ehrlicher Abe	Patrick and Linda Cross
1983	Dual Ch. Checkmate's Challenger	John and Irene Voglein
1984	FC Gretchen Pride	Bill Bussey
1985	FC Windswept's Little Big Man	Frank Alexander
1986	FC Uodibar's Koonas	John Rabidou
1987	Liebchen Buddendorff	Mary Finley
1988	Flashdance Ginny	Robert Howe
1989	FC Stuka of the Night	Stanley Rys
1990	FC Sanjo's Sin City Slicker	Steve Harrold
1991	Desert Dutch	Don Lloyd
1992	FC Rawhide's Clown	Dierk Davis
1993	FC Rawhide's Clown	Dierk Davis
1994	NFC Rawhide's Clown	Dierk Davis
1995	FC Heide's Mighty City Slicker	Robert Thompson
1996	FC Alamo Magic	Frank Alexander

Appendix G

GERMAN SHORTHAIRED POINTER CLUB OF AMERICA HALL OF FAME

1980

FC Albrecht's Countess Tena

Ch. Adam v. Fuehrerheim

DC Blick v. Grabenbruch

NFC/FC Blick v. Shinback

DC Cede Mein Dolly der Orrian

Esser's Chick

A/C Dual Ch. Gretchen v. Greif

FC Greif v. Hundscheimerkogel

DC Kay v.d. Wildburg

NFC/DC Moesgaard's Dandy

Ch. Oak Crest's Rick v. Winterhauch

DC Oxton Bride's Brunz v. Greif

NFC Rip Traf v. Bess

DC Rusty v. Schwarenberg

FC v. Thalberg's Fritz II

Ch. Yunga War Bride

1981

FC Tip Top Timmy

DC Oxton's Minado v. Brunz

Ch. Gretchenhof Moonshine

DC Frei of Klarbruck, UDT

A/C FC Radbach's Bimbo

Arta v. Hohreusch

Mars v. Ammertal

Bob v. Schwarenberg

NFC Patricia v. Frulord

A/C FC Lutz v. Dem Radbach

MFC Bobo Grabenbruch Beckum

Int. FC Moesgaard's IB

FC Windy Hill Prince James

DC Baron Fritz v. Hohentan

A/C Ch. Fliegen Meister's Gunner

FC Checkmate's Dandy Dude

1982

A/C DC Arrak v. Heisterholz

NFC/DC Dandy Jim v. Feldstrom

DC Biff Bangabird

DC Richlu's Dan Oranien

Gretchenhof Tallyho

Ch. Warrenwood's Kandy Kane

FC/1967 NAFC Moesgaard's Coco

Big Island Junker

Ch. Rocky Run's Stoney

FC/AFC Ammertal's Kitt v. Shinback

1983

FC Hugo v. Bergeskante

Ceres of Hidden Hollow

1984

DC Robin Crest Chip, CD

A/C Ch. Fieldfine's Count Rambard

FC Ammertal's Lancer "D"

1985

FC Uodibar's Boss Man

A/C Ch. Conrad's Brio

1986

A/C Ch. Gretchenhof Columbia River

A/C Ch. Jillard of Whispering Pines, CD

Ch. Lieblinghaus Snowstorm

1987

Ch. Adam's Hagen v. Waldenburg

DC Erick v. Enzstrand

Ch. Nock's Chocolate Chip

FC/1963 NFC Moesgaard's Angel

1988

Ch. Windsong's Misty Memories

FC Moesgaard's Angel's Deejay

FC/AFC Stoney's Jake v. Hewletts

1989

A/Mex Ch. Kaposia's Waupun II

FC Kaposia Chief of Oak Crest, CD

FC/AFC Tip Top Savage Sam

FC Shilo v. Hessenwald

DC Kaposia's Firebird

1990

Ch Strauss's Happy Go Lucky

A/C Ch. Wentworth's Happy Wanderer

A/C Ch. Weinland's Matinee Idol

FC/AFC Hidden Hollow's Ronlord Ruler

1991

FC Jigg's White Smoke

FC/AFC/NAFC P. J. Wildfire

1992

DC Esser's Chick v.d. Wildburg

1993

A/C Ch. Sure Shot's Bounty Hunter, UDT, MH, TT, AD

1994

FC Sundance Gypsy Lee

DC/Can. Ch. NMK's Britannia v. Sibelstein

A/C Ch. NMK's Placer Country Snowbird

1995

Ch. Schatzi v. Heiligsepp, CD

DC and K.S. Ybold Rothenuffeln

FC Big Oak's Bumper

FC/AFC Brown L

NFC/DC Erlicher Abe

1996

DC/AFC/Can. Ch. Shillrest's Impressive, A/C, CDX, MH

A/C Ch. Cheza's Riverside Imp, A/C, CD

FC Checkmate's Dude's Bigfoot

1997

NFC/NAFC/AFC Beier's Evolution

FC/AFC Dixieland's Rusty

Ch. Kingswood's Maximilian

NFC/DC/AFC Leibchen Buddendorff

Ch. Up N' Adam's Barbara, CD, JH

GUIDELINES FOR DOGS
NOMINATED TO HALL OF FAME

1. The dog must be deceased—mandatory.
2. The dog must be registered with the AKC—mandatory.
3. The dog should have completed an AKC title—strongly preferred.
4. The dog should have produced titled offspring—strongly preferred.

   Males: 10 Ch., 5 FC, or 2 OTCH

   Females: 3 Ch., 2 FC, or 2 OTCH
5. The dog could be classified as one of the early Foundation dogs of the GSP breed.
6. The dog should have contributed substantially to the breed, not only in performance, but as a producer.
7. The dog should have left an everlasting impression on the GSP breed in America.

Index